War In Peace

Volume 10

War In Peace

The Marshall Cavendish Illustrated Encyclopedia of Postwar Conflict

Editors-in-Chief
Ashley Brown
Dr. John Pimlott

Editorial Board
Brig-Gen. James Collins Jr (USA Retd.)
Vice-Admiral Sir Louis Le Bailly KBE CB
Ian V Hogg; David Floyd
Professor Laurence Martin
Air-Vice Marshal SWB Menaul CB CBE DFC AFC

MARSHALL CAVENDISH
NEW YORK, LONDON, TORONTO

Reference Edition Published 1985

Published by Marshall Cavendish Corporation
147 West Merrick Road
Freeport, Long Island
N.Y. 11520

Printed and Bound in Italy by L.E.G.O. S.p.a. Vicenza.

British Library Cataloguing in Publication Data

Brown, Ashley
    War in peace : the Marshall Cavendish
    illustrated encyclopaedia of post-wa conflict.
    1. History, Modern—1945-   2. War -History
    —20th century
    I. Title   II. Dartford, Mark
    909.82   D842

    ISBN 0-86307-293-3
        0 86307 303 4   vol. 10

Library of Congress Cataloging in Publication Data

Main entry under title:

War in peace.

    Includes bibliographies and index.
    1. Military history, Modern—20th century.   2. Military
art and science—History—20th century.   3. World politics—1945-
I. Marshall Cavendish Corporation.
U42.W373 1984   355'.009'04   84-19386
ISBN 0-86307-293-3
        0 86307 303 4   vol. 10

Editorial Staff

Editor	Ashley Brown
Editorial Director	Brian Innes
Editorial Manager	Clare Byatt
Editorial Editors	Sam Elder
	Adrian Gilbert
Sub Editors	Sue Leonard
	Simon Innes
Artwork Editor	Jonathan Reed
Artwork Buyer	Jean Morley
Picture Editor	Carina Dvorak
Picture Consultant	Robert Hunt
Design	EDC

Reference Edition Staff

Editor	Mark Dartford
Designer	Graham Beehag
Consultant	Robert Paulley
Indexers	F & K Gill
Creation	DPM Services

Editorial Board

Contributors

David Blue served with the CIA in various countries of Southeast Asia, including Laos, and is a writer on and a student of small wars.

Gordon Brook-Shepherd spent 15 years in Vienna, first as lieutenant-colonel on the staff of the British High Commission and then as a foreign correspondent for the *Daily Telegraph*. A graduate in history from Cambridge, he is currently Chief Assistant Editor of the *Sunday Telegraph*.

Jeffrey J. Clarke is an expert on recent military history, particularly the Vietnam War, and has written for the American Center of Military History.

Major-General Richard Clutterbuck OBE has been Senior Lecturer in politics at Exeter University since his retirement from the army in 1972. His works include *Protest and the Urban Guerrilla, Guerrillas and Terrorists* and *Kidnap and Ransom*.

Alexander S. Cochran Jr is a historian whose area of research is modern Indochinese affairs with particular reference to the war in Vietnam since 1945. He is at present working in the Southeast Asia Branch of the Center of Military History, Department of the Army.

Colonel Peter M. Dunn is a serving officer in the USAF. His doctoral thesis is on the history of Indochina during the mid-1940s.

John B. Dwyer served both with the infantry and with armoured units in Vietnam. He was editor and publisher of the Vietnam veteran's newsletter *Perimeter* and has been a writer and correspondent for *National Vietnam Veteran's Review* for the past few years. His particular interest are Special Forces and Special Operations.

Brenda Ralph Lewis has specialised in political and military history since 1964. She s a regular contributor to military and historical magazines in both Britain and the United States.

Hugh Lunghi served in Moscow in the British Military Mission and the British Embassy for six years during and after World War II. He was interpreter for the British Chiefs of Staff at the Teheran, Yalta and Potsdam conferences, and also interpreted for Churchill and Anthony Eden. He subsequently worked in the BBC External Services and is a former editor of *Index on Censorship*.

Charles Messenger retired from the army in 1980 to become a fulltime military writer after 21 years service in the Royal Tank Regiment. Over the past 10 years he has written several books on 20th century warfare, as well as contributing articles to a number of defence and historical journals. He is currently a Research Associate at the Royal United Services Institute for Defence Studies in London.

Billy C. Mossman is a well-known American writer and historian. He is currently working on a volume on the Korean War for the US Army Center of Military History.

Bryan Perrett served in the Royal Armoured Corps from 1952 to 1971. He contributes regularly to a number of established military journals and acted as Defence Correspondent to the *Liverpool Echo* during the Falklands War. His recent books include *Weapons of the Falklands Conflict* and *A History of Blitzkrieg*.

Chapman Pincher is one of England's leading authorities on international espionage and counter-intelligence. He is the author of political novels and books on spying, the most recent of which is *Their Trade is Treachery*, which deals with the penetration of Britain's secret services by the Russian secret police.

Yehoshua Porath is a noted scholar at the Hebrew University in Jerusalem. He has made a special study of the Palestinian problem and is the author of two books on the subject, the most recent of which is *The Palestinian Arab National Movement 1929—39*, which was published in Britain in 1977.

Contributors

Antony Preston is Naval Editor of the military magazine *Defence* and author of numerous publications including *Battleships, Aircraft Carriers* and *Submarines*.

Brigadier-General Edwin H. Simmons, US Marine Corps, Retired, is the Director of Marine Corps History and Museums. At the time of the Inchon operation and the Chosin Reservoir campaign, he, as a major, commanded Weapons Company, 3rd Battalion, 1st Marines. Widely published, he is the author of *The United States Marines*.

Ronald Spector is an expert on Vietnam and has recently completed a book on that subject for the Center of Military History in the United States.

Andres Suarez served in the Cuban ministry of education from 1948—1951, took part in the Cuban revolution, and served in the ministry of housing from 1959. From 1965, he has been Professor of Latin American Studies at the University of Florida. Other publications include *Cuba and the Sino—Soviet Rift*.

Sir Robert Thompson KBE, CMG, DSO, MC is a world authority on guerrilla warfare, on which he has written extensively. He was directly involved in the Emergency in Malaya in the 1950s and rose to become permanent Secretary for Defence. From 1961 to 1965 he headed the British Advisory Mission to Vietnam and since then he has advised several governments, including the United States, on counter-insurgency operations Sir Robert Thompson is a Council member of the Institute for the Study of Conflict, London. His books include *Defeating Communist Insurgency* and *Revolutionary War in World Strategy, 1945—69*.

Patrick Turnbull commanded 'D' Force, Burma during World War II. His 29 published works include a history of the Foreign Legion.

Contents of Volume

The turning of the tide

International terrorism, 1973-78

The growth of international terrorism in the late 1960s and early 1970s was tightly linked to the Palestinian struggle to achieve a homeland at the expense of the Israelis. The decision of George Habash's Popular Front for the Liberation of Palestine (PFLP) to embark on a campaign of spectacular plane hijacks in the wake of the Arab defeat in the Six-Day War of 1967 set the ball rolling, and Yassir Arafat's Fatah – through its front organisation Black September – joined in after 1971. Terrorists of the New Left in Europe and Japan were drawn into the international campaign, as well as receiving training from the Palestinians for their domestic operations.

But by 1973 the leaders of the PFLP and Fatah had come to have severe doubts about the effectiveness of international terrorism. Such dramatic coups as the hijackings to Dawson's Field in 1970 and the Munich Olympics hostage-taking in 1972 had very effectively brought the Palestinian cause to the notice of world opinion, but they had also awoken intense hostility to the Palestinian movements both in the West and among the leaders of the more conservative Arab states. It was also far from obvious how such tactics could lead to the eventual establishment of a Palestinian state. Arafat and Habash were deeply divided over their attitude to conservative Arab regimes – Habash saw the Palestinian cause as part of a general revolutionary process in the Arab world – but by 1973 they were agreed that the time for terrorism was over. Fatah's Black September campaign was called off and Habash disassociated the PFLP from the terrorist activities of Wadi Haddad, the notorious head of the movement's 'External Operations'.

But, even if they were totally sincere – which at least in the case of Habash many have doubted – the two main Palestinian leaders were in no position to stop the wave of international terrorism which they had largely started. A network was in place, trained terrorists were available, and political backing (plus finance) would come from some radical Arab states. The scene was set for a continuation of terrorism in which the Palestinians and other Arabs were to find themselves the object of attacks as often as were the Israelis and their backers.

The focus for inter-Arab conflict was the question of the attitude to take towards negotiation with Israel. Especially after the Yom Kippur War of October 1973, many Arab leaders felt that diplomacy could lead towards their objectives, but this involved tacitly or explicitly accepting the existence of an Israeli state in some shape or form. The most radical Arab states and Palestinian groups persisted in refusing to accept the existence of Israel in any form. Arafat, as head of

The airports of Western Europe, such as Orly airport, Paris, were frequent targets for terrorist attacks in the 1970s. Top: A Palestinian moves through Orly with an RPG-2 rocket in January 1975. The rockets missed their target; despite several attempts, no airliner was ever shot down in this way. Above: All Western countries stepped up the arming and training of their security forces to counter terrorism. These French police at Orly carry a special long-barrelled version of the MAT-49 sub-machine gun.

Right: A burnt-out Pan Am airliner at Rome airport is guarded by police after one of the most ferocious terrorist attacks ever witnessed. On 17 December 1973 five members of the Libyan-backed NAYLP carried out an incendiary attack on the aircraft on the ground, burning 32 passengers to death.

The playboy of terror

Ilich Ramirez Sanchez, known as Carlos the Killer, was born on 12 October 1949, the eldest son of a Venezuelan communist and millionaire. In 1968 his father's contacts gained Carlos entry to the Patrice Lumumba University in Moscow, but his reckless and wealthy life-style was ill-suited to the Soviet Union. Within a year he was expelled from both the university and the country.

After a short spell in London, Carlos left for the PFLP camps in the Middle East where so many terrorists of his generation received their training. The PFLP needed non-Arab operatives in Europe to organise their international actions; Carlos was sent back to London to await the moment for action, remaining unnoticed by the authorities behind his facade as a wealthy socialite and womaniser.

In 1973 Carlos was 'activated' by Wadi Haddad, moving to Paris. His style was dramatic: he loved to get into the action himself, and was delighted when his existence became public knowledge in 1975. During the OPEC kidnap he announced himself to the hostages as 'the famous Carlos', and he collected press-cuttings about himself. But his notoriety necessarily limited his usefulness as a terrorist in the field. After the death of Wadi Haddad in 1978, Carlos appears to have moved into the service first of

FILIACION
PERSONAL DESCRIPTION

Above: An identity photo of Carlos.
Bottom: The arms found in his Paris flat.

Colonel Gaddafi and then of President Assad of Syria. It was thought that Carlos might have retired into private life by 1983, but in December of that year the bombing of Marseilles railway station was apparently once more his work.

The fascination exercised by Carlos had resulted from the contrast between his ruthless dedication to the revolutionary cause and his flagrant taste for luxurious living. Neither his tastes nor his spectacular exhibitionist style have recommended themselves to other professionals in the world of terrorism, but Carlos's abilities as an organiser and executor of operations has been unquestioned.

the Palestine Liberation Organisation (PLO), became fully committed to a diplomatic approach, reaching a pinnacle of achievement when he was invited to address the UN General Assembly in November 1974. Those Palestinians opposed to Arafat's line were meanwhile organised by the Iraqi regime into a 'Front of Palestinian Forces Rejecting Surrenderist Solutions'. The PFLP and the PFLP-General Command were among the groups forming this Rejection Front.

It was not the so-called Rejection Front itself that was responsible for the continuation of terrorism after 1973, however, but three distinct centres of support for the rejectionist principle. One was Iraq, whose Ba'athist rulers obtained the services of Sabri al Banna, better known as Abu Nidal, former Fatah representative in Baghdad and a leading member of Black September who refused to stop his activities when that movement was wound up. Another major source of terrorist initiatives was Libya under its eccentric and excitable ruler, Colonel Muammar Gaddafi. He set up the National Arab Youth Organisation for the Liberation of Palestine (NAYLP) as his terrorist arm, at first like the Iraqis using the services of a Black September defector, Ahmed Abdel Ghaffar, known as Abu Mahmoud.

The third main centre of terrorism after 1973 was the network connected with Wadi Haddad. PFLP External Operations had established a close working relationship with the Japanese Red Army, the German Baader-Meinhof Red Army Fraction and a number of otherwise unattached international terrorists. One of these, the Venezuelan Ilich Ramirez Sanchez, known simply as Carlos, took over control of the European part of the network in June 1973 after the Israelis assassinated his predecessor, Mohammed Boudia. This truly international terrorist web was to be responsible for carrying out some of the most

Above right: Yassir Arafat, once regarded as the arch-terrorist leader, addresses the UN as representative of the Palestinian people, 13 November 1974.

Above: Wadi Haddad, head of the PFLP External Operations network, was behind many of the most spectacular terrorist incidents, including the Dawson's Field hijackings in September 1970, the OPEC kidnapping in December 1975, and the Mogadishu hijack in October 1977. Disowned by the PFLP leader George Habash after 1973, he continued to exploit the connections established between the Palestinians and the terrorists of other countries, notably the Baader-Meinhof group and the Japanese Red Army, until his death in 1978.

spectacular operations of the 1970s.

The Libyan-backed NAYLP began operations in August 1973 with a machine-gun and grenade attack on passengers waiting to board a TWA flight from Tel Aviv which had just landed at Athens airport; five passengers were killed and 55 wounded. But worse was to come: on 17 December five NAYLP terrorists ran onto the tarmac at Rome airport and lobbed a thermite bomb into a taxiing Pan Am airliner, burning 32 passengers to death. The terrorists then hijacked a Lufthansa aircraft, shooting an airline worker in the process, and flew via Damascus to Kuwait. In Kuwait they were induced to surrender to the authorities and later, under interrogation, apparently revealed that the aim of the operation had been to disrupt Arab-Israeli negotiations that were about to begin in Geneva. The Fatah leaders of the PLO were furious over the Rome attack; the five terrorists were handed over to the PLO and tried by a 'revolutionary court'. Abu Mahmoud, Gaddafi's ex-Fatah terrorist leader, became a marked man. The following year he imprudently visited the Lebanon where he was picked up by Fatah's security section, led by Arafat's deputy Abu Iyad, and executed by a Palestinian firing squad.

Meanwhile Carlos had initiated his terrorist career in December 1973 with the attempted assassination of a leading Zionist in Britain, Teddy Sieff. A month later he was involved in the bombing of an Israeli-owned bank in the City of London. By August 1974 he was operating in Paris, car-bombing supposedly pro-Israeli media targets. At the same time, Wadi Haddad's External Operations network was continuing its connection with the Japanese Red Army, which had so dramatically surfaced in the Lod airport massacre of May 1972. At the end of January 1974, in a series of linked actions on opposite sides of Asia, Palestinian and Japanese terrorists attacked Shell fuel installations and seized hostages in Singapore while another group took over the Japanese embassy in Kuwait. All the terrorists involved were eventually flown to Haddad's traditional base, Aden. Carlos became involved with the Japanese connection in September 1974, when he played a large part in organising a Japanese Red Army takeover of the French embassy in the Netherlands which successfully achieved the release of a Japanese operative in French custody.

Meanwhile hijackings and attacks on airliners continued, chiefly carried out by Libyan-backed bands. In March 1974 a British VC-10 was hijacked on its way from Bombay to London, landed at Amsterdam and finally blown up on the ground. The following October a TWA airliner was blown up in flight over the Aegean, killing all 88 passengers. A further hijacking of a British Airways airliner followed in November. Carlos attempted to get in on the act by organising – or perhaps himself carrying out – two missile attacks on El Al airliners taking off from Orly airport, Paris, in January 1975. The first attack resulted in damage to one aircraft on the ground, and the second a week later was interrupted by security guards: after a gunfight and the seizing of hostages, the terrorists involved were able to negotiate their way onto a flight to Iraq.

A climate of terror

While these attacks had no precise political objectives besides the maintenance of a general climate of terror – and the circular goal of obtaining the release of terrorists captured in the course of previous operations – the critical divisions within the Arab world became the pretext for more precisely motivated actions. In October 1974 Arab heads of state were gathered for a summit conference in Rabat, capital of Morocco, with on the agenda a proposal to confirm the PLO as the sole representative of the Palestinian people and, in effect, to give Yassir Arafat a veto on any peace settlement in the Middle East. Opposition to this move centred on King Hussein of Jordan, whose own territorial demands were in conflict with the Palestinian claim to the West Bank of the Jordan. As the summit met, Moroccan security authorities received a tip-off from the Israeli secret service that led to the arrest of 15 men who were on a mission to assassinate Hussein and possibly other conservative Arab leaders. Abu Iyad, Arafat's deputy and former head of Black September, was reportedly implicated in this plot – remarkable if true, since Arafat himself was actually at the conference. Whether because of the threat to his life or not, King Hussein surprisingly withdrew his opposition to the PLO's claims and Arafat achieved another diplomatic triumph.

The most spectacular of all terrorist operations against the Arab conservatives, however, came the following year, in 1975, and was the work of the Wadi Haddad-Carlos network. Carlos had only narrowly escaped capture in June when Michel Moukharbel, his liaison officer with Haddad, inadvertently led the French police to his flat. Carlos escaped after killing two of the policemen and Moukharbel, whom he suspected of treachery, but his identity was now known to the world's police forces. Perhaps for this reason Haddad decided to use Carlos in person when he planned to kidnap 11 of the most powerful men in the world, the oil ministers of the Organisation of Petroleum Exporting Countries (OPEC), who would be meeting in Vienna in December.

In the view of Haddad and other rejectionists, OPEC had betrayed the Palestinian – and indeed, the Arab – cause by its failure to put its oil wealth sufficiently at the disposal of their cause and its reluctance to use the 'oil weapon' to crippling effect against the West. The particular objects of their hostility were the oil ministers of Iran (Jamshin Amouzegar) and Saudi Arabia (Sheikh Yamani). The terrorists' plan was to kidnap the ministers, extort a declaration of support for the Palestinians, and execute Yamani and Amouzegar. On 21 December six terrorists – Carlos, Baader-Meinhof members Hans Joachim Klein and Gabriele Kröcher-Tiedemann and three Arabs – penetrated the OPEC building with remarkable ease. Three men were killed mounting a forlorn last-minute resistance to the kidnap, and once the terrorists had their hostages they controlled the situation. Only one terrorist, Klein, was wounded by Austrian police.

A statement from the terrorists was broadcast and they were allowed to leave Austria with their hostages in a DC-9. Their intention was to fly from country to country, dropping an oil minister off at each stop, until only the intended victims were left to be shot on arrival at the final destination, Aden. At the first stop in Algiers, however, difficulties mounted, and Carlos soon agreed to accept an unspecified sum of ransom money in return for the release of all the hostages.

Throughout the kidnap, Carlos boasted to Sheikh Yamani of the capacity of the organisation to mount further operations, and predictably in June 1976 came the next spectacular – the hijacking of an airbus to Entebbe in Uganda, by a mixed group of Germans and Palestinians. The terrorists felt so secure that Haddad himself went to Uganda to supervise proceedings, but the outcome was a turning-point in the history of terrorism – a successful assault by the Israelis which freed the hostages, and inflicted heavy losses on their captors. It was a sign of things to come.

In October 1977 it was the turn of Wadi Haddad's Palestinians to pay their debt to the Baader-Meinhof group who had given them so much help, but the hijacking of a Lufthansa aircraft to Mogadishu in Somalia once more resulted in disaster for the terror-

The seizure of the OPEC oil ministers, meeting at their headquarters in Vienna on 21 December 1975, was a high point of international terrorism. It was also Carlos's only public appearance. Left: Wounded terrorist Klein is carried from the OPEC building. Below left: Traces of the brief gun-battle inside the building. Below: Carlos (in light raincoat and beret, centre) shepherds the oil ministers onto a bus provided by the authorities. Bottom: At the airport, the ministers are moved onto a plane bound for Algiers.

When Egyptian forces tried to emulate Israel's success at Entebbe with a commando assault on a hijacked airliner at Nicosia, Cyprus, in February 1978, the results were disastrous. Above: Three of the 15 Egyptian commandos shot dead by the Cypriot National Guard, who defended the airport against the raiders. Right: Leaders of the commando force at their comrades' funeral.

ists. The West German GSG9 counter-terrorist squad, with a little help from the SAS, successfully assaulted the aircraft, and none of the hijackers' demands were met.

Haddad and the tactics he had pursued were in sharp decline. In February 1978 a final operation was mounted, this time against an Arab enemy. Two Palestinian assassins killed an Egyptian editor known to be in favour of Egypt's reconciliation with Israel, in Nicosia, Cyprus. They then hijacked a Cyprus Airways airliner which, after taking off, was forced to return to Nicosia. There the Egyptians tried to carry out their own version of the Israelis' raid on Entebbe, sending in a commando force, but they had failed to secure the agreement of the Cypriot authorities and were badly mauled by the Cypriot National Guard at the airport.

On 1 April 1978 Wadi Haddad died of cancer in a hospital in East Germany. His death marked the end of a spectacular stage in the history of terrorism, even though terrorist in-fighting between conflicting Arab groups remained very much alive. The Iraqi-backed Fatah defector Abu Nidal had formed a group known as Black June – after the Syrian offensive against Palestinians in the Lebanon in June 1976 – and engaged in a war of assassination, first against the Syrians and then against representatives of the PLO, which was still pursuing the possibility of a negotiated settlement involving the possible co-existence of a Palestinian and an Israeli state. The tempo of killings mounted through 1978: in January the PLO's leading diplomat in London, Said Hammami, was shot dead and in June the PLO representative in Kuwait suffered the same fate. Through July and August Iraqi diplomats were attacked by the PLO and PLO offices by Black June in Paris, Beirut, London and Karachi.

This sordid and bloody conflict marked as well as anything the demise of terrorism as a strategy for changing the world. A spectacular coup might still be attempted to draw attention to a cause, but the idea of international terrorism as a road to the overthrow of the existing power system was finished – destroyed by internecine feuding and more effective government action.

R. G. Grant

Israel triumphant

The raid on Entebbe

At 0900 hours on 27 June 1976 Air France Flight 139 took off from Tel Aviv bound for Paris. The aircraft, an A-300 airbus, made an intermediate stop at Athens; when it took off again shortly after noon there were four terrorists among the 12 crew and 256 passengers aboard, two of them belonging to the German Baader-Meinhof gang – Wilfried Böse and Gabriele Kröcher-Tiedemann – and two of them members of the Popular Front for the Liberation of Palestine (PFLP). They had studied the security arrangements at Athens airport and detected a flaw which permitted them to smuggle grenades and automatic weapons aboard the aircraft.

At 1210 hours the terrorists hijacked Flight 139 and, following a carefully prepared plan, diverted it to Benghazi. Here the aircraft remained for the next six-and-a-half hours, during which it was refuelled – out of humanitarian concern for the hostages, according to Colonel Gaddafi – before becoming airborne again. It flew steadily south during the night, crossing the Libyan Sahara and the Sudan, and at approximately 0315 hours on 28 June the A-300 touched down at Entebbe International Airport in Uganda.

The choice of Entebbe as a destination was determined by the known attitudes and character of Uganda's ruler, Field-Marshal Idi Amin Dada. Although in the first years of his rule Amin had received extensive aid from the Israelis – they had helped train the Ugandan Army, hence the Israeli paratroopers' wings that Amin proudly wore on his many uniforms – under

the influence of Colonel Gaddafi the Ugandan ruler had become a sworn enemy of Israel. Officially Amin adopted a neutral attitude towards the hijackers, but in fact they were welcomed. Leading Palestinians were at the airport to meet the aircraft when it arrived, as were units of the Ugandan Army. The hostages were shepherded into the airport's old terminal building.

The hijackers' demands did not become clear until 29 June, when they were made public by Uganda Radio. The price of freedom for the hostages was to be the release of 53 terrorists, of whom 40 were imprisoned in Israel, six in West Germany, five in Kenya, one in France and one in Switzerland.

Israel, the nation most affected, had always made it perfectly clear that she would never compromise with terrorism, and that she was quite prepared to shed the blood of her own citizens to prove the point. For example, in May 1974 terrorists had made captive the pupils of a school at Maalot in Galilee; the Israeli Defence Forces (IDF) had stormed the building and killed the gunmen, but 22 children had died in the exchange of fire. At Entebbe, however, it seemed as though whatever happened Israel could not win, for only 105 of the hostages were Jewish, and the Israeli government simply dare not take risks with the lives of the remainder.

Curiously, it was the terrorists themselves who squandered the one priceless advantage they had over the Israelis. Without considering the full implications of the act they segregated the non-Jewish hostages

A jubilant crowd welcomes back the 105 liberated hostages and their rescuers at Lod airport, Tel Aviv, on 4 July 1976. The long-distance raid to free the hostages held at Entebbe airport in Uganda was an extraordinary display of skill and daring which gave a considerable boost to Israeli morale.

Top right: Israeli Chief of Staff Lieutenant-General Mordechai Gur (left) and Major-General Dan Shomron, who planned the raid on Entebbe. Bottom right: Idi Amin Dada, president of Uganda, in front of a wrecked Israeli tank during a visit to Egypt in 1976. Amin's anti-Israeli feeling was an important element in the hijackers' plans, but the Israeli paratroopers' wings on his uniform testify to a previous close relationship with the Israelis.

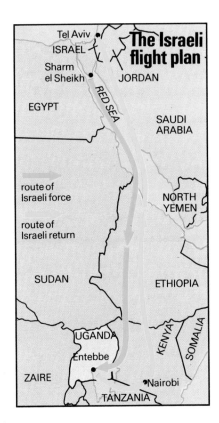

and, as a gesture to world opinion, allowed them to continue their journey to France. Not only were the released hostages able to provide a great deal of valuable information concerning the military situation at Entebbe, all of which was passed on to Israel, but also the Israelis were now free to concentrate on the plight of their own people without further international complications. Nonetheless, the terrorists were still in control of the overall situation. The Israeli government therefore temporised, announcing that the imprisoned terrorists would be released, but that the necessary arrangements could not be concluded before 4 July. This the hijackers accepted. Meanwhile the Israelis desperately sought a military plan to liberate the hostages before that date.

No place for failure

The feasibility of a raid had been under discussion since 28 June, but the difficulties were enormous, especially since the objective lay over 5000km (3000 miles) distant. The Israeli chief of staff, Lieutenant-General Mordechai Gur, felt that the consequences of failure would be so catastrophic that he would not even consider recommending such a mission unless it had a reasonable chance of success. After the release of the non-Israeli hostages, however, Gur, Prime Minister Yitzhak Rabin and Minister of Defence Shimon Peres were prepared to examine a plan prepared by Major-General Dan Shomron, the director of infantry and paratroops.

The basis of Shomron's plan was a night landing at Entebbe by four C-130 Hercules transport aircraft, which would then disgorge troops and the appropriate transport vehicles to give them a high degree of ground mobility. In order to elude detection on the inward flight, the first Hercules would come in directly behind a scheduled British cargo flight. The troops detailed to carry out the raid on the ground were divided into five groups: Group 1 to secure and illuminate the runway; Group 2 to seize the old

terminal building and release the hostages; Group 3 to seize the new terminal building; Group 4 to secure the airfield, prevent interference by several of Amin's armoured units which were known to be present in Kampala, 30km (20 miles) distant, and destroy the Ugandan MiG-17 and MiG-21 fighter aircraft on the airfield itself, thereby inhibiting pursuit; and Group 5 to evacuate the hostages and see them into the waiting Hercules, which would either be refuelled on the spot or at Nairobi in neighbouring Kenya.

The degree of resistance which might be expected remained an unknown quantity. The IDF knew that the post-independence Ugandan Army was descended directly from the efficiently-run regiments of the King's African Rifles, and that their own men had given it more recent training. It was felt that, despite giving the appearance of having reverted to an armed mob, Amin's troops might put up a very stiff fight. Due allowance had to be made for heavy casualties and with this in mind a Boeing 707, equipped as a

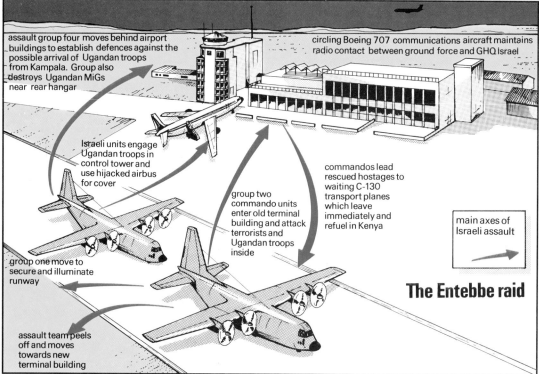

assault group four moves behind airport buildings to establish defences against the possible arrival of Ugandan troops from Kampala. Group also destroys Ugandan MiGs near rear hangar

circling Boeing 707 communications aircraft maintains radio contact between ground force and GHQ Israel

Israeli units engage Ugandan troops in control tower and use hijacked airbus for cover

group two commando units enter old terminal building and attack terrorists and Ugandan troops inside

commandos lead rescued hostages to waiting C-130 transport planes which leave immediately and refuel in Kenya

group one move to secure and illuminate runway

assault team peels off and moves towards new terminal building

main axes of Israeli assault

The Entebbe raid

Above left: Israeli military vehicles drive out of a Hercules transport. Mobility on the ground was an essential feature of the Entebbe operation. Above: Israeli paratroopers in training dismount at speed from a Hercules. It was the elite qualities of Israel's best troops that made the raid on Entebbe possible.

into the leading Hercules with a view to confusing the Ugandans during the first vital few minutes. A rehearsal of the raid took place during the evening of Friday, 2 July, using a model, and at 1530 hours the following afternoon the four Hercules transports took off in succession from Sharm el Sheikh at the southern tip of the Sinai peninsula, followed by the two 707s. By 1600 hours all elements of the raiding force were airborne.

Their route took them south down the middle of the Red Sea. They flew at high altitude without attracting undue attention in either the Egyptian or Saudi Arabian radar stations. For most of their journey, however, they would be flying close to the Sudan and in the normal course of events they would be at high risk from the moment they made the necessary alteration in course to the southwest. On this occasion, however, luck was running with them, for the previous day an abortive coup in the Sudan had led to all but one of the country's radar installations being closed down, and that presented little threat. The aircraft droned on across Africa, their crews more concerned about the prospect of the bad weather known to be developing in the vicinity of Lake Victoria than the possibility of Sudanese intervention. Some way short of the objective, the hospital 707 peeled off *en route* to head for Nairobi.

The lynch-pin of Shomron's plan lay in landing the first Hercules directly behind the scheduled British cargo flight, as the latter would not only absorb the attention of the Ugandan radar operators but also mask the noise made by the Israeli aircraft. The timing had to be exact, and it was. Seven hours after take-off, the Israeli force was approaching Entebbe through rain-laden skies, listening to the British captain acknowledging the control tower's instructions. Shomron's C-130 slotted in behind the freighter, its pilot imagining that he would have to make a difficult instrument landing. As altitude was lost, however, the rain stopped and Entebbe airport lay brilliantly illuminated ahead.

The assault begins

Immediately on touch-down the Hercules' legendary short-landing capability was put to good use. The aircraft slowed down and the runway group tumbled out in sequence, taking with them alternative lights in case the Ugandans turned off their own landing system. As it transpired, there was no need for these as the radar operators had not spotted the intruder and no alarm had been raised; for this mistake they were promptly shot by the enraged and humiliated Idi Amin.

The Hercules rolled on towards a darker area of the airport and while the British freighter taxied towards its bay, the Mercedes and two Land Rovers, containing the group which was to assault the old terminal, were driven down the ramp and set off for their objective.

The assault group was led by Netanyahu, who travelled in the Mercedes. It seemed that the Ugandans were not altogether taken in by the deception plan, for 100 metres from the terminal two sentries orderd the car to stop at gun-point. Netanyahu and another officer opened fire with silenced pistols, hitting one of the men, and the group drove on to within 50 metres of the building. From this point the Israeli commandos went in on foot. The hostages were all lying down in the main hall and many were

Above inset: Lieutenant-Colonel Jonathan Netanyahu, a young paratroop officer with a distinguished service record, was the only member of the raiding party killed during the operation.

hospital aircraft, would fly directly to Nairobi, Kenya – one of the few African countries friendly to Israel – while the raid was in progress. Simultaneously, a second 707 would circle Entebbe and act as a flying communications link with General Headquarters in Israel. The raid was to be commanded by General Shomron himself, while the all-important task of seizing the old terminal building and releasing the hostages would be the responsibility of Lieutenant-Colonel Jonathan Netanyahu, a young, dashing and resourceful paratroop officer who had already distinguished himself during the Six-Day and Yom Kippur Wars.

Shomron was only too aware that his plan contained no margin for error. It was, however, the only option open to Israel other than complete surrender to the terrorists' demands, and was therefore adopted. Intelligence sources continued to piece together a picture of the situation at Entebbe, while those who would actually be involved in the operation studied photographs and plans of the airport – which had been modernised by the Israelis during their days of friendship with Amin. As far as possible, everything was done to reduce the element of risk. It was known, for example, that Idi Amin had once arrived at Entebbe in a black Mercedes car escorted by a Land Rover, and similar vehicles were obtained and loaded asleep. Four terrorists had been left to guard them, one on the right, two on the left and one at the back of the hall; all were standing and were instantly identified by their weapons. Completely surprised, they were quickly killed and the assault wave swept on up the stairs, having been warned by the hostages that there were more terrorists and Ugandan troops on the floor above. Orders were that if the Ugandans opened fire they were to be treated as an armed enemy, but otherwise they were to be permitted to escape or surrender; but for the terrorists there was no mercy. Many were shot dead at close quarters while still half-asleep. Altogether, 35 Ugandan soldiers and 13 terrorists were killed – including Böse and Kröcher-Tiedemann – during the operation. Some 60 Ugandan soldiers are believed to have escaped from the building.

Total victory

Seven minutes after the first Hercules landed the second touched down, followed by the third and the fourth. As the ramps were lowered, jeeps and personnel carriers sped across the tarmac to perform their allotted tasks. The group under Colonel Matan Vilnai assaulted the new terminal buiding, which was hastily abandoned by the Ugandans, 15 of whom surrendered and were locked inside a room after being disarmed.

Amin's troops seemed totally confused by events and incapable of mounting a coherent reaction. The only determined resistance came from the control tower, a burst of fire from which killed Netanyahu just outside the old terminal. Vilnai's unit quickly eliminated this centre of opposition with concentrated machine-gun and RPG fire.

Colonel Uri Orr's group was now free to set about embarking the hostages in the waiting Hercules. For various technical reasons Shomron was advised to defer refuelling until the force had reached Nairobi and, having obtained approval of this departure from

the original plan via the airborne command post circling overhead, he despatched the first of the transports, laden with hostages, at 2358 hours – at this point only a mere 57 minutes had passed since the raid had begun.

The team detailed to eliminate the Ugandan MiGs spent a lively few minutes with their machine guns, turning eight of them into balls of flame. In comparison, the anti-tank teams which had moved out towards the perimeter had a very dull time of it. No reinforcements, armoured or otherwise, appeared from the direction of Kampala. Shomron remained with the rearguard until the outposts were pulled in and at 0054 hours the last Hercules lifted off; as it did so, the Ugandans finally extinguished the runway lights.

In addition to Netanyahu, three hostages had been killed during the assault despite shouted warnings to keep down, and a small number of the raiders had been wounded. At Nairobi these were transferred to the hospital aircraft and, after being refuelled, the Israelis were on their way home by 0408 hours. By now, it could safely be assumed that airspace along the Sudanese border would not be available, so their route took them out over the Indian Ocean, round the Horn of Africa and up the Red Sea.

The arrival of the aircraft at Ben Gurion airport was accompanied by scenes unique in Israel's history. Crowds surged forward with gifts of flowers and champagne, there were tears of relief and joy for the released hostages, and the returned paratroopers were carried shoulder-high.

The Entebbe Raid will always remain a high point in the history of airborne forces, despite the fact that so many elements in the Israeli plan were interdependent and that good luck was virtually an essential ingredient. Such a venture could not even have been contemplated without troops and aircrew motivated and trained to a quite extraordinary degree.

Bryan Perrett

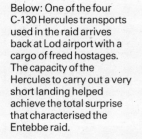

Below: One of the four C-130 Hercules transports used in the raid arrives back at Lod airport with a cargo of freed hostages. The capacity of the Hercules to carry out a very short landing helped achieve the total surprise that characterised the Entebbe raid.

Mogadishu

A victory for counter-terrorism

By the middle of 1977 the majority of Western governments had made inroads into the problems posed by urban terrorist organisations and had, in the process, formed specially trained groups to combat them. In the United Kingdom, for example, the Special Air Service (SAS) Regiment's Counter Revolutionary Warfare Team had developed weapons and techniques which were particularly suitable for use in situations where terrorists were holding their victims hostage, while in Germany the massacre of Israeli athletes at the Munich Olympic Games had led to the formation of the Grenzschutzgruppe 9 (GSG9) anti-terrorist squad under Ulrich Wegener.

It was in Germany that urban terrorism showed its most vicious face in the form of the ruthless Baader-Meinhof Red Army Fraction. By August 1977 most of the group's leaders were behind bars but a wealthy industrialist, Hanns-Martin Schleyer, was kidnapped and held to ransom as a hostage for their release. It was soon clear that the Bonn government was not going to submit to this demand and the terrorists decided to increase the pressure by hijacking a German passenger aircraft. Since Entebbe security had been tightened up at most of the world's major airports, but a careful study by the terrorists revealed that at Palma, Majorca, it was still possible for a hijack team to smuggle its weapons aboard an aircraft.

The Baader-Meinhof group had performed a number of services for Palestinian terrorists in the past – for example, their participation in the Entebbe hijack – and now it was the turn of their Palestinian colleagues to return the compliment. The hijacking team was to be led by Zohair Akache, a Palestinian with several killings already to his credit, who called himself 'Captain Mahmoud'.

At 1300 hours on 13 October Lufthansa Flight LH181 from Palma, Boeing 737 *Charlie Echo*, lifted smoothly from the tarmac under the control of Captain Jürgen Schumann, setting course for the southern coast of France and thence home. An hour later air traffic controllers heard Schumann report that his aircraft had been hijacked and that he had been ordered to fly to Rome. Simultaneously, the voice of Mahmoud broke in, announcing the *Charlie Echo* was now flying under his supervision.

The 737, fitted only with medium-range communications equipment, swung away to the southeast, contact with its base in Germany becoming more and more tenuous as the distance between the two opened up. In the end, all messages had to be relayed through other Lufthansa aircraft which happened to be in the area and were fitted with long-range radios. The terrorists now made known their demands, which included not only the release of the Baader-Meinhof

The Mogadishu hijacking

1. 1400 hours 13 October 1977 Lufthansa flight LH181 hijacked and ordered to Rome.
2. Aircraft refuelled at Rome airport and flies to Larnaca, Cyprus.
3. Terrorists then order flight to Bahrain and on to Dubai.
4. GSG-9 and SAS teams also fly to Dubai and recce the aircraft disguised as ground crew.
5. Aircraft then flown to Aden where empty fuel tanks force unauthorised landing. Pilot shot by terrorist leader.
6. After refuelling, co-pilot continues flight and lands at Mogadishu.
7. GSG-9 and SAS teams arrive in Mogadishu on 17 October and following morning storm plane killing three terrorists and successfully rescuing hostages.

route flown by hijacked aircraft

leaders, but also a £9 million ransom for the aircraft, its 79 passengers and its crew. In Rome, while the aircraft was being refuelled, Schumann managed to drop four cigars from the flight-deck window, a sign which was correctly interpreted as meaning that there were four terrorists aboard.

However, before the authorities could react, *Charlie Echo* was airborne again and heading for Cyprus. Permission to land at Nicosia was refused on the grounds that the airport had closed down, but the 737 touched down at Larnaca. Here, the terrorists were asked to give up their plan, first by the Cypriot foreign minister and then by the local representative of the Palestine Liberation Organisation. Mahmoud reacted wildly, yelling that he was not interested in anything the intermediaries had to say; he threatened to have the aircraft blown up on the spot unless it was refuelled instantly. His threat was taken very seriously and in due course *Charlie Echo* took off once more, landing briefly at Bahrain on the Gulf before making a further short hop as far as Dubai. This proved to be a critical mistake, for Dubai was one of the United Arab Emirates which had very close links with Britain; it was, moreover, one area of the world with which the SAS had an especially close association. In the meantime, however, the hostages were forced to stay put in the sweltering heat of the Gulf.

By now the German response was gathering momentum. A 30-strong GSG9 team had flown to Larnaca but arrived just as *Charlie Echo* was taking off. They returned to Germany via Turkey but when it became clear that Dubai was Mahmoud's intended destination a second GSG9 team under Wegener himself flew directly there, landing at first light on 15 October. Simultaneously, a senior member of the government had visited London to ask the British prime minister, James Callaghan, to use his influence to obtain permission for GSG9 to go into action on sovereign Dubai territory. It seems unlikely that the Germans were aware of the extent of SAS involve-

ment in Dubai, which went as far as the training of the Royal Guard by former SAS personnel, and they were certainly delighted when Callaghan offered the services of an SAS liaison team, consisting of Major Alastair Morrison and Sergeant Barry Davies. Assembling a crate of flash-bangs – harmless stun grenades – the two men set off at once by jet for Dubai.

Who should break the siege?

When they arrived they found that the local authorities had placed polite but strict curbs on GSG9's activities, but the British team was able to ease these so that the Germans, disguised as airport personnel, were at least able to make a detailed reconnaissance of the aircraft. The government of Dubai was arguing that its own troops should be used to break the siege, an insistence which found favour with neither the British nor the Germans. Both pointed out that while the Royal Guard's efficiency as an infantry unit was not in question, it had not received the specialist training necessary for anti-terrorist operations.

Meanwhile, Mahmoud had promised to blow up the aircraft and his hostages during the morning of 16 October unless his demands were met. The chief German negotiator, Hans-Jürgen Wischnewski, was in touch with him through the control tower radio but the terrorist leader was clearly in no mood for reasoned discussion. Then, with a mere 40 minutes left to the expiry of the deadline, the 737 took off.

At first its destination remained unknown. The aircraft was refused permission to land in Oman and it continued to fly southwest across Arabia's Empty Quarter in the direction of Aden, capital of the People's Democratic Republic of Yemen. Neither that country's Marxist rulers nor its legion of Soviet and East German advisers had any wish to become involved in the affair, so they also refused permission to land, blocking the main runway. Unfortunately, by now *Charlie Echo*'s fuel tanks were almost dry and Schumann was forced to make the best landing he

Previous page: Ulrich Wegener, the commander of GSG9, expresses his satisfaction after the successful completion of the mission to free the hostages of the Mogadishu hijacking. GSG9 had been specifically created for this type of operation after the botched handling of the Munich Olympics hostage-taking in 1972.

Below: Officials pick up the body of the captain of the hijacked Lufthansa flight, Jürgen Schumann, from the tarmac at Mogadishu. Schumann (inset left) was shot by the terrorist leader, Zohair Akache, after he had allegedly communicated with the authorities during a refuelling stop at Aden, and his body was thrown out of the plane when it reached its final destination. Insert above right: One of the terrorists crouches in a doorway of the aircraft.

could. Worried that the nose-wheel had sustained damage in the process, he disembarked briefly to carry out a cursory inspection, and then climbed back aboard. Screaming that the Captain had been communicating secretly with the authorities, Mahmoud forced him to kneel and then shot him dead.

Wegener and his team, accompanied by the two SAS men, had flown on from Dubai but the South Yemen government adamantly refused to let them land, even when offered German economic aid, and they were forced to divert to Jiddah in Saudi Arabia.

Next morning, 17 October, Mahmoud made co-pilot Jürgen Vietor fly the refuelled *Charlie Echo* to Mogadishu, the capital of Somalia. Advised of this development, Wegener and his team flew there from Jiddah, joined after dusk by the original GSG9 team which, after first returning to Germany, had been standing by in Crete waiting for the situation to stabilise again.

If it was at all possible, the Germans wanted to secure the release of the hostages and the aircraft without recourse to violence and they had brought the ransom money with them in a large box. As the dialogue between the control tower and Mahmoud progressed, however, the terrorist leader once more threatened to blow up the 737 unless all his demands were met, and to emphasise the point he had Schumann's body thrown onto the tarmac to lie under the African sun. To buy time, the negotiators told Mahmoud that 11 terrorists held in German gaols would be released and flown out to Mogadishu. Mahmoud responded by announcing that, pending the arrival of the prisoners from Germany, his deadline would be put back to 0230 hours on 18 October. In the meantime, he warned the Germans not to be devious and told them not to make dangerous comparisons with the Entebbe rescue the previous year.

There was now no alternative but to storm the plane and at the personal request of German Chancellor Helmut Schmidt, President Siad Barre of Somalia authorised GSG9 to take whatever steps were necessary. The two SAS men, Major Morrison and Sergeant Davies, were still with Wegener, and helped him draw up the plan for the attack.

The assault began at 0150 hours on 18 October. While the two hijackers on the flight deck were engaged in conversation by the control tower, the Anglo-German assault team, their faces blackened, moved stealthily out towards the aircraft. Then, at 0207 hours, an ignited oil drum was rolled in front of the aircraft, distracting the attention of the terrorists in the cabin. At the same time, the attackers placed stepladders up to the emergency doors. Morrison and Davies burst into the aircraft from both sides of the fuselage and tossed their flash-bangs into the interior. The German commandos surged past into the flat silence created by the detonation of the stun grenades, shouting at the hostages to keep down. The ensuing firefight lasted for eight minutes. Inside the main cabin the Germans engaged one gunman forward and another aft, hitting both. Mahmoud appeared in the door to the flightdeck and was shot down, as was the fourth terrorist. At the end, Mahmoud and two of his comrades lay dead or dying, while the fourth member of their team, a woman, was seriously wounded. One commando, a stewardess and four passengers were slightly injured. The interior of the cabin had been doused with aviation fuel and alcohol by the hijackers prior to the attack, but miraculously this had not ignited during the fighting.

There was a bloody postscript to the hijacking, however. Within hours of the successful freeing of the hostages, the imprisoned leaders of the Baader-Meinhof gang were found dead in their cells. In revenge those members of the gang still at liberty murdered Hanns-Martin Schleyer, the kidnapped industrialist. His body was found in the boot of a car, six days after the gun battle at Mogadishu.

Yet none of this detracted from the technical success of the GSG9/SAS operation. Mogadishu demonstrated in the most dramatic way possible that international terrorism could be met and defeated by international means. **Bryan Perrett**

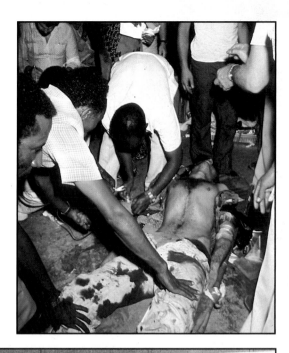

Right: One of the hijackers lies dying after being riddled with bullets during the assault on the airliner by the GSG9 and SAS force. Three of the four terrorists involved were killed.

Below: The 79 passengers arrive back in Frankfurt after their ordeal as hostages. Bottom: Ulrich Wegener (centre) and the West German minister of the interior inspect the GSG9 group on its return from Mogadishu. The operation made GSG9 German national heroes overnight.

Key Weapons

ELECTRONIC WARFARE:

THE AIR WAR

One of the most important aspects of modern air combat is electronic warfare. In the 1930s and 1940s, the availability of radar and reliable radio sets provided a means to use airpower more effectively through detection of enemy aircraft, control of interceptors, navigation and the more accurate delivery of munitions by bombers. These first-generation avionics (as airborne electronics are termed) were so effective that by 1945 no major air force could operate without them. The spread of avionics naturally stimulated the development of electronic counter-measures (ECM).

Radar functions by the transmission of a beam of electro-magnetic waves into space and the reflection of any part of that signal by an object in its path. The reflected signal can be used to gauge distance, bearing or location, depending on the role of the particular radar system. But the accuracy of this information can be undermined by deliberately distorting the returning radar 'echo'. This 'active' ECM or 'jamming' is intended either to blot out the signal completely or to provide a false one in its place.

Active ECM equipment takes a number of forms, one of the most common being a device that creates electronic noise. This is intended to swamp the enemy receiver to the point where it can no longer discern the true signal (the effect of static on a domestic radio set is a good example of the same principle). Noise jammers are very effective and can be divided into two types: the spot jammer and the barrage jammer. Spot jammers operate against a precise and fixed radio/radar frequency while barrage jammers cover a spread of such frequencies. The spot jammer allows the maximum jamming power to be brought to bear on a specific target; the barrage jammer can be used against a range of targets or a 'frequency agile' system (one which can transmit on a number of frequencies and change rapidly from one to another).

Another type of active ECM is the deception jammer. This normally consists of a receiver which takes in the enemy radar transmission and amplifies it, transmitting it back at an artificially delayed time. This creates a false target at a range or position different from that of the real target. A development of this system is the reverberation jammer which creates numerous false targets.

Passive ECM systems are those which do not involve the emission of a signal. Most warplanes are now fitted with a simple warning receiver which alerts the crew if the aircraft has been detected by a hostile radar. But the simplest and most widely used passive counter-measures technique is the dropping of 'chaff'. This usually comprises coated glass-fibre needles cut to a length which is a proportion of the wavelength of the radar at which it is aimed. Clumps of chaff are dropped from the aircraft and, on hitting the airflow, blossom into a radar-reflecting cloud. The radar set focuses on this cloud and sees what appears to be a large number of targets creating echoes, thus obscuring the actual target aircraft. Chaff was first used in World War II – when it was known in English as Window (the Japanese called it *Giman-shi* which means 'deceiving paper') – by Japanese bombers during May 1943 over Guadalcanal, with devastating results. It remains today an extremely potent but simple counter-measure.

The nature of the electronic warfare installation an aircraft carries is dependent on the size of the particular airframe and also the type of hostile emitter it is

intended to counter. Large aircraft such as the American B-52 and B-1 bombers or the Soviet Tu-22M bomber carry a 'suite' of such equipment internally. Such installations are multi-functional and feature a range of active jammers tailored to specific threats (such as the Northrop AN/ALQ-155 or the ITT ALQ-172 against radar), reception equipment to warn of the appearance of hostile signals (the ALR-46 in the B-52), extensive computer control to speed and maximise the system's response, and chaff dispensers (AN/ALE-24 or AN/ALE-27, for example). The latest development in counter-measures is the introduction of an airframe which is designed to give the least possible radar image (known as the radar cross-section) and is built incorporating radar absorbent materials – the 'stealth' technology. The sophisticated ECM systems built into modern aircraft require specialised operators and the electronic warfare operator has become a vital member of the crew of many aircraft.

Not all electronic warfare systems are defensive; all the emissions from the electronic apparatus used

Top: A US unmanned reconnaisance aircraft mounted on top of an ST-71. Above: Two drones beneath a B-52. Above right: A Tornado prototype P02 with a West German EL/73 deception jammer under the wing. Right: The Marconi Skyshadow ECM pods on this Tornado are carried on the outer wing pylons. Below right: A US Marine Sea Cobra with an ALE-29A chaff dispenser mounted above the weapons pylon. Below: Inside the Hughes APG-63 radar of an F-15A. Previous page: Harrier GR Mk3s carrying ARI 18223 radar on the tail-fin and projecting rearwards, operating in front and rear arcs.

by modern aircraft and other weapons systems reveal their position, and this can be exploited by a potential attacker. Airborne early warning, maritime patrol and anti-submarine warfare aircraft are now fitted with electronic support measures (ESM) equipment comprising sensitive receivers designed to pick up radiations emanating from other ships and aircraft and to provide a fix on them as a back-up to conventional search radars.

Many electronic warfare items can be easily seen on current warplanes. For example, the box-like feature on the tail rudder-fin of many RAF aircraft houses the antenna for a radar warning system – the Marconi ARI 18223 on the Jaguar and the Harrier, or the similar ARI 18228 on the Phantom and the Buccaneer. Examples of podded jammers include the Marconi Sky Shadow to be seen on Tornado aircraft and the widely used American-produced Westinghouse AN/ALQ-101 and -131 units. These systems are now being given digital processors in an attempt to achieve higher performance and greater flexibility. Chaff systems are slightly less visible – for example, the F-16's AN/ALE is mounted internally – but the French Alkan counter-measure dispersal pods are carried externally on the Mirage and the Jaguar.

There are also either in production or in operation dedicated electronic warfare platforms and electronic intelligence (ELINT) aircraft. ELINT aircraft are some of the most secret electronic warfare machines of the present day. In a situation of 'Cold War' the eavesdropping performed by these aircraft is vitally important. As well as listening-in to the enemy's communications traffic, ELINT aircraft are used to build up a library of knowledge on the enemy's radar equipment and frequencies. This can be vital information when designing jammers and a useful source of intelligence about enemy operational procedures and dispositions. Only a few air forces currently have an ELINT capability, and the largest capacity is naturally enough in the possession of the United

States and the Soviet Union. Both the USAF and the USN operate such aircraft as the Boeing RC-135 family and the Lockheed U-2 and TR-1, while the Navy flies the Lockheed EP-3E Orion from its land bases and the Douglas EA-3B Skywarrior from its carriers. The Soviet Navy operates the Antonov An-12 Cub-B, and the Tupolev Tu-16 Badger-D and -F in an ELINT mode. The Soviet Air Force uses the two Tu-16 models. Within Nato, aside from the American systems, both the RAF and the West German Navy are known to have ELINT planes, flying, respectively, the Nimrod R1 and modified Breguet Atlantics. Further afield, both Israel and Japan are also known to have such a capacity.

Perhaps even more exclusive are the dedicated electronic warfare aircraft, machines whose primary function is that of electronic jamming. They are especially useful for stand-off jamming, which is the blanketing of all significant radar in a specific area, valuable for covering fighter strikes. American forces

Top left: This USAF F-4C has an AN/ALQ-119 ECM pod mounted on the inner wing pylon. Developed to protect strike aircraft, the AN/ALQ-119 is both a noise jammer and a deception jammer. Above: The TU-95 Bear has a Bee Hind radar in the tail, above the rear gunner's position. Left: The AV-8B Harrier carries American electronics and an internal chaff dispenser. It can carry an AN/ALQ-164 ECM pod.

Centre right: Made by Electronica SpA of Italy, this ELT/460 noise jammer is designed for installation on high performance ground attack aircraft and fighters. Right: The ELT/555 airborne deception jammer, here carried under the wing of an MB-339K, is also produced by Electronica SpA. It is designed for use against SAM, AAM and AA radars. The ELT/555 can be mounted on the MiG-21, as well as on the Phantom, Mirage and other Nato aircraft.

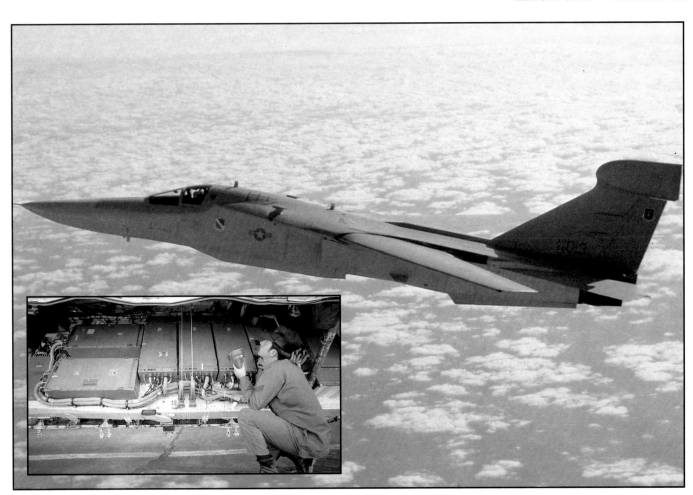

Above: The EF-111A carries its ALQ-99E jamming transmitters in the weapons bay and the fin-tip pod contains the receiver and antennae.
Insert: The electrical system of the EF-111A that powers the jammers.

operate the Grumman EF-11A Raven in the USAF and the Grumman EA-6B Prowler in the USN and USMC, both using the AN/ALQ-99 jamming system. The Soviet Navy uses the Tupolev Tu-16 Badger-H and -J; the Soviet Air Force the Yakovlev Yak-28 Brewer-E and the Mil Mi-4 Hound-C and Mi-8 Hip-J and -K helicopters in the electronic jamming role.

The impact of electronic warfare cannot be overestimated as it has played a major role in three conflicts since 1945. During the American bombing of North Korea between 1951-53, World War II jammers such as the AN/APQ-9 barrage type and the AN/APT-2 and AN/APT-5 spot types were used to jam North Korean radar which was proving effective against B-29 bombing raids. The Vietnam War was the scene of major US efforts to counteract the radar-guided SA-2 Guideline missile and its Fansong radar. The Hughes ALQ-71 pod was built in response to the threat posed by these Vietnamese AA measures. During the B-52 raids of December 1972, Republic F105G Wild Weasels – aircraft designed to identify hostile radars and launch anti-radiation missiles against them – were used in conjunction with large amounts of chaff to defeat the SAM defences of Hanoi and Haiphong. The effectiveness of these tactics can be shown by the results. The USAF flew over 700 sorties during an 11-day period between 18-29 December 1972. An average of 64 B-52s appeared over the Hanoi area every night except Christmas Day and although between 750 and 1000 SA-2s were launched at them, only 15 B-52s were brought down.

Most recently, electronic warfare showed its effectiveness in the Beqa'a Valley in Lebanon. On 9 June 1982, Israeli planes attacked Syrian SA-6 batteries, destroying 17 and severely damaging two more. Remotely piloted vehicles were used in conjunction with E-2 Hawkeye surveillance aircraft to ascertain the radar frequencies of the Syrian weapons. Then Shrike air-launched and Wolf ground-launched anti-radiation missiles were fired at the SAM batteries. This successful operation allowed the Israelis to achieve air supremacy over Lebanon and demonstrates the importance of effective electronic warfare in any future conflict.

Below: The Atlantic ATL-2 is the latest development in the Atlantic family of aeroplanes. It is well-equipped with electronic warfare equipment, with ECM pods on the wings and a radar detector carried internally; the crew of 12 contains an ECM-ESM operator.

Right: The Italian-made ELT/156 warns when the aircraft is illuminated by search or tracking radar.
Below: The Grumman EA-6B is a four-seat variant of the A-6 Intruder with five AN/ALQ-99 jamming pods under the wings and fuselage.

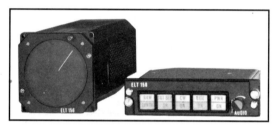

New allies, old enemies
The superpowers adapt to change in Southeast Asia

The fall of Saigon in April 1975 (below: an NVA soldier on the roof of the former US embassy) altered the balance of power in Southeast Asia. The US feared for the stability of its remaining friends in the region (above: meeting in Manila in 1981, left to right, men only, US Vice-President Bush, Vice President Malik of Indonesia, Prime Minister Prem Tinsulanonda of Thailand, Prime Minister Lee Kuan Yew of Singapore, and President Marcos of the Philippines).

The frantic helicopter-borne evacuation of the US embassy in Saigon in April 1975, was only the dramatically televisual symbol of a realignment of strategic relations in Southeast Asia that had been under way since the visit of US presidential adviser Henry Kissinger to Peking in July 1971. The United States had by that time recognised the futility of its massive commitment of ground forces to an Asian war it had not the slightest hope of winning.

President Richard Nixon drew the necessary conclusion that the diplomatic pursuit of adjustments to the regional balance of power would provide a more economical and effective alternative to the heavy, vote-losing casualties which the United States was suffering in Vietnam. Having belatedly recognised the significance of the decade-old Sino-Soviet split, the US jettisoned that part of its Cold War ideological baggage labelled 'monolithic communist bloc', and sought through improved relations with the People's Republic of China to limit the damage that might be caused to US interests by a communist victory in Indochina. The rapprochement with

Peking had the added advantage of bringing into play a regional balance to the Soviet Union, which would have implications for the global superpower confrontation.

The results of these developments were that, first of all, mainland Southeast Asia could be seen more objectively as fundamentally peripheral to American interests; secondly, the theory of promiscuously falling dominoes, which had provided the public rationale for the whole US military involvement in Southeast Asia, could be discreetly abandoned; and thirdly, China shifted the emphasis of its policy towards the region from one of excluding US influence to one of opposition to penetration of the area by the Soviet Union.

Having burnt its fingers in Vietnam, and reassured by its new relationship with Peking, the US seemed content, during the mid-1970s, to rely upon a security axis anchored on Japan, and stretching from South Korea through Taiwan to the Philippines and Indonesia. The focus of this axis was in the northeast, but it also provided the United States with allies and bases

in the southeast region from which secure communications between the Pacific and Indian Oceans could be guaranteed.

The stability of US influence in Southeast Asia was dependent, however, on the continued tenure of power by regimes favourable to the West in the Philippines, Indonesia, Malaysia and Thailand. In the Philippines, the Americans' main ally in the region and site of an important US Seventh Fleet base at Subic Bay, the government of President Ferdinand Marcos in Manila faced mounting opposition in the late 1970s and early 1980s, not only from the guerrilla forces of the communist New People's Army and the Muslim Moro National Liberation Front, but also from liberal opinion in the urban centres. The martial law regime established in 1972, which gave Marcos almost dictatorial powers, was severely shaken in 1983 by the violent protests which followed in the wake of the murder at Manila airport of leading opposition politician, Benigno Aquino, as he returned to the Philippines from exile in the United States. Since the Philippines could rely on the United States for its external defence, it could devote its own defence effort to counter-insurgency with a reasonable chance of holding firm, but it was more difficult for the Americans to help Marcos handle the potentially explosive urban liberal discontent.

Indonesia, though not directly linked by treaty to the United States, is also an important factor in American perceptions of the Southeast Asian power equation. The regime of President Suharto, established in 1966 in reaction to an attempted communist coup, is dominated by the military, itself predominantly Javanese. There is widespread disaffection with the Suharto government within Indonesia, espe-

cially in the outlying islands of the far-flung Indonesian chain. The persistence of the Fretilin guerrilla movement in East Timor is an example of the internal security problems which Indonesia might potentially face on a wider scale in the future. The islands of Indonesia straddle some of the most important waterways in the world, and despite recent criticism in the US Congress of alleged human rights violations by the Suharto regime, the United States remains vitally interested in its continued stability.

Malaysia, like the Philippines, is essentially concerned with problems of internal security, and in this respect its armed forces are amongst the most experienced in the region. Apart from the period of Confrontation with Indonesia during the 1960s, the Malaysian armed forces have been engaged in an almost constant campaign against the guerrilla forces of the Malaysian communists since the end of World War II. Although the communist threat has been negligible since the end of the Emergency in 1960, by which time British forces had successfully suppressed a large-scale communist guerrilla campaign, elements of the communist forces remain active along the Thai border.

A more serious internal security problem has been faced by Thailand, which confronts a communist insurgency, allied with ethnic minorities in the northeast of the country, and backed by the Vietnamese as a counter to Thai support for the anti-Vietnamese forces operating in Kampuchea. The Thai military government finds itself under pressure from all sides: from Vietnam, from its Association of South East Asian Nations (Asean) allies who would prefer a compromise settlement with Vietnam, and from its internal enemies, and is undoubtedly the weakest link

Right: Muslim guerrillas in the south of the Philippines. Most of the West's allies in Southeast Asia were troubled to some degree by insurgent movements, provoked by ethnic differences, poverty, or the corruption of those in power.

Below: The assassination of Philippine opposition leader Benigno Aquino at Manila airport on 21 August 1983. Aquino's body is lifted into an airport security (AVSECOM) vehicle as other security officers (right) menace the journalist photographing the event from inside the aircraft. On the left lies the body of Rolando Galman, shot by the security forces immediately after the killing of Aquino. According to the official version of events, Galman was the assassin, but he is widely believed to have been framed for a murder actually carried out by the security forces themselves.

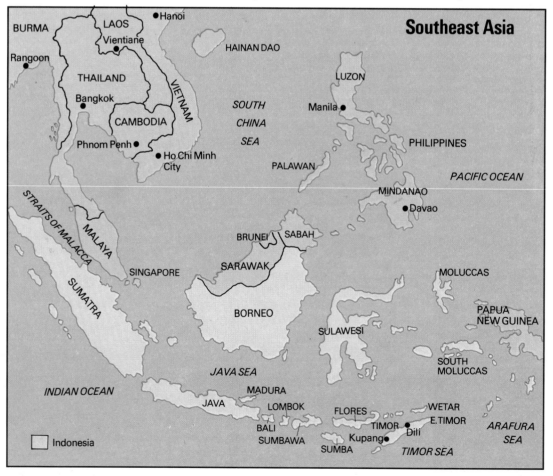

Southeast Asia

in the chain of pro-Western countries in the region.

The most serious regional conflicts after 1975 occurred, however, as a result of the pattern of power established by the American withdrawal and communist victory in Indochina. Vietnam, reunited and militarily strengthened after the collapse of the Saigon regime, reasserted its traditional claim to leadership in Indochina. The latent conflict between the Vietnamese and the Khmer of Kampuchea (formerly Cambodia) re-emerged almost immediately after the fall of Saigon and Phnom Penh to the communists, and border clashes developed to a serious scale.

Asean, which includes Thailand, Singapore, Malaysia, Indonesia and the Philippines, called for the establishment of a 'zone of peace, freedom and neutrality' in Southeast Asia, but the Vietnamese, who regarded Asean as a tool of the United States, rejected this proposal, countering with the offer of a series of bilateral treaties of friendship.

Soviet influence

While these negotiations dragged on, the confrontation between Vietnam and Kampuchea, which was backed by China, became increasingly serious, and Vietnam turned in 1978 to the Soviet Union, hoping by this means to counter the threat of Chinese intervention in support of the Khmer Rouge. In June 1978, Vietnam became a full member of the Council of Mutual Economic Assistance (Comecon), the East European equivalent of the EEC, and in November 1978, Vietnam and the USSR signed a Treaty of Friendship and Cooperation. Reassured by the security clauses of this agreement, Vietnam moved swiftly against the Khmer Rouge, invading Kampuchea and installing a pro-Hanoi government there in January 1979. China reacted by mounting an indecisive punitive invasion of the northern border provinces of Vietnam in February-March 1979, provoking Hanoi actively to encourage the departure of its ethnic Chinese minority. Soon the steady stream of 'boat people' had transformed a localised conflict into a major international issue.

The shock-waves of these events spread throughout the region, and introduced a potential split in the ranks of Asean, between those states, such as Singapore and Thailand, which aligned themselves with China and feared Vietnamese expansionism, and those, such as Malaysia and Indonesia, which having large Chinese minorities themselves tended to be more suspicious of the long-term growth of Chinese influence in the region.

This essentially regional conflict provided the justification for the continued involvement of external powers in the area. The Soviet Union, in particular, profited by extracting the use of military bases on Vietnamese territory as the price of its continued support. Soviet vessels, such as the aircraft carrier *Minsk* and its supporting units, made regular use of the American-built facilities at Cam Ranh Bay, while Soviet Tu-95D reconnaissance aircraft, based at Da Nang, were able to monitor naval movements throughout the region.

The end of US combat involvement in Southeast Asia has clearly not led, therefore, to a reduction in superpower involvement in the region. The United States, the Soviet Union and China remain extensively committed in Southeast Asia, although in a new pattern dictated by local conflicts. **Robin Corbett**

Taking to the hills

Resistance to Indonesia in East Timor

The April 1974 left-wing coup in Portugal set off a chain-reaction of decolonisation which spread throughout Portugal's overseas empire. In Angola, Mozambique and Guinea-Bissau nationalist movements were in a position to take power and establish independent states. In the small Portuguese colony of East Timor, however, no such national liberation movement existed to which the Portuguese could hand over power, and the creation of Timorese political parties was the first effect of the ripples spreading outwards from Lisbon.

The fundamental issue which divided the Timorese parties was that of whether or not an independent East Timor would be a viable proposition. The União Democrática de Timor (UDT) felt that continued, though independent, association with Portugal was the best solution, while the Associação Popular Democrática dos Timorenses (Apodeti) stood for full integration into neighbouring Indonesia as an autonomous province. The only party which called for immediate and total independence was the left-wing Frente Revolucionária Timorense de Libertação e Independência (Fretilin).

From the beginning, however, external forces showed an interest in the colony's future. As early as September 1974, President Suharto of Indonesia and Prime Minister Gough Whitlam of Australia were reported to have agreed, at a meeting in Java, that incorporation into Indonesia would be the most satisfactory solution. Discussions between Portugal, the UDT and Apodeti at a conference in Macao on 26–28 June 1975, led to an agreement on the gradual decolonisation of East Timor, providing for continued Portuguese sovereignty until October 1978, with elections to a People's Assembly to be held before that, in October 1976.

The UDT, however, was at the same time holding talks with Indonesia, which was increasingly hostile to the possibility of an independent East Timor, fearing that it might fall under the control of Fretilin, which the Indonesians regarded as a communist organisation. On 6 August 1975, the president of the UDT declared: 'We are realists. If we want to be independent we must follow the Indonesian political

Above: A Fretilin patrol on the border with West Timor shortly before President Suharto (below) ordered his troops to invade. Well-armed with G3 and Mauser rifles from stocks of the former Portuguese garrison, Fretilin was able to crush its internal opponents during a short, fierce civil war (right).

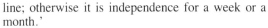

line; otherwise it is independence for a week or a month.'

Internal rivalries spilled over into full-scale civil war when the UDT staged a coup on 11 August 1975. Fighting broke out between Fretilin, which was relatively well armed with equipment supplied by the local Portuguese garrison, and the UDT, which was supported by Apodeti and the smaller Kota and Trabalhista parties. Accepting that they were powerless to control the situation, the Portuguese began to organise an evacuation of their forces, and by early September, after a period of fierce street-fighting, Fretilin was in complete command of the capital, Dili, and claimed to be in control of the whole colony. Having established its own administration, Fretilin proclaimed the independence of the Democratic Republic of East Timor on 28 November 1975.

Indonesia, whose province of West Timor bordered the Portuguese colony, had been watching these developments with alarm, and there were several reports of troop concentrations along the border, although the Indonesians claimed their soldiers were only engaged in manoeuvres and road-building projects. Then, on 7 December 1975 a force of some 6000 Indonesian paratroopers, described officially as 'volunteers', invaded East Timor under cover of naval gunfire.

Fretilin resistance to the invasion was so strong that Indonesia was forced to send in a second wave of troops on 25 December in order to secure control of Dili. Withdrawing to the hills, Fretilin embarked on a guerrilla war against the Indonesian armed forces and claimed in January 1976 to retain control of some 80 per cent of the country.

The anti-Fretilin Timorese parties were meanwhile cooperating with the Indonesians, and formed a provisional government on 17 December 1975, led by Arnold dos Reis Araujo, a member of Apodeti. Early

in 1976, the Indonesians set up a 28-member representative council in East Timor, and on 31 May this council called on President Suharto to incorporate the ex-Portuguese colony into Indonesia. On 14 August Suharto duly proclaimed East Timor, renamed Loro Sae, Indonesia's 27th province.

Fighting continued, however, and the Indonesian forces seem to have acted with great brutality towards the local population, with even the vice-chairman of the provisional government, Francisco Xavier da Cruz, admitting in February 1976 that some 60,000 East Timorese had lost their lives since the UDT coup of August the previous year. A former Australian consul in East Timor, James Dunn, estimated in a report published in February 1977 that the Indonesian Army had massacred up to 100,000 Timorese after the invasion of 1975, including half of the former colony's 7000-strong Chinese community. Information on the situation in East Timor was limited, however, since the Indonesian authorities imposed a ban on all foreign journalists, and refused entry to the International Red Cross.

The international reaction

The international reaction to the Indonesian occupation of East Timor was uneven and contradictory. Portugal, for example, immediately cut all diplomatic links with Djakarta, and insisted that it retained sovereignty over East Timor. A report published in Lisbon in 1981, however, disclosed that Portuguese officials had indicated to Indonesia, at a meeting held in Hong Kong in June 1975, the willingness of Portugal's left-wing military rulers at that time to accept an incorporation of East Timor into Indonesia.

Australia, which had also apparently encouraged the Indonesian annexation of East Timor, nevertheless adopted a critical attitude towards the invasion. But an Australian Foreign Ministry report of June

1977 spoke of Indonesia's incorporation of the former Portuguese colony as an 'irreversible fact', and on 20 January 1978 Australia formally recognised East Timor to be a province of Indonesia. New Zealand has likewise supported Indonesian claims to East Timor, as have several of Indonesia's allies in the Association of South East Asian Nations (Asean).

The United Nations, on the other hand, consistently condemned Indonesia, and resolutions passed by the UN Trusteeship Committee, the General Assembly and the Security Council called for Indonesian withdrawal and a recognition of the right of self-determination of the people of East Timor.

Throughout 1976 and 1977 fighting continued, and while an Indonesian offer of an amnesty in August 1977 encouraged large numbers of Fretilin supporters to surrender, it also triggered off a power struggle within the organisation, which resulted in the replacement of Francisco Xavier do Amaral, president of both Fretilin and the Democratic Republic of East Timor, by the hard-line Nicolau dos Reis Lobato.

Isolated guerrillas

While Indonesia continued to claim that only a small, unimportant remnant of Fretilin fighters remained active, in fact the Indonesian Army mounted a major offensive in 1978, in an effort to force the Fretilin guerrillas into isolated areas and then to starve them into submission. The Indonesian offensive relied heavily upon locally recruited conscripts and militia, though the latter appear to have proved unreliable, often going over to the guerrillas with their weapons. The shock troops of the offensive were elite Indonesian commando units, however, and it was reported that tanks, napalm, heavy area-bombing and de-

foliants were being employed.

The offensive appears to have achieved a large degree of success and to have decimated the Fretilin leadership, Lobato himself being killed on 1 January 1979. All reports agree, however, that the civilian population were the worst sufferers, and thousands died of starvation. Indeed, comparison of the last official Portuguese census figures for East Timor, published in 1974, and figures published by Indonesia in November 1979, reveals a decline in population of over 130,000, to a total of 522,433.

By the early 1980s, it was widely believed that Fretilin resistance was more or less over and that Indonesian control was being consolidated. In fact, it now appears that during this period Fretilin was recovering under the new leadership of José Gusmão Sha Na Na, and that guerrilla activity persisted, though at a lower level of intensity.

By March 1983, secret negotiations between Fretilin and the Indonesian authorities had led to a ceasefire, which raised speculation that a political settlement might be possible. In August 1983, however, a 50-strong group of the Indonesian-organised Civil Guard, who according to some reports may have been former Fretilin guerrillas, ambushed 14 Indonesian soldiers and took to the hills. The attack provoked a massive response from the Indonesian Army. Up to 8000 men, including a large number of fresh reinforcements, were deployed in a renewed offensive.

In spite of its relative obscurity, the struggle for control of East Timor is potentially of great significance. The island of Timor lies astride the Straits of Ombai-Wetar, which provide a vital route for US nuclear missile submarines moving between the

Above: Local, poorly-armed militia units provided a back-up to regular Fretilin forces. This group, armed with Mausers and bows and arrows, is receiving instructions from a Fretilin officer at a road-block outside Dili during the civil war. Above right: The first Fretilin president of East Timor, Francisco Xavier do Amaral. Deposed by a more hard-line faction in 1977, he was later killed in a clash with Indonesian troops. Far right: Fretilin soldiers tend a wounded comrade.

Right: At a secret conference in March 1983, Indonesian officers (left) and Fretilin representatives negotiate a ceasefire agreement. An Indonesian offensive during 1978 severely mauled Fretilin forces, but after a period of reorganisation, guerrilla operations again provided a serious problem for the Indonesians during the early 1980s.

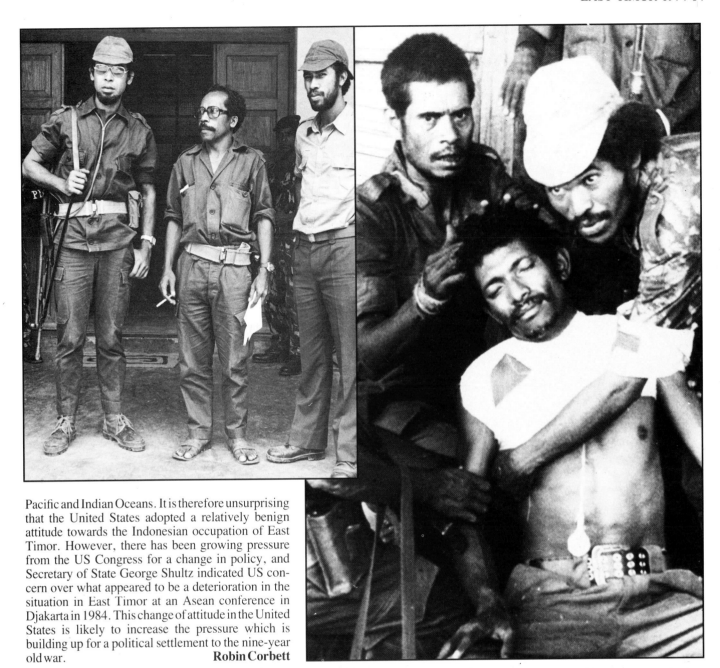

Pacific and Indian Oceans. It is therefore unsurprising that the United States adopted a relatively benign attitude towards the Indonesian occupation of East Timor. However, there has been growing pressure from the US Congress for a change in policy, and Secretary of State George Shultz indicated US concern over what appeared to be a deterioration in the situation in East Timor at an Asean conference in Djakarta in 1984. This change of attitude in the United States is likely to increase the pressure which is building up for a political settlement to the nine-year old war. **Robin Corbett**

The forgotten people

South Moluccan exiles turn to terror

After a bitter war of national liberation, the Netherlands East Indies achieved independence as the United States of Indonesia on 27 December 1949. Initially a confederal republic, Indonesia included within its territory the islands of South Molucca, the inhabitants of which had been converted to Christianity by the Dutch, in whose Royal Netherlands Indies Army (KNIL) many of them served.

Immediately after independence the Indonesian government made moves towards the establishment of a unitary state; this alarmed the Moluccans, who responded by proclaiming an independent Republic of the South Moluccas (Republik Maluku Selatan – RMS) on 25 April 1950. Indonesia, however, did not recognise the RMS and proceeded to incorporate the South Moluccas into a unitary Republic of Indonesia in May 1950. Scattered resistance was led by the president of the RMS, Dr Christian Sumotil.

Meanwhile, in Makassar, capital of the island of Sulawesi, Moluccan troops of the KNIL – which had not yet been disbanded – participated in an armed rebellion against the Indonesian government. The rebellion was suppressed, but the Moluccan troops who had participated in the rising then refused to be demobilised by the Dutch in Indonesia. Thus in 1951 they were transported with their families to the Netherlands, where they were demobilised and housed in temporary camps. The community of some 15,000 experienced enormous problems of assimilation, dreaming rather of a return to an independent South Moluccas.

Resistance to Indonesia in the South Moluccas effectively ended when Dr Sumotil was captured in 1963, but the growing militancy of young South Moluccans in the exiled community was revealed by the series of attacks upon Indonesian targets in the Netherlands which followed the execution of Dr Sumotil in 1966. In 1975, the Free South Moluccan Youth Organisation (Vrije Zuidmolukse Jongeren – VZJ) decided upon a strategy of violent action, and broke away from the moderate RMS 'government-in-exile' headed by Dr Jan Manusama. Following an unsuccessful attempt to kidnap Queen Juliana of the Netherlands, the VZJ mounted two attacks in December 1975 which brought it worldwide attention.

On 2 December, seven armed Moluccans hijacked a train near the village of Beilen, killing the driver. They took the passengers hostage and demanded to be flown to where they could join the Fretilin movement on East Timor. They also called for the release of all Moluccan prisoners in the Netherlands, and for talks on the independence of the South Moluccas, to be held under UN auspices.

Two days later, another group of six Moluccans occupied the Indonesian consulate-general in Amsterdam, taking a number of Dutch and Indonesian hostages. The intensity of South Moluccan bitterness was brutally shown on 4 December, when the train hijackers shot one of their hostages and threw his body out onto the railway tracks. Negotiations continued, however, and the hijackers gradually released all of their hostages, surrendering on 14 December, to be followed five days later by the group in the Indonesian consulate.

A second train hijack, this time coordinated with the occupation of a primary school, took place on 23 May 1977. The Rotterdam-Groningen express was halted near the village of Onnan by a group of nine armed Moluccans, who released about half of the 100 passengers, holding the rest as hostages. At the same time, four Moluccans entered the primary school in nearby Bovensmilde, taking about 100 children and five teachers prisoner. Police and troops sealed off the area, while the Moluccans made known their demands, which included the release of all South Moluccans imprisoned for earlier incidents, and for a Boeing 747 to be made ready at Schipol airport.

The terrorists threatened to kill their hostages, but the Dutch government ruled out any negotiations until all the children had been released. Meanwhile, three officers of the British SAS arrived in the Netherlands to advise the Dutch government on the sieges.

In spite of the release of the schoolchildren on 27 May, the Dutch government decided that it must end the sieges by force, and at dawn on 11 June 1977 Marines stormed the school and the train simultaneously. The troops released the remaining

Left: Indonesian troops advance past the bodies of supporters of Moluccan independence during the fighting which accompanied the incorporation of the Moluccas into Indonesia in 1950. Below: Young Moluccans in the Netherlands express their support for the terrorists in 1977, in front of the emblem of the South Moluccan Republic. None of these young people had ever seen the homeland of which they dreamed.

The assault on the hijacked train, 11 June 1977

The operation to free the 51 hostages began at 0453 hours with six F-104 Starfighters screaming in at treetop height, dropping smoke canisters and making repeated passes over the train in order to confuse the terrorists and mask the actual assault. Down below, a pink flare fired over the train gave the signal for the assault group of Dutch Marines to advance.

Giving repeated warnings over loud hailers for the hostages to remain calm and keep down, the troops rushed the train, spraying automatic fire into the driver's compartment, where they knew the Moluccan terrorists were concentrated. Within moments the front of the train was a bullet-riddled wreck, and six of the nine terrorists lay dead.

Blowing off the doors with plastic explosives, the Marines entered the train, searching from carriage to carriage for the remaining terrorists. The hostages, concentrated in the second and fourth compartments, had obeyed the instruction to stay down, but in the confusion of the battle, a 19-year-old girl and a 40-year-old man were killed in the crossfire as they stood up when the Marines burst in.

Within 10 minutes everything was over. The surviving hostages were taken to hospital, along with two injured terrorists and two wounded Marines. The train, peppered with bullet holes, was towed slowly away.

Below: The bullet-scarred train after the assault by Dutch Marines in which six terrorists and two hostages died.

Right: A masked terrorist keeps watch as hot food is delivered to the children taken hostage at Bovensmilde primary school in May 1977.

schoolteacher hostages without casualties, but at the train six South Moluccans and two hostages were killed. Over 5000 Moluccans attended the funeral of the dead terrorists on 14 June 1977, and rioting accompanied the trial of the remaining terrorists.

In a further incident on 13 March 1978, three Moluccans took 71 hostages in government offices in Drenthe, near Assen, and demanded the release of 21 Moluccans who had been imprisoned for previous attacks. Five passers-by were wounded and one hostage shot dead. The siege ended the next day with an assault by specially-trained Dutch Marines.

The Dutch government acted decisively during each of these incidents, and subsequent prison sentences were heavy. The Netherlands have, however, shown great sympathy for the underlying causes of Moluccan terrorism, and the government has acted to improve housing conditions, employment opportunities and education facilities. The Dutch have also established an agreement with Indonesia, whereby Moluccans are encouraged to develop links with relations remaining in the Moluccas, and given financial assistance to return there to live. Former leaders of the VZJ have also visited Indonesia, and have spoken of the need to forget the sterile dream of independence, and for Moluccans to return home in order to help overcome the underdevelopment of their homeland. **Robin Corbett**

Muslims and Maoists

Guerrilla war in the Philippines

Ferdinand Marcos was elected president of the Philippines in 1965, ruling by decree under a state of martial law from September 1972. Over the years charges of corruption and electoral malpractice grew more insistent against his regime, culminating in the worldwide criticism directed at Marcos after the murder of Benigno Aquino, a leading opposition politician, as he arrived at Manila airport in August 1983.

But the most serious threat to President Marcos's power has come from guerrilla wars being waged by the Moro National Liberation Front (MNLF) in the south of the country and the Maoist New People's Army (NPA) in the north. Initially it was the Moro rebellion which posed the greater threat.

The original Spanish colonists of the Philippines discovered the Moros, a fiercely independent Muslim people, on the islands of Mindanao and the Sulu archipelago. The Moros looked traditionally to the Malays to the southwest, with whom they had cultural and economic links, and their animosity towards the north was intensified when the Christianised Filipinos served as willing auxiliaries of the Spanish in the long and vicious wars during which Spain sought to subjugate the Muslim sultanates of the south.

The Moro wars continued intermittently from 1578 until 1898, when the Spanish-American War led to the replacement of Spain by the US as the colonial power in the Philippines. This change left unsettled, however, the question of whether, and on what basis, the Muslim south would be incorporated into the new American possession.

Faced by large-scale Philippine guerrilla opposition on Luzon, the United States initially adopted a policy of non-interference towards the Moros, being unwilling to provoke further armed opposition. After

1901, however, when the Philippine-American War ended, America gradually increased its presence in the south, instituting direct rule with the aim of its total integration into the Philippines. This aim, which received the enthusiastic support of Philippine nationalists, was seen by the Moros as a threat not only to their political autonomy, but also to their religion.

The result was large-scale fighting, in which poorly armed and unorganised Muslims faced an increasingly numerous and well equipped enemy. The initial rebellion having been ruthlessly suppressed, the United States adopted a policy of divide and rule, subsidising friendly Muslim leaders, and pursuing the aim of assimilation by means of a modern, Americanised education system.

The limited self-government granted to the Philippines in 1935 merely meant the arrival of new Philippine administrators for the Moros, along with growing numbers of Christian settlers into the relatively underpopulated south, attracted by fertile land, rich mineral deposits and exploitable timber reserves.

The significance of Philippine independence in 1946 was likewise limited for the Moros, who continued to experience semi-colonial rule from Manila. Though there were isolated uprisings during the 1950s, the post-independence period was one of general retreat by the Muslims, faced with the growing pressure of large-scale Christian migration from the north, and a regime totally unsympathetic to their problems. By the early 1970s, the population balance in whole provinces of the traditionally Muslim south had shifted in favour of the Christians, and was in danger of doing so in several more.

Added to the inroads of what the Muslims saw as

Above: Armed with American World War II-vintage Garand rifles and MI carbines, a group of Muslim guerrillas fords a stream while on patrol. The Bangsa Moro Army, based amongst the Muslim population of the southern Philippines, posed a serious threat to the regime of President Marcos during the mid-1970s.

Top right: Demonstrators in Manila call for a boycott of the May 1984 parliamentary elections. Urban protest against the rule of President Ferdinand Marcos (right) grew dramatically after the murder of opposition politician Benigno Aquino in August 1983.

Christian land-grabbing, the strong centralist government of President Marcos, even more powerful under martial law, was seen as a direct threat to their way of life. Based on tribalism and Islam, Moro society had in many ways cut itself off from the social and economic advance being experienced by the Philippines generally. This only increased the Muslim sense of grievance, and fuelled the flames of insurrection.

It was in those areas where neither Christians nor Muslims clearly dominated that the first acts of communal violence occurred. Clashes between rival gangs of Christian 'Ilagas' and Muslim 'Barracudas' during 1970-71 led to both Muslims and Christians fleeing to areas where they felt more secure, further strengthening the barriers between them.

Fighting became serious after Philippine troops massacred a group of Muslims travelling to the polls during the November 1971 election. It was against this background that the MNLF emerged as the successor to the more amorphous Mindanao Independence Movement. The MNLF was led by the young left-wing academic, Nur Misuari, who within a month of the declaration of a nationwide state of martial law in September 1972 launched the Front's military wing, the Bangsa Moro Army, into a full-scale insurrection for an independent Moro state. The insurrection, reportedly financed and armed by Libya and relying on the near-by state of Sabah in Malaysia for support and sanctuary, spread rapidly, and MNLF forces were in control of large parts of Cotabato Province and the Sulu archipelago by March 1973.

Military resources

Then as now, the Philippines spent a smaller proportion of its Gross National Product on defence than any other member of the Association of South East Asian Nations (Asean), and the Armed Forces of the Philippines (AFP) numbered only 58,000 at the time of the declaration of martial law. MNLF forces, which by 1973 totalled an estimated 50,000 men, were often able to attack AFP outposts in overwhelming numbers, inflicting heavy casualties and forcing the AFP

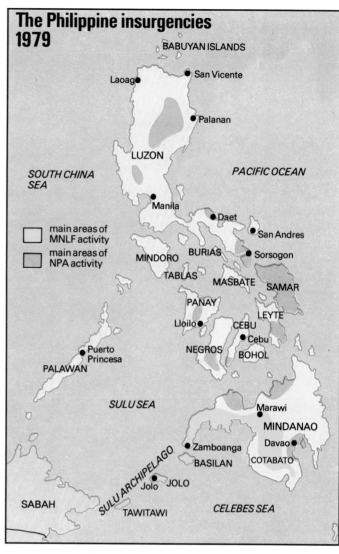

The Philippine insurgencies
1979

□ main areas of
   MNLF activity
▨ main areas of
   NPA activity

Above: Private armies
have become a feature
of life in the Philippine
countryside. These
members of a group
known as 'Charlie's
Angels', one armed with a
Browning Automatic Rifle,
are involved in operations
against guerrillas of the
Maoist New People's Army
in the northern Philippines.
Of questionable military
value, such private armies
are mostly employed by
local landowners to police
their estates.

to retreat into the main administrative centres, while
large areas of the countryside, as well as many towns
and cities, fell into MNLF hands.

A further wave of guerrilla activity came in February 1974, when MNLF forces occupied the city of
Jolo for several days, only withdrawing when subjected to a combined naval and aerial bombardment.
By 1975, however, the scale of guerrilla operations
had begun to decline, though it was clear that the
MNLF was capable of sustaining the war almost
indefinitely.

Realising the improbability of a purely military
solution, and subject to growing pressure from Islamic countries in the Middle East, whose influence had
increased enormously following the oil crisis of 1974,
President Marcos opened peace negotiations with the
MNLF in Saudi Arabia in late 1974. Marcos made
great efforts to develop contacts with the Middle
Eastern backers of the MNLF, hoping to prove to
them that the Moros were not being threatened with
genocide, as had been claimed by the MNLF. Though
this first round of negotiations proved fruitless, contacts were maintained, and several Islamic fact-finding missions visited the Philippines. Negotiations
were re-opened in Tripoli in December 1975, after a
visit to Libya by Imelda Marcos, wife of the president, during which she was able to convince Colonel
Muammar Gaddafi of the sincerity of Philippine
interest in a just political solution.

The resulting agreement provided for a ceasefire,
to be followed by the introduction of autonomy for 13
provinces in the southern Philippines. President Marcos, however, interpreted the agreement to be conditional upon the result of a referendum to be held in
the affected provinces, the question being phrased in
terms of a yes or no to MNLF rule. Given that
Christians formed a majority in eight of the provinces,
with a population of 6,500,000 to the Muslims'
4,000,000, the resulting rejection of the autonomy
plan was predictable. For the MNLF, which had
called for a boycott of the referendum, this was a
serious setback, and it returned to its demand for total
independence.

In spite of this, the ceasefire was largely observed,
broken only from time to time by skirmishes between
the AFP and MNLF forces. The war entered a new
stage, however, on 10 October 1977, when an MNLF
unit massacred a group of 36 unarmed Philippine
officers, including the Commander of the First Army
Division, Teodulfo Bautista, on Jolo Island. The AFP
reacted swiftly, mounting a campaign of reprisals
against the MNLF on Basilan and Jolo islands. Large
areas were mined, air strikes were employed and
free-fire zones declared. Civilian casualties were
heavy. In December 1977, AFP forces discovered
and destroyed the MNLF national headquarters in the
dense jungle north of Zamboanga City. Fighting
reached its peak in January 1978, when eight batta-

lions of AFP troops stormed the heavily defended cliff-top fortress of Usman Sali, the MNLF commander responsible for the October massacre.

While this tough military response indicated the ability of the AFP to contain the Muslim insurgency, President Marcos also went ahead with a series of political initiatives, offering amnesty and financial assistance to MNLF guerrillas who surrendered and holding peace talks with MNLF leaders in the Philippines.

The government also went ahead with the introduction of two autonomous zones in east and west Mindanao, which it hoped would satisfy the demands of the Muslim population for greater control of their own affairs, as well as reassuring them that they would not be subject to increasing Christian domination.

The MNLF, meanwhile, experienced internal difficulties, splitting into three separate factions. The first, led by Nur Misuari and based in Libya, was probably the largest, though it had become isolated from the local MNLF leadership in the Philippines. Nur Misuari's position was weakened by the decline in active support from Libya for the rebellion in the

Top left: Moros prepare to ambush an army patrol. Relatively well-armed, their main source of supply is the Philippine Army.
Above: After the ambush, the guerrillas concentrate on collecting the weapons and ammunition of the dead soldiers. Top right: A Moro fighter, fatally wounded during the ambush, has paid with his life for the weapons.

Left: A mountain base of the communist New People's Army, which now constitutes the most serious military threat to the Philippines. Notice the cultivated area around the tents from which the guerrillas obtain their food.

Below: The Philippine Army, though better armed and supplied than the guerrillas, and greatly expanded since the beginning of the current insurgency in the early 1970s, still faces serious problems of indiscipline and corruption.

Philippines, partly as a result of the successful diplomatic offensive by President Marcos. The second group, which was based in Cairo, was led by Hashim Salamat, who broke away from Misuari in 1977. Salamat was in favour of a negotiated settlement with the Philippine government. The smallest group, the Bangsa Moro Liberation Organisation, led by Salipada Pendantun and based in Saudi Arabia, was rumoured to receive encouragement from the Philippine government, which was interested in deepening any split within the Muslim rebellion.

By the 1980s the New People's Army (NPA) had taken the place of the MNLF as the main security threat to the Manila regime. The NPA is the military wing of the Maoist Communist Party of the Philippines, Marxist-Leninist, which was formed in 1968 as a result of the Sino-Soviet split. The NPA was founded in March 1969, and its first operational base was in Tarlac Province, central Luzon, an area with a rich tradition of peasant insurgency and a former stronghold of the communist Huk guerrillas. Forced later to move its main base to Isabela Province, in the northeast of Luzon, the NPA grew steadily, claiming to have 2000 men under arms by 1971.

The introduction of martial law in 1972, and the development of a government programme of land reform were temporary setbacks for the NPA, but it continued to find recruits. Increased AFP efficiency, as well as splits within the NPA leadership, led to a series of reverses for the communists in the period 1975-78. Chinese support was withdrawn as part of Peking's rapprochement with Washington. Many NPA leaders were captured by the AFP and the guerrillas were forced to reorganise, adopting smaller military units and spreading their operations into new areas.

Progress was slow and careful, but by the early 1980s the NPA was estimated to have between 7000 and 11,000 regular troops, backed by thousands of part-time militia. Reports indicated that the NPA might have formed a tactical alliance with the MNLF, the two movements cooperating in operations against the AFP. The NPA was also reported to have extended its activities into Mindanao, in areas bordering the provinces affected by the MNLF rebellion. Operating in two-thirds of the Philippines' 77 provinces, the NPA is causing the United States serious concern regarding the stability of its most important ally in Southeast Asia. **Walter Hoffmann**

Marcos's men

In response to the MNLF and NPA insurgency, the Philippine Forces increased their manpower enormously, the army by 1984 numbering some 60,000 men, equipped with Scorpion light tanks, mechanised infantry combat vehicles, and armoured personnel carriers. The navy, with 28,000 men, including 9600 Marines, has played a relatively minor role in the war with the MNLF, being responsible for the interception of vessels carrying arms and supplies to the rebels, as well as for supporting land operations with naval bombardments. The Marines have, however, been extensively used against the NPA guerrillas.

The air force, like the navy, is relatively small, as the Philippines, with no hostile neighbours and no land borders to protect, rely heavily on the presence of US forces at the Subic Bay naval base and Clark air force base, both on the island of Luzon. The air force is, therefore, basically a counter-insurgency force, equipped with F-8 Crusaders, F-5A/F-5B Freedom Fighters, and SIAI-Marchetti SF-260 and T-28 Trojan counter-insurgency aircraft. The Philippine Air Force also uses Bell UH-1 Iroquois helicopters.

The brunt of the fighting against the guerrillas has been borne by the 43,500-strong Philippine Constabulary (PC), supported by the 46,000-strong Integrated National Police. The PC is equipped with light infantry weapons, roughly comparable to those available to the MNLF, and relies on the army and Marines for support when heavier weapons are necessary. The army and Marines tend only to be involved in large-scale operations.

Key Weapons

ELECTRONIC WARFARE:

THE LAND WAR

Throughout the history of land warfare, the commander with the better lines of communications has always had a major advantage over his opponent; however sophisticated the weaponry deployed, it is severely hampered if the operator cannot be instructed when and where to fire, and if the commander cannot coordinate the actions of the various elements at his disposal. The emergence of reliable radio equipment during World War II revolutionised battlefield management; the success of the German tactic of Blitzkrieg depended heavily on the availability of effective electronic communications. Since that time, all the world's armies have come to rely on radio as their primary communication tool. Apart from communications equipment, another factor in the growth of the so-called 'electronic battlefield' has been the use of radar to detect personnel and vehicles on the ground and the use of direction-finding equipment to locate emitters of radio and radar signals.

There can be little doubt as to the effectiveness of available electronic equipment. This effectiveness has generated a need for counter-measures, to which radio and radar are extremely vulnerable. A communications net can be disrupted by jamming, and simply monitoring the transmissions of an enemy whose radio security is lax can reveal valuable intelligence. Also, a group of monitoring stations can be used to locate accurately a divisional headquarters, for example, by its radio transmissions, allowing it to be attacked and thereby paralysing an important subsection of the overall command structure. Both Nato and the Warsaw Pact have recognised the opportunities of electronic warfare and have provided their ground forces with an array of equipment designed to attack the enemy's sensory and communications systems and to provide signals intelligence (SIGINT).

The Soviet Army has adopted the name 'radio-electronic combat' for electronic warfare. They have organised specialised units at army and front level to carry out the electronic offensive. The basic units are the Signals Interception Battalion and the Radio-electronic Combat Battalion.

The Signals Interception Battalion acts as an intelligence-gathering and radio direction-finding force. According to recent estimates, such a unit comprises 433 officers and men and 114 trucks, divided between an HQ Company and Radio Intercept, Radio Direction-Finding and Radar Intercept Companies. The Radio Intercept Company has an establishment of 97 officers and men and is equipped with 28 SR-50-M intercept receivers covering the VHF/UHF bands and aimed at FM-voice communications. The Radio Direction-Finding Company is slightly larger with an establishment of 118 officers and men operating 16 radio direction-finder sets drawn from the SR-19-V, SR-20-V and SR-25-V types. Together, these three sets can give accurate bearings on HF to VHF AM/FM-voice communications. The Radar Intercept Company had the largest establishment of the three, with 123 officers and men operating 15 radar intercept systems. These will be either the SB-20-V covering the 50MHz–11GHz frequency bands, or the SM-21-V covering the 50MHz–10GHz frequencies.

The Radioelectronic Combat Battalion represents the offensive capability within the Soviet Army's electronic warfare units. These handle the actual jamming of enemy systems and, manned by 492 officers and men, are made up of three radio jamming

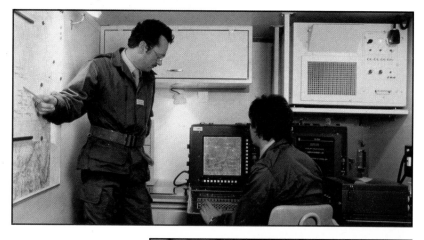

Previous page: The US TEAMPACK, here mounted on a Dragon 300 vehicle, is used to pinpoint hostile transmitters. Above: The heart of the 'electronic battlefield' will be command, control and communications centres (C^3) – like this French installation – analysing information from the frontline.

Right: A French infantryman with a TRC 743 field data terminal attached to his radio. Below: Men of the US 82nd Airborne Division deploy communications equipment on Grenada in 1983.

Left: The Transportpanzer-1 (TPZ-1) Eloka is fitted with an EK33 jammer and a 15KW generator to provide power. Other electronic warfare variants of the TPZ-1 are the mobile radar model and the command and communications model.

Below: The French AMX30 AA tank with the Oeil Vert radar. This is a pulse doppler system and works in either distant surveillance mode (out to 15 km – 9 miles) or close-in mode (out to 6.5 km – 4 miles). The radar operates on the 1710-1750MHz frequencies.

and one radar jamming companies. The radio jamming units have an establishment of 105 officers and men operating four radio intercept sets, four direction-finders, 12 radio jammers and three multichannel jammers. The radar company is manned by 93 officers and men and is equipped with 10 radar intercept/direction-finding sets and 11 jammers.

Both types of battalion are highly mobile, with all their equipment being either vehicle-mounted or towed. The threat posed by this capability, backed up by further capacity mounted in Mi-4 Hound and Mi-8 Hip helicopters, is taken very seriously by Nato. Some observers believe that the Soviet system could reduce battlefield communications to the level of 1916, an extremely serious proposition when it is considered how reliant Nato is on radio communications. The capabilities of Soviet radioelectronic units were illustrated in Europe during the intervention in Czechoslovakia in 1968 when the Warsaw Pact forces involved employed chaff and barrage-jamming techniques, forming a vast electronic screen along the borders between Czechoslovakia and West Germany. This effectively masked the troop movements and airlifts.

The main contingent of Nato's land electronic warfare units is provided by the US Army. In each of its 16 frontline divisions there is an organic electronic warfare/intelligence battalion which combines the roles of the Soviet units already described. The US Army has not yet adopted a standard table of organisation and equipment for its electronic warfare units. As

might be expected, these battalions are furnished with a wide range of sophisticated equipment. Three important current systems are the AN/MLQ-34 TAC-JAM communications jammer, the AN/MSQ-103 signals intercept/direction-finding system and the EXJAM expendable jammer.

The first of these, the MLQ-34, is designed to disrupt and deceive enemy communications links. The system as a whole comprises a number of receivers for target identification, high-powered transmitters and a controlling computer, the entire package being mounted on an M-548 tracked cargo-carrier chassis. Each transmitter is capable of generating a multi-kilowatt signal over a broad frequency range, making the system a powerful and flexible electronic warfare tool. Produced by GTE Sylvania, 17 TAC-JAMs have been completed and the US Army has a further 31 systems on order.

The MSQ-103 TEAMPACK equipment is a mobile system designed to identify and locate hostile communications transmitters. Used at the divisional level, TEAMPACK covers the 500MHz-50GHz frequency band and can be mounted on a range of vehicles including the XM-1015 tracked chassis, the M-35 utility truck and the jeep. Included within the system is built-in computer-processing and a wideband data link for the transmission of received material back to a control/analysis centre. MSQ-103 is in current use with the US Army and will become the service's basic electronic warfare receiving equipment.

The EXJAM system currently under development by Fairchild Weston represents the leading-edge of American electronic warfare technology. Essentially a 'throw-away' system, EXJAM is made up of a number of transmitters mounted in a 155mm artillery shell. Once fired, each transmitter package is ejected at pre-set intervals and falls to earth along the flight path. On hitting the ground, the unit imbeds itself, deploys an antenna and begins transmitting a jamming signal almost immediately. EXJAM was field-tested during 1983/1984 and a manually-emplaced variant is also being developed.

Left: A TEAMPACK AN/MSQ-103A installed on the back of an XM-1015. TEAMPACK is an extremely versatile system, which can be mounted on many different kinds of vehicles.

Right: The battlefields of the future will see great use of remotely-piloted vehicles, like this Compass Cope-R, for reconnaissance and target observation as well as jamming and direction-finding. An RPV can carry a wide range of communications and surveillance equipment, tailored for specific mission requirements.

Alongside its ground-based units, the US Army makes extensive use of airborne electronic warfare platforms such as the RU-21 series Beechcraft Utes, the EH-60A Black Hawk helicopter and the RV-1 series Grumman Mohawk. Such aircraft carry a wide range of systems including the Cefly Lancer and Guardrail signals intercept/direction-finding equipment on the RU-21, the Quick Fix jamming system on the EH-60A and the Quick Look surveillance system on the RV Mohawk.

The British Army operates a combined intelligence/electronic warfare system, believed to be concentrated in the 30th Royal Signals Regiment. This formation has the additional role of maintaining communications security, monitoring the army's own signals traffic to ensure that no information of value to an enemy is transmitted because of lax operator techniques. The British are reticent about discussing current operational equipment. Two known examples of UK systems are the Marconi S373 and the

Below: The launching of an Aquila remotely-piloted vehicle, the choice of the US Army for battlefield reconnaissance and electronic warfare. Made by Lockheed, it is still in the prototype stage, and had great difficulty meeting the US Army's requirements.

MEL/Ferranti Barbican units. Both systems are vehicle-mounted, the S373 providing multi-band jamming and surveillance capability and the Barbican carrying out radar classification, analysis and direction-finding.

The S373 uses a number of high-powered transmitters feeding twin parabolic antennae mounted in a 'double bubble' radome which can be hydraulically raised or lowered. The system operators are housed in a container mounted behind the radome on the carrier vehicle, a standard 4-tonne Bedford truck. The system is also provided with a self-contained intercept capability and both voice and data-link communications channels.

Barbican uses a similar vehicle as a base and is highly automated, needing only a single operator. A full Barbican system would comprise three intercept stations, all joined by voice/digital data-link channels to a central control. Frequency coverage is believed to be between one and 18GHz. Both these systems are currently in the development stage and no information as to their eventual use in service has been released.

Outside Nato and the Warsaw Pact, the most experienced nation in electronic warfare is Israel. Precise details of Israeli equipment remain obscure, but it is believed that the country has a wide range of locally produced intercept and jamming equipment. These are highly mobile, being mounted on a variety of wheeled and tracked vehicles. Some examples of equipment are the EL/K 7010 ground-based mobile VHF jammer and the ELBIT MN-53 ESM system to intercept and identify radar emitters. Israel is unique in being the only country currently making operational use of an electronic warfare drone, the Mastiff remotely-piloted vehicle, which is employed for communications surveillance.

The future line of development of electronic warfare on land may be indicated by a new US project developing a digital electronic warfare capability for tanks. A threat-warning system incorporating sensors and display might provide greater survivability on the battlefield. The advantages of attaining 'electronic supremacy' over the opposition on the battlefield leaves little doubt that further developments in the use of electronic support and counter-measures will be forthcoming. Finding the enemy quickly will be especially important with the spread of precision-guided munitions, making a first strike more destructive.

Top: The Barbican intercept receiver, made by MEL, is installed on a Bedford 4-tonne truck.
Above: An aerial delivered seismic intrusion detector (ADSID), used extensively by the US in Vietnam, especially to give early warning of an infantry threat to firebases. Left: A Soviet Mercury Grass VHF communications system.

Empire in turmoil
The Ethiopian revolution and its aftermath

When Haile Selassie came to the throne of Ethiopia in 1930, he inherited a state which could claim a continuous existence going back some 2000 years. The mythical dynastic history of the 'King of Kings' went back even further, to King Solomon and the Queen of Sheba. During the 19th century, when the rest of Africa was divided up between the European powers, the Emperors of Abyssinia, as it was then known, not only kept their independence but strengthened and expanded their rule.

At the time of Haile Selassie's accession, the country was bordered to the northeast by the Italian colony of Eritrea, which in 1935 became the base for an Italian occupation of Ethiopia. Selassie went into exile until 1941, when he was reinstalled by the British, victorious over the Italians throughout the region. The status of Eritrea and part of the Somali-inhabited Ogaden region to the southeast remained in doubt until after World War II. Eritrea came effectively under Ethiopian rule from 1952, and the British-administered area of the Ogaden was handed over to Ethiopia in 1955.

Despite the legitimacy conferred by a long tradition, the imperial throne came increasingly under attack in the changing postwar world. The archaic structures of a feudal state and society were ill-adapted to an economy being slowly transformed by contact with the world economic system, and opposition developed in many diverse quarters to Selassie's absolute rule exercised through his puppet parliament. Armed resistance in Eritrea grew after 1960 when the region lost its autonomy and was reduced to the status of a province. In the Ogaden the traditional hostility of the local nomadic population to central government also took on a new dimension from 1960, when the formation of Somalia gave the Somalis an independent homeland. Somalia aspired to incorporate all the Somali-inhabited areas in neighbouring states, a project favoured by Ethiopia's Somali subjects in the Ogaden.

To counter the guerrilla movement in Eritrea and the threat of Somali irredentism, Ethiopia was forced to embark on the expansion and modernisation of its armed forces. The source of military aid, modern equipment and training was the United States, which by the 1970s was devoting more of its military aid budget to Ethiopia than to the rest of Africa put together. By 1970 the Ethiopian Army consisted of four infantry divisions – each division 8000 strong – an armoured brigade, a commando battalion and a parachute battalion; the embryo of an air force had also been conceived, comprising a squadron equipped with American F-5s.

This armed force proved quite adequate to contain the Eritrean insurgency and deter Somalia from intervention in the Ogaden, but it could not defend the imperial regime against other sources of opposition – indeed, it was itself a major seat of discontent. Unrest simmered in all ranks, but especially among the junior officers, many of whom had been on training courses

Above: Ethiopian leader Colonel Mengistu Haile Mariam reviews an Addis Ababa parade with Cuba's Fidel Castro in March 1977. Faced with Eritrean insurgency and Somali invasion, Ethiopia relied heavily on the use of Cuban troops.

Above: Emperor Haile Selassie, whose corrupt and inefficient regime was overthrown by the army in September 1974. Deposed and arrested, Haile Selassie died in prison in August 1975.

Above: Power in post-revolutionary Ethiopia was in the hands of the Derg, a committee drawn from the army. Between 1974 and 1977, its three leading members were Mengistu (left), Brigadier-General Teferi Banti (centre) and Lieutenant-Colonel Abate Atnafu (right). Both Banti and Atnafu fell victim to Mengistu in the intense power struggles of 1977.

in the United States. Contact with the outside world had made them angrily aware of the archaic Ethiopian promotion system which denied attainment of senior rank to all but the members of the aristocracy. They were also aware that those at the top were in many cases using their exalted position to line their pockets, an abuse the government made no attempt to eliminate or punish.

Years of inconclusive fighting in remote areas under considerable hardship had sapped the soldiers' morale, but they were above all sensitive to the general current of hostility to the government in most areas of Ethiopian society that had swelled to a flood by 1974. A new middle class had developed in the towns, including students and intellectuals, which resented the backwardness of their country. In the countryside poverty-stricken peasants were responsive to spreading agitation calling for 'land to the labourers'. The government's inability to respond adequately to the famine of 1972-74, in which some 200,000 peasants may have died, was a final revelation of the regime's moral and political bankruptcy.

The storm finally broke in mid-January 1974. First, the garrison of Neghelle, a remote post in Sidamo Province, mutinied over living conditions. Officers sent to enquire into the causes were imprisoned and forced to live off the men's rations. On 10 February air force personnel at the Debre Zeit base near Addis Ababa went on strike over pay. Four days later students and teachers staged noisy demonstrations objecting to the proposed curtailing of envisaged educational reforms. The following week the capital's taxi drivers rioted over a threatened 50 per cent increase in petrol prices. The month closed with a major uprising in the ranks of the 2nd Division over pay, conditions of service, and alleged administrative corruption.

Time for a change

For the first time since his accession in 1930 Haile Selassie, by then 82 years old, felt it would be wise to make some concession to popular opinion. The universally unpopular prime minister, Aklilu Habte Wold, was sacked from the position he had held for the past 13 years, to be replaced by a die-hard aristocrat, Endalkatchew Makonnen. But this move was to do nothing to relieve the tension since, though voicing support for the 'people', Makonnen was hoping to shift much of the power from the Emperor to his own clique of great landowners, the Ras.

To begin with, certain appeasing gestures were made. The forces' demands on pay and living conditions were granted. A general strike threatened by the Confederation of Ethiopian Labour Unions (CELU) was averted by giving official permission for government employees to form trade unions. The proposed rise in the cost of petrol was postponed indefinitely and talks were promised on land reforms. On the other hand, no steps were taken to probe into corruption in the services and demands for the arrest and trial of suspect senior officers were ignored.

Student demonstrations, strikes and peasant re-

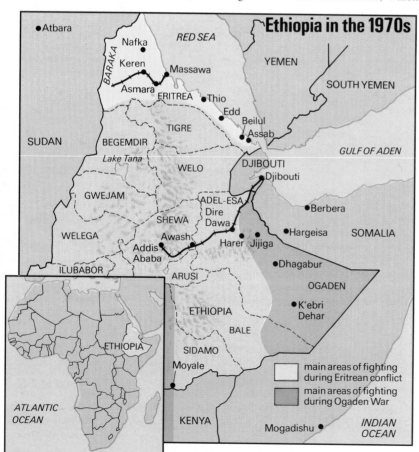

Ethiopia in the 1970s

Above: The Derg's policy of land reform and its appeal to Ethiopian nationalism made it enormously popular with the peasants, seen here during a demonstration in Addis Ababa.

Below: Under serious pressure from Eritrean guerrilla movements and the Somali invasion of the Ogaden, the Derg rapidly increased the size of the Ethiopian Army and rearmed with equipment supplied by the Soviet Union. The troops below are carrying Soviet SKS 7·62mm rifles.

volts continued until June, when there occurred a decisive development in the army, with simultaneous mutinies in the 2nd, 3rd and 4th Divisions, led by junior officers and NCOs. A number of higher-ranking officers were arrested and a Coordinating Committee of the Armed Forces – known as the Derg, from an Amharic word for 'committee of equals' – was set up, consisting of 126 members, none at the time above the rank of major. The Derg quickly established itself as the most powerful body in the country under the dynamic leadership of an ordnance officer of peasant origin, Mengistu Haile Mariam.

It was the Derg which staged the final act of the overthrow of the old regime. On 12 September, an officer drove to the imperial palace to read an act of deposition to the emperor, who had for some time been living in almost total isolation. The octogenarian ruler was then arrested and taken to a cell in the 4th Division jail where he remained until his death the following August.

Mengistu's first victim

The Derg at first invited an ex-general, Aman Andom, to take over the country as head of a Provisional Military Government, but this gesture proved an abysmal failure. Andom was not prepared to act as a figurehead, and was fundamentally out of sympathy with much of the Derg's radical programme of nationalisation, land reform and nationalism (which took the form of resistance to separatist movements). From the start Andom clashed bitterly with Mengistu, especially over the question of the proposed execution of former officials and senior officers jailed by the Derg, and over the advisability of a negotiated settlement to the Eritrean question, which Mengistu opposed.

On 22 November Mengistu delivered a furious condemnation of those he termed 'counter-revolutionaries'. That same night the general's house was surrounded by a squadron of tanks and blown to pieces, Andom himself perishing in the ruins. Next day the order was issued for the execution of the political prisoners, among them the former prime minister, Aklilu.

The control of the country now passed directly to the Derg, constituted as a Provisional Military Administrative Council (PMAC), but Mengistu still held back from taking full power, and Brigadier-General Teferi Banti became head of state. Although the PMAC programme had a strong left-wing element – Ethiopia was declared a socialist state in December 1974 – it was chiefly marked by intense nationalism, its slogan coined by Mengistu being *Ethiopia Tikden*, best translated as Ethiopia First. Opposition to separatism was combined with a total rejection of civilian participation in government. Thus many of those forces which had threatened the old regime – Eritrean and Somali separatists, and radical students, intellectuals and trade unionists in the towns – also menaced the Derg government.

During 1975 the energies of urban radicals were turned aside as they dispersed into the rural areas on a concentrated campaign of political education among the peasantry. But in 1976, in an endeavour to consolidate an anti-military front, various civilian factions formed the Ethiopian People's Revolutionary Party (EPRP) with its own combat wing, the Ethiopian People's Revolutionary Army (EPRA), determined to launch a campaign of urban terrorism to break the Derg's hold on power and establish a civilian Marxist regime. The first EPRA bombs exploded in Addis Ababa on 30 April 1976, and by the autumn of that year the EPRP had become the Derg's major problem, even more directly threatening than the full-scale war being fought in Eritrea.

A splinter group from the EPRP, the MEISON (All Ethiopian Socialist Movement), allied itself with the Derg against the urban guerrillas and provided an armed militia to cooperate with special military security detachments set up to hunt down EPRA members. Elements of MEISON were suspected of complicity in a narrowly failed attempt to assassinate Mengistu in September 1976, however, demonstrating how the mounting pressure was creating splits within the Derg and among its supporters.

In February 1977 Mengistu moved against his opponents in the Derg. After head of state Teferi Banti had delivered an anti-Mengistu speech, the two men

Left: Student demonstrators burn an effigy of Prime Minister Aklilu Habte Wold in March 1974. Radical student protests were an important factor in the overthrow of Haile Selassie. Below: Police repression, which the students first encountered under Haile Selassie, was to worsen when the Derg took power.

Right: Differences between Mengistu's Derg and the civilian leftist parties degenerated into a brutal campaign of murder on the streets of Addis Ababa. Rival assassination squads fought a vicious war, leaving their victims' bodies on public display.

met on 3 February for discussions. The meeting developed into a violent quarrel which in turn degenerated into a shoot-out: Banti and seven of his men were killed. The Derg met on 11 February and appointed Mengistu the new head of state with a potential rival, Colonel Abate Atnafu, as his deputy. Atnafu would also fall victim to Mengistu the following November, reportedly for opposing the tightening links with the Soviet Union.

1977 was the crucial year in the Derg's struggle both to defeat separatism and to crush internal opposition. Mengistu unleashed what he himself termed a 'Red Terror' against his radical enemies on the streets of Addis Ababa. The campaign of counter-terror against individual members of the EPRP expanded into mass killings. On 1 May militia drafted in from the country opened fire on students preparing a May Day protest, killing some 500, after which gangs of militia raided students' homes, arresting and subsequently executing a further 400. As the EPRP fought back Addis Ababa became a nightly battleground. Meanwhile Somali pressure on the Ogaden developed into a full-scale invasion as Somalia sought to exploit the chaotic conditions in Ethiopia. The summer of 1977 saw a remarkable series of Somali advances which threatened to drive the Ethiopians completely from the Ogaden. In Eritrea, town after town fell to separatist guerrillas. Even supporters of the old regime, organised from exile in London, succeeded in infiltrating units into the western province of Begemdir.

Eritrean fiasco

An initial attempt by the Derg to expand the army in response to military threats had failed disastrously. Profoundly worried by the set-backs registered in the field during operations against the Eritreans, Mengistu had proclaimed a 'general mobilisation'. A force of 300,000 men was raised, hastily and poorly equipped, given only the most rudimentary basic training, and then thrown into the field as an 'autonomous' army. Later Mengistu admitted that he had hoped that sheer weight of numbers would prevail. The experiment proved to be one of his few mistakes. After suffering appalling losses, this horde was hastily

withdrawn to be employed from then on in an internal security role.

In May 1977, however, Mengistu visited Moscow and returned with a promise of military aid that was to retrieve the situation. Initially, despite the declaration of a socialist state, the Derg had continued to receive American military aid. But already before the fall of Haile Selassie's regime, the United States had begun to have doubts about its commitment to Ethiopia. Originally adopted as a conservative bar to the expansion of left-wing influence in the Horn of Africa – seen as strategically important because of its control of the narrow entrance to the Red Sea – support for Ethiopia had been devalued as the government exploited it for a war against Eritrean separatists in which the United States had no interest. Nothing in the development of Ethiopian politics after the overthrow of the emperor encouraged the Americans to increase their backing. The Mengistu regime finally established in February 1977 was distasteful to the US government of President Jimmy Carter because of its left-wing tendencies and its contempt for human rights. On 27 April the Pentagon announced the blocking of all arms supplies to Ethiopia and the beginning of the supply of 'defensive weapons' to its neighbours Sudan and Somalia.

By turning to the Russians, however, Mengistu was able to extract far greater support than the Americans would ever have offered. The Soviet Union had been supplying Somalia, backing its left-wing

October 1977, but all to no avail. By the end of 1977 the military balance in the Ogaden had tipped totally against Somalia and the Ethiopians were able to chase the Somali Army from their territory in 1978 – although pressure from both superpowers halted any possible Ethiopian invasion of Somalia.

A 'wave of madness'

At the same time, the Derg ruthlessly achieved control of the situation in Addis Ababa. During the months of December 1977 and January 1978, the EPRA and MEISON fought bloody battles in the streets of the capital, while special Derg counter-terrorist squads hunted down both sides. By the end of this 'wave of madness', as it has been described, the prisons were overflowing and thousands had died, but Mengistu and the Derg were firmly in control.

Only in Eritrea was the Derg unable durably to assert its authority, despite an immensely expanded army. In 1984 it was reckoned that the strength of the Ethiopian Army was at least 100,000 regulars backed by a reasonably trained territorial force of between 150,000 and 200,000 men. The air force had expanded to 3500 men with 113 combat aircraft – mostly MiG-17s, but with one squadron of MiG-23s. The foreign presence was estimated at 1400 Russians, a combat division of 13,000 Cubans and 250 East Germans, many of whom operate aircraft and man the more sophisticated heavy weapons. Yet despite the expansion of the Ethiopian armed forces into probably the biggest and best equipped in black Africa, the Eritrean insurgency remained unrepressed.

Into the 1980s Mengistu established his rule on ever firmer bases. Having crushed the opposition civilian radicals, he worked towards establishing a mass party which would make Ethiopia a Soviet-style single-party state. Outside of Eritrea, no apparent serious threat to the regime remained.

Patrick Turnbull

Above: Ethiopia's new military rulers soon saw the student militants as dangerous rivals for power and moved to suppress them. Here soldiers guard students arrested during a demonstration.

regime, but the Soviets had no time for Somali territorial ambitions. The highest aim of Soviet diplomacy in the region was to achieve a federation of Ethiopia, Somalia, Eritrea and the South Yemen, under Soviet tutelage, which would have given Russia mastery of the Red Sea. Attempts to create such a grand alliance foundered precisely on Somali territorial claims. In May 1977, given the chance to swap influence over Somalia for influence over Ethiopia, the Soviet Union jumped at the chance.

Soon military hardware, Russian and East German military advisers and Cuban combat troops were flowing into Ethiopia. Somalia, on the other hand, was disappointed in its hope for Western support. In a desperate bid to seduce the West, President Siad Barre even allowed German and British counter-terrorist squads to operate in his capital, Mogadishu, against hijackers who had flown an airliner there in

The struggle for Eritrean independence

The Italian colony of Eritrea, established on the Red Sea coast of Africa in 1899, came under temporary British administration in 1941 when Italy's East African empire fell to Allied troops. Postwar divisions between the great powers prevented the United Nations arriving at a more permanent solution to the question of Eritrea's future until 1952, when it was agreed that it should be federated with neighbouring Ethiopia. The large degree of autonomy originally granted to Eritrea under this arrangement was gradually eroded by the autocratic regime of Emperor Haile Selassie, however, until the dissolution of the Eritrean parliament and outright annexation were pushed through in 1962. Eritrean resistance to Ethiopian domination had already begun during the 1950s, and by September 1961 the Eritrean Liberation Front (ELF), founded in 1960, had opened an armed struggle for total independence.

Liberators divided

Based originally amongst Eritrea's large Muslim population, the ELF, backed by Syria and Iraq, was able to tie down a large proportion of the Ethiopian armed forces throughout the 1960s. Its conservative nationalism was gradually radicalised from the mid-1960s onward, as it attracted increasing numbers of the predominantly urban Christian population to its ranks. The latent divisions between radical and conservative, Muslim and Christian, led in 1970 to the first of the major splits which have consistently bedevilled the Eritrean national liberation movement. A group led by Osman Saleh Sabbe broke away from the ELF to form the more radical Eritrean People's Liberation Forces (EPLF), which received the backing of the Palestine Liberation Organisation and Iraq.

Serious fighting between the various Eritrean factions weakened the opposition to Ethiopian control of Eritrea, which nevertheless grew during this period as a result of the economic crisis experienced by the province following the closing of the Suez Canal after the Six-Day War of 1967, and the general dissatisfaction with the regime of Haile Selassie which was developing throughout Ethiopia.

That dissatisfaction erupted into a wave of strikes and student demonstrations, in Asmara, capital of Eritrea, as well as in Addis Ababa, in 1974, leading to a take-over by left-wing officers. Ethiopia's new military rulers were well aware of the difficulties to be faced in achieving a purely military solution to the Eritrean insurgency, and General Aman Andom, who became head of state in September 1974 and was himself an Eritrean, made peace overtures to the Eritrean nationalists. Opposition from within the Derg led to a violent split in the ruling group, however, and Andom was killed during an armed assault on his home on 23 November.

The tenuous possibility of a peaceful compromise to the Eritrean conflict disappeared in January 1975, when a joint ELF-EPLF attack was launched on Asmara. Though the Ethiopians repelled this offensive with great brutality, the Eritrean guerrillas fol-

Revolt o

The experience, organisation and modern armament of the Eritrean guerrillas (above), shown here displaying their AKM assault rifles, contrasted sharply with the poorly equipped, unorganised militia hurriedly put together by the Ethiopians and sent off, poorly trained, to crush the Eritrean rebellion. Armed with a collection of Soviet World War II PPSh and PPS sub-machine guns (right), the peasant militia was soon routed and fled.

he Red Sea

lowed up this experiment in joint operations with a string of successes, gradually extending their control over the Eritrean countryside. While the Derg continued to make vague noises throughout 1975 indicating a desire for negotiations, the lack of any concrete proposals convinced the Eritreans that only military victory would win them total independence. 1976 saw new guerrilla successes in Eritrea, which the Derg attempted to counter by mobilising a mass peasant militia. Though greatly outnumbering the Eritrean guerrilla forces, this militia was poorly trained, little more than an armed horde. Largely Christian, and motivated by the promise of land in Eritrea, the militia's march on the war-torn province took on the confused aspect of a religious crusade with colonial overtones.

Transported to the Eritrean border, the militia was isolated, badly supplied and without clear leadership. The Eritreans were able to exploit this confused situation in May 1976, when they mounted a number of attacks on militia assembly points, inflicting heavy losses and creating utter panic amongst the untrained Ethiopian peasants, sending thousands of them fleeing southwards.

The source of weakness

This rout of the militia offensive marked a decisive seizure of the military initiative by the Eritreans, who now began to extend their control from the countryside into the towns, bottling up the Ethiopian garrisons, and making movement without heavy armoured support highly dangerous. By December 1977, the Ethiopians were trying desperately to retain control of Asmara and the Red Sea ports of Massawa and Assab, while the Eritrean separatists were in command of the whole of the rest of the province. Divisions within the Eritrean nationalist ranks, which had split again in 1976 to produce a third separatist organisation, the ELF-PLF, continued to constitute a fatal source of weakness, however, particularly once the revolutionary regime in Addis Ababa began to improve its relations with the radical Arab states and East European countries which had been the Eritreans' principal backers.

The Ogaden War of 1977-78, which might have been expected to provide a classic diversion of Ethiopian forces, allowing the Eritreans to consolidate their grip on their liberated areas, in fact enormously strengthened the Derg, which was able to channel patriotic sentiment into the creation of a new mass army; at the same time the left-wing military rulers in Addis Ababa became convinced that they must turn to the Soviet Union and Cuba for assistance. Massively supplied with modern Soviet weapons, trained by East European instructors, and backed by large numbers of Cuban combat troops, the Ethiopians were not only able to liberate the Ogaden from Somali forces, but also to turn to preparations for a new offensive in Eritrea. The Eritreans' chance of winning total independence began to recede as Ethiopian forces massed for the assault.

Although Fidel Castro's hesitation over involvement in the Eritrean conflict deprived the Ethiopians of the direct support of Cuban troops, the re-arming and re-organisation of the Ethiopian armed forces, carried out by the Soviet Union and its allies, allowed Addis Ababa to begin the reconquest of its rebellious province. One by one the towns held by the Eritreans fell to superior Ethiopian forces, and the Eritreans

were forced to revert to guerrilla tactics. The Ethiopians were unable to inflict a decisive defeat on their opponents, however, and continued to face a long-term insurgent problem.

The town of Nafka, in northern Eritrea, provided an example of the limits of Ethiopian success, and the tenacity of Eritrean resistance. Persistent Ethiopian attempts to recapture the town were repulsed, and an assault in 1979 was so decisively defeated that the Ethiopian survivors were forced to fight their way to the sea, where they were evacuated by Soviet warships.

Attempts to retake Nafka were resumed in 1981, again without success, and in January 1982 Colonel Mengistu Haile Mariam, Chairman of the Ethiopian Derg, announced preparations for a new operation, to involve 10 divisions, totalling some 120,000 men. Nafka was to be taken in a pincer movement, but having become a symbol of Eritrean resistance, it was strongly defended. Sited in easily defended broken ground which precluded the use of Ethiopian armoured vehicles, Nafka was surrounded by a double line of Eritrean trenches, with dug-outs and strongpoints sited to take maximum advantage of the ground.

Resolute resistance

The siege of Nafka lasted four months, during which the town was subjected to intense daily artillery and aerial bombardment. The resolutely-held trenches repulsed every Ethiopian infantry assault, however, until the Ethiopian commander was obliged to admit defeat and give the order to withdraw. The Ethiopian offensive was also smashed in the Barka sector, where the Eritreans were able to recapture the important rural centre of Helhal, near Keren.

This battle saw some of the bitterest fighting of the whole war, but the strength of their armoured formations and their total command of the air enabled the Ethiopians to maintain their grip on the open, flat ground, making extensive use of napalm, phosphorus and cluster bombs. The Eritreans also insisted that they had been subjected to nerve-gas attacks, and produced photographs of their troops manning positions wearing gas masks. Nevertheless, Ethiopia has consistently denied these allegations.

By mid-1982, the Ethiopian offensive had fizzled out, leaving the Eritreans in a slighty stronger position than had been the case for a number of years, but the question of how to resolve a conflict which had lasted for over 20 years, costing an estimated 100,000 lives, remained unanswered. While the most satisfactory solution would seem to be a return to federation with a guaranteed and extensive degree of autonomy for the Eritreans, the problem of different social and political systems co-existing within such a federation remained. While the relatively advanced and democratic situation in Eritrea during the 1950s contrasted strongly with the feudalistic autocracy of Haile Selassie's Ethiopia, the revolutionary regime now in power in Addis Ababa would be equally suspicious of what it might now regard as a moderate, pro-Western Eritrea, standing between it and access to the Red Sea. The vital economic and military importance of access to Eritrea's Red Sea ports remains the key factor in Ethiopia's continued determination to resist Eritrean secession, and in ensuring the maintenance of Soviet military assistance for Addis Ababa.

Patrick Turnbull

Left: An Ethiopian militiaman armed with an obsolete Soviet-manufactured 7·62mm DP light machine-gun. Bottom left: During 1976-77, Eritrean forces inflicted a series of major defeats on the Ethiopians, and captured large amounts of equipment. Here Eritrean guerrillas set up a captured 122mm howitzer.

Right: Eritrean guerrillas survey a knocked out Soviet-made BTR-60PB armoured personnel carrier. Soviet equipment was decisive in stemming the tide of Eritrean advances. Below: The guerrillas made extensive use of camels in the harsh Eritrean terrain.

The Ogaden War

The Somali invasion of Ethiopia

One of the first acts of Somalia, when it achieved independence in July 1960, was to demand the re-drawing of its frontiers to include those areas of neighbouring Ethiopia, Kenya and Djibouti inhabited by ethnic Somalis. The largest area claimed by Somalia was the southern Ethiopian province of the Ogaden, which was largely desert and inhabited predominantly by Somalis. The Ethiopian Emperor Haile Selassie rejected the claim, and declared a state of emergency in the Ogaden, concentrating his troops along the Somali border.

This state of tension erupted into open warfare in 1964, when fighting broke out between Ethiopian and Somali forces. Ethiopian military superiority soon made itself felt, however, and the confrontation ended with the resumption of negotiations.

Post-independence Somalia faced serious internal problems, which temporarily diverted attention from the problem of the Ogaden. Domestic discontent reached boiling point on 15 October 1969, when the president of the Somali Republic was assassinated by one of his own guards. Six days later, the commander-in-chief of the armed forces, Major-General Mohammed Siad Barre, assumed power as the new president in a bloodless coup. One of the main goals of the new government, which proclaimed Somalia a socialist state in October 1970, was the incorporation of all Somali-populated areas into a unified nation.

As sterile negotiations with Ethiopia dragged on, Siad Barre began to supply aid to militant Somalis within the Ogaden, who were able to stage a number of successful attacks on isolated Ethiopian units in the province. Disappointed by the results of the 1974 revolution in Ethiopia, which deposed Haile Selassie but brought to power a group of nationalist left-wing army officers, who were just as committed to the preservation of the unity of the Ethiopian empire, Siad Barre turned to consideration of a military solution to the Ogaden dispute.

Somalia missed its best opportunity to strike at Ethiopia during the period of internal conflicts and chaos which followed the 1974 revolution, because at that time the Somali armed forces were diverted to emergency relief work as a result of the tragic drought which struck the whole region during the mid-1970s.

Left: Ogaden tribeswomen display their enthusiastic support for the West Somali Liberation Front.

The Somali armed forces (below), although well trained and equipped by their Eastern bloc advisers (right: Hungarian officers in Mogadishu before the Ogaden War), were no match for the Ethiopians once the Soviet Union transferred its support to the other side.

By early 1977, however, encouraged by the series of heavy defeats which the Ethiopian Army was suffering at the hands of separatist guerrillas in Eritrea, and by the murderous struggle in Addis Ababa between the ruling body, the Derg, under Colonel Mengistu Haile Mariam, and civilian leftist groups, Barre concluded that the time had come to strike the decisive blow.

Realising the political importance of not being branded as an aggressor by either the United Nations or the Organization of African Unity – whose foundation stone was the sanctity of the frontiers bequeathed by colonialism – Barre refrained from officially com-

mitting the Somali Army to the Ogaden, but Somali troops almost certainly participated, alongside forces of the West Somali Liberation Front (WSLF), when between 3000 and 6000 men invaded the Ogaden from Somalia in May 1977. The WSLF, which had been founded in 1975, was based among the Somali population of the Ogaden, and claimed the right of secession for the territory south of a line running from Moyale on the Kenyan border, through Awash, south of Addis Ababa, to Djibouti – an area of some 625,000 square km (240,000 square miles), inhabited largely by ethnic Somalis.

Somalia's decision to prise the Ogaden away from

Left: An Ethiopian M41 tank, put out of action by Somali forces during their advance into the Ogaden.

Below: A column of Cuban-manned T55 tanks moves southward in the Jijiga sector. By early 1978, Cuba was estimated to have some 15,000 troops serving in Ethiopia, and an airlift of Cuban troops into the Somali rear had been decisive in turning the tide of the war.

Above: A group of Somali guerrillas guard a captured 14.5mm ZPU-2 anti-aircraft machine gun. Although the WSLF had been active in the Ogaden for some time before 1977, the regular Somali Army was responsible for the main operations of the Ogaden War.

Ethiopia by armed force was based on a faulty estimation of the international situation, however. The most important factor lay in the superpower alliances of Ethiopia and Somalia, which Barre judged to be stable and in Somalia's favour. In fact, however, the Ethiopian revolution had set off a regional chain-reaction, which by 1977 was causing a realignment of alliances. Ethiopia had been a close ally of the United States under Haile Selassie, and the Ethiopian armed forces had been trained and equipped by America. But the leftward drift of the Derg and its increasing resort to terroristic methods of rule alienated the administration of President Jimmy Carter in Washington, which halted all arms supplies to Addis Ababa on 24 February 1977. This weakening of Ethiopia's backing in the West would undoubtedly have been to Somalia's advantage, had it not coincided with a strengthening of the Mengistu regime's links with the Soviet Union.

Moscow, which had been allied to Somalia since 1974 by a Treaty of Friendship and Cooperation, viewed with sympathy the radical course being adopted by the Derg. An Ethiopian delegation to Moscow in December 1976 was able to negotiate the purchase of over $100 million worth of arms, the first shipments of which began to arrive in Ethiopia in May 1977, along with a group of Soviet military advisers and instructors. Meanwhile, by rationing supplies of arms to Somalia, Moscow planned to avoid a full-scale war in the Horn of Africa. The Soviet Union sought to gain maximum advantage from the situation by proposing a regional federation of pro-Moscow states, to include Somalia, Ethiopia and South Yemen. An attempt to mediate on this basis by Cuba's Fidel Castro in March 1977, foundered because of Somali insistence on the settlement of its claim to the Ogaden as a precondition of its participation in the proposed federation.

In June 1977, the WSLF stepped up its campaign in the Ogaden, cutting the Djibouti-Addis Ababa railway line at several points. The success of this offensive decided Siad Barre to commit the Somali Army to an invasion of the Ogaden on 24 July, though the fiction that no regular Somali forces were involved was maintained.

Throughout the early stages of their advance into the Ogaden, Somali forces had the advantage of operating close to their bases, and amongst a population which was overwhelmingly sympathetic to them. The Ethiopians, on the other hand, were isolated and disorganised, and their morale was low as a result of the purges and chaos which had resulted from the 1974 revolution. Within a few days, Somali units had taken the south Ogaden towns of K'ebri Dehar and Daghabur, as well as the important army and air force base at Gode, and were advancing northward on Jijiga and Harer.

Somalia suffered a major setback in early August, however, when the United States, which had promised to supply Mogadishu with 'defensive' weapons as recently as 15 July, and may even have implied more active encouragement of a Somali attack on Ethiopia, became alarmed at the implications of association with the Somali invasion and cancelled the agreement. The Soviet Union, meanwhile, continued to move closer to the Mengistu regime, which proclaimed a state of war between Ethiopia and Somalia, ordered a general mobilisation, and pressed ahead with the formation of a mass peasant militia. This militia, along with the rapidly expanded regular armed forces, was trained by Soviet and Cuban military advisers in the use of the Soviet weapons which had begun to arrive in May 1977.

Somalia continued to enjoy an unbroken string of successes in the field, and by the time Mengistu had issued his mobilisation order, the whole of southern and central Ogaden was in Somali hands. Heavy fighting was taking place around Harer and Dire Dawa, though the Ethiopian Air Force, flying from a base at Dire Dawa, was able to blunt the Somali advance, allowing the army, supported by large numbers of militia, to stabilise the front.

By September, the Somalis were poised for an assault on Jijiga, the most important Ethiopian base in the whole province. Its retention was of such importance that Mengistu himself is reported to have flown to the town to exhort its garrison to resist to the last man if necessary. After fierce fighting, the Somalis overran the outer defences, inflicting some 3000 casualties upon the Ethiopian defenders, who fell

back into the town itself. The siege continued with attacks by the Somali Air Force, but Ethiopian morale was already low, and the will to resist had evaporated. On 12 September the garrison surrendered, though a number of troops managed to slip away through the Somali lines and fell back on Harer, the Ethiopians' last stronghold in the Ogaden.

The high-point of Somali success came in November, with attacks on Harer, but this also proved to be the turning-point of the war. The rapid advance had dangerously extended the Somali lines of supply, and had taken them into areas where the population was not as naturally sympathetic to their cause. The Ethiopians, on the other hand, were now fighting nearer to their own base, and were not only defending soil that was more clearly identifiable as Ethiopian, but had also begun to mobilise the energies unleashed by the revolution.

More decisively perhaps, the early Ethiopian defeats seem to have convinced the Soviet Union to increase the scale of its arms supplies to the Derg. Realising that Moscow had decided to give all-out backing to the Ethiopians, Somalia cancelled its treaty with the Soviet Union on 13 November 1977, expelled all remaining Soviet advisers, and closed down all Soviet military facilities, such as the naval base at Berbera. Mogadishu also severed its diplomatic relations with Havana, although it maintained them with Moscow.

The Soviet airlift

On 26 November 1977, United States intelligence detected the first wave of a massive Soviet airlift, which over the coming months was to provide Ethiopia with surface-to-surface missiles, T55 and T62 tanks, 122mm BM-21 rocket launchers, fighter aircraft and transport helicopters, as well as huge quantities of smallarms and ammunition. With the new weapons came increasing numbers of Soviet and Cuban advisers, as well as large numbers of Cuban combat troops, who by early 1978 were estimated to number some 15,000. It was reported that the Cubans had been airlifted directly from Angola, where they had been involved in support of the Marxist government.

As well as Russians and Cubans, East German military instructors, reportedly flying combat missions in Soviet-supplied MiGs, and South Yemeni troops, including a number of tank crew, were also present on the Ethiopian side as the fighting in the Ogaden became more intense. The increasing weight of Soviet influence in Addis Ababa was indicated by the fact that the direction of Ethiopian military operations in the Ogaden was now in the hands of a committee with included five senior Soviet officers – among whom was General Grigori Barisov the effective operational commander – nine Cubans, led by General Arnaldo Ochoa Sanchez, commander of the Cuban forces in Ethiopia and former Cuban commander in Angola, and two South Yemenis.

Stiffened by the first Cuban contingent of 500 troops to reach the front, the Ethiopian defenders of Harer were able to throw back the repeated Somali attacks, and the Ogaden War entered a phase of attrition, in which the ever-increasing Ethiopian superiority in manpower and war material was to prove decisive.

General Barisov, formerly a senior adviser to the Somali armed forces, ordered a counter-attack

against Somali positions on 21 January 1978, and the Ethiopians, newly trained and equipped, spearheaded by Cubans, and with strong air and artillery support, were able to establish a new defensive perimeter around Harer and Dire Dawa. By February they were ready for an all-out assault. The Ethiopian offensive launched on 3 February became bogged down in torrential rain, however, and the Somalis used the opportunity to withdraw over the Gara Marda Pass to positions around Jijiga. On 5 March, Jijiga fell to a renewed Ethiopian assault, this time involving a Cuban force of 70 tanks which had been lifted by helicopter to the Somali rear.

Siad Barre, who on 11 February had announced the official entry of Somali forces into the Ogaden War, realised now that he was facing not only a decisive and crushing defeat in the Ogaden, but also the possibility of an Ethiopian invasion of Somali territory. He therefore began the immediate withdrawal of all Somali heavy equipment from the Ogaden, and on 9 March 1978 announced the total withdrawal of Somali troops.

The Ethiopian and Cuban advance rolled southward inexorably, supported by the Ethiopian Air Force, which had already won total command of the air. Fighting was reported to have ceased on 14 March, but guerrillas of the WSLF continued to harass the Ethiopian and Cuban forces in the Ogaden.

The danger of an Ethiopian invasion of Somalia was averted, however, reportedly due to Soviet influence. Moscow was interested in maintaining the status quo in the Horn of Africa, for continued tension between Somalia and Ethiopia was the most effective way of ensuring the continued dependence of the Derg upon Soviet and Cuban backing. Moscow, and its proteges in Addis Ababa, must also have taken note of a statement by US Secretary of State Cyrus Vance on 10 February, which made evident the readiness of Washington to recommence the supply of arms to Mogadishu should Ethiopia invade Somalia.

Tension along the Somali-Ethiopian border persisted, however, into the 1980s and while the WSLF continued to be active, inflicting steady losses on Ethiopian troops stationed in the Ogaden, a large Cuban unit remained present in the mountains around Harer, ready to move should the situation deteriorate. Somalia, meanwhile, repeatedly claimed that Ethiopian aircraft had mounted attacks against targets in Somalia, inflicting heavy civilian casualties.

Patrick Turnbull

Above: Soviet Antonov An-12 Cub transport aircraft at Dire Dawa. Deprived of American arms supplies after February 1977, Ethiopia turned to the Soviet Union and Cuba for military assistance. Soviet weapons and advisers began to arrive in May 1977, and in November a massive airlift of military equipment began which allowed Ethiopia rapidly to expand its armed forces and go over to the offensive. By March 1978, the Somalis had been swept from the Ogaden.

ELECTRONIC WARFARE:

THE SEA WAR

The seaborne applications of electronic warfare can trace their origins back to the Russo-Japanese War of 1904-05 when both sides used intercept receivers to monitor signals and also made attempts to jam them. By the end of World War II, naval electronic warfare had settled into two main areas – electronic support measures (equipment designed to receive, identify and locate hostile radio and radar emissions) and offensive jamming equipment (for disrupting and degrading enemy electronic sensors and communications gear).

In the decade and a half following 1945 more importance was placed on electronic support measures rather than on jamming as the availability of seaworthy radar sets revealed new possibilities in long-range ship and aircraft detection in both fair and foul weather, by day or by night.

The emphasis of electronic warfare at sea changed dramatically, however, with the emergence of the radar-homing missile during the early 1960s. The sinking of the Israeli destroyer *Eilat* led to a major re-examination of the situation in the field of naval electronic warfare. On 21 October 1967 the *Eilat* was blockading Port Said when an Egyptian Komar-class missile boat at anchor in the harbour launched its SS-N-2 Styx missiles against the Israeli ship. Hits were scored and the *Eilat* sank as a result of the damage; being an ex-World War II destroyer of the British Z-class, it was not equipped with any radar or jamming devices effective against these postwar Soviet missiles.

This new breed of weapon posed an enormous threat to surface ships: the missiles' high speed left many conventional air defence weapons incapable of engaging them and their radar-guidance made them very accurate. The emphasis in electronic warfare at sea hence shifted to efforts to deceive missile radars.

One effective electronic counter-measure (ECM) is the transmission of a jamming signal or the generation of a false return signal to the missile's radar with the intention of making the weapon fall short or wide of its intended target. Chaff has also been widely used. Chaff is a reflective material, fired from launchers, designed to provide radar with a confusing signal. Speed is the most important feature of any counter to anti-ship missiles; the chaff employed at sea is known as 'rapid bloom', since it forms the reflective cloud very quickly. At sea, chaff is used in three modes, depending on the range of the threat when detected. At extreme and medium ranges chaff is deployed in either 'confusion' or 'distraction' mode; in both cases large numbers of clouds of chaff are discharged in the hope that the missile will lock-on to one of these. These two modes are especially useful for dealing with large-scale missile attacks. At the closest ranges 'centroid' mode is used: in this case a large mass of chaff is deployed very close to the ship to provide a more attractive signal to the incoming missile.

The use by the Egyptians of passive (receiving) radar-homing missiles during the 1973 October War was a sign of the approaching obsolescence of a whole generation of electronic tactics. Passive radar-homing missiles such as the AS-5 Kelt use the target's own radar transmissions or jamming signals as guidance; against such systems only switching-off the transmission being homed onto will disturb the guidance system, but the latest generation of missiles in this category have the facility to 'remember' the

target's location even though the target may have shut-down all its transmitters.

Another, highly secret, sector of naval electronic warfare is the field of intelligence-gathering or SIGINT (SIGnals INTelligence). The Soviet Navy has a large number of 'trawlers' equipped with an extensive array of listening devices to analyse transmissions from ships nearby. These vessels are regularly in attendance at Nato naval exercises. It has been reported that a number of Soviet Golf-class submarines have also been given SIGINT equipment. The Americans also have SIGINT ships, the most

Previous page: The mainmast of the amphibious assault ship USS *Inchon* carries SPS 10 surface search radar, satellite communications devices and Tacan (tactical analysis) beacons. Above: A Soviet SIGINT ship, the Moma-class *Jupiter*. Below: A chaff rocket being loaded into a Shield chaff launcher, built by Plessey.

newsworthy of which was the USS *Pueblo*, captured by the North Koreans in 1968. The information gathered by these vessels proves most useful in designing electronic counter-measures against the missiles of the opposition. The equipment installed on these ships has less sophisticated counterparts on ordinary warships for the detection of enemy signals under war conditions. To reduce the chance of discovery by enemy sensors, a ship will operate in EMCON (EMission CONtrol) mode which involves shutting down the radar and radio to the minimum necessary.

Currently, naval electronic warfare equipment is being produced by the two superpowers and in a number of smaller countries. The United Kingdom is probably Europe's largest producer of electronic warfare hardware. Four types of chaff launchers are in production in the UK: Corvus (which comes in an eight-tube unit), Barricade (six sets of triple tubes), Shield (three-barrelled modules which may be combined to make up to 12 launch tubes), and Protean (up to four groups of nine launchers carrying four magazines of 36 chaff grenades each). There is also a chaff shell for the 4·5in gun common to most larger British ships. For electronic support the UK produces three major systems: SCIMITAR (system for countering interdiction missiles and target acquisition radars) can jam SSMs (surface-to-surface missiles) or ASMs (air-to-surface missiles) over the 8-16GHz frequency range; Susie is a passive intercept receiver which detects all types of pulsed radar transmissions over the 2-16GHz frequency; and Cutlass detects signals in the 1-18GHz range. Electronic support systems like Susie and Cutlass normally have a data processor to compare the signal to a radar library of patterns for identification.

Some other examples of European electronic war-

fare equipment are the French Thomson-CSF TMV 433 which detects incoming missiles and attempts to jam them and the French Dagaie chaff system. The West Germans also produce a chaff system – the Hot Dog/Silver Dog – which is a capable of firing infra-red decoy grenades as well. Italy's Elettronica SpA produces the Newton naval electronic warfare system consisting of the ELT/211 electronic support system, the ELT/311 jamming transmitter and the ELT/521 deception jammer. Sweden produces an ingenious chaff system called the EWS-900 which uses a pneumatic operation to launch chaff missiles.

Above and below: The Matilda radar warning system. The masthead array (above) is connected to the display unit and the processor unit (shown with the masthead array below) either on the bridge or in an operations room. Below left: A Protean chaff launcher carried on the bow of a patrol boat.

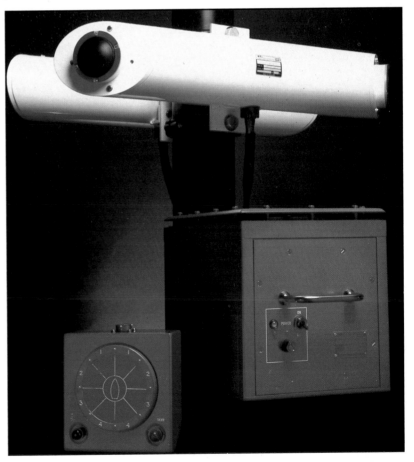

Left: The LN 66 navigation radar of the USS *Inchon*. The *Inchon* also carries SPS 58 (3D-search), SPS 40 (air-search) and SPS 10 (surface-search) radars.

The USSR's equipment in this field is shrouded in secrecy, with only names easily available such as Side Globe which is carried by the Moskva, Kresta and Kara-classes and is known to be an ECM system; the Kresta-class is also known to be carrying the Bell Clout ECM system.

More is known about the United States' electronic warfare systems. One of the latest developments is the Raytheon AN/SLQ-32 which comes in three variants. The (V)1 type warns, identifies and direction-finds incoming radar-guided SSMs or ASMs. The (V)2 is the same as the (V)1 with the additional capability of

detection of the source radar of the incoming missiles. The (V)3 provides further refinements by allowing the jamming of the missile. The (V)1 is designed for smaller ships such as Knox-class frigates, the (V)2 for the Spruance, Kidd and Oliver Hazard Perry-classes and the (V)3 for larger ships such as cruisers and aircraft carriers. The United States also produces the Mk33 Mod O chaff system. This uses a Mod O six-tube fixed launcher which operates on DC power; as the ship's electricity is AC a converter is necessary for the operation of the launcher. The manufacturer, Hycor, produces a Gemini cartridge containing both infra-red flares and chaff. The Mk33 system is to be replaced by the Mk36 system in the future. The US Navy also uses the AN/SLQ-17 deception jammer, which automatically tracks signals from missiles.

Within Nato a number of bodies have been established concerned with electronic warfare. These include the US Joint Electronic Warfare Center comprising participants from the US Army, Navy and Air Force. In the UK, a Maritime Electronic Support Group has been set up at Royal Navy Air Station Yeovilton to help train Nato naval forces in electronic warfare conditions.

Below left: The operations centre of the SLQ-32 electronic warfare system. Below: The antenna array of the SLQ-32 system; multiple-beam antennae are used to give coverage in all but the lowest frequency wavebands.

Far left: The Head Light B radar (centre) of a Soviet Kresta-II class cruiser; also visible (left) is the rear antenna of the Head Net C paired array. Left: The USS *John A Moore* has a typical combination of radars. The forward mast carries an SPS-49 long-range air-search radar on top, and aft of the middle mast is an SPG-60 fire-control radar.

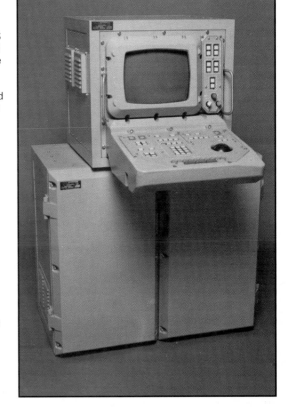

Right: The display console and processing unit of the Elettronica Newton ECM system. The Newton system has a modular format which makes it extremely versatile.

The Falklands campaign in 1982 may have shown how large a role electronic warfare will play in any future conflict, and the dangers of a lack of electronic warfare capability. HMS *Sheffield* was well-equipped with electronic support measures and a decoy launcher, yet in the short time between the Argentinian Super Etendard firing its AM39 Exocet missile and the weapon hitting the ship, none of this equipment could help. At the time of the attack, the Type 996 search radar was switched off to avoid giving the ship's position away and to enable satellite signals traffic to be transmitted. To compensate for this blindness, HMS *Sheffield* was linked to the carrier HMS *Hermes'* radar which plotted the strike formation but wrongly identified the flight as being made up of Mirage aircraft. The computer element was slow to react to the missile as the Exocet's radar operates on the same frequency as some British equipment and the computer was, in any case, programmed to regard the type as friendly, not as a threat. The result of all this was that the first any of the *Sheffield's* crew knew of the attack was when the missile's exhaust plume was spotted four or five seconds before impact; there was

no time to take any defensive measures. The fate of this sophisticated modern warship at the hands of a simple missile reinforced the attitude that more attention must be paid to countering the threat of the anti-ship missile.

The effectiveness – and one of the hazards – of using chaff was also illustrated in the Falklands by the sinking of the *Atlantic Conveyor*. Argentinian Super Etendards spotted a large target and launched their Exocet missiles. The target was HMS *Invincible*. The attack was detected by the radar of one of its escorting ships, and, after the fleet was alerted, every naval vessel nearby fired off Corvus chaff rockets and opened fire with their AA armaments. The missiles were successfully decoyed, but then they locked on to the nearby *Atlantic Conveyor* and sank it.

Iraq's use of the anti-ship missile in the Persian Gulf against merchant shipping demonstrates the high vulnerability of ships not equipped with an electronic warfare capability. For those ships with such hardware, increasing sophistication and speed of response will be demanded for their electronic warfare equipment.

Below: HMS *Sheffield*, sunk on 3 May 1982, off the Falkland Islands. The Falklands War showed the vulnerability of surface ships to sea-skimming missiles like the Exocet. Insert: A Harpoon missile being fired from an Asroc launcher. The radar-homing system of the Harpoon is 'frequency agile', rapidly changing frequency to defeat attempts to jam the guidance and thus make the missile fall wide of its target.

Interested parties

Western intervention in black Africa

When France and Britain gave independence to most of their African colonies between 1958 and 1964, they did not abandon all involvement in the internal politics of the new states. Both ex-colonial powers, and private companies based there, retained extensive economic interests in Africa, including rights to mineral resources which were sometimes of considerable strategic importance as well. These economic interests required stability and an at least modestly well-disposed government if they were to function profitably and maintain stable supplies of raw materials to the home country.

Guaranteeing stable governments in post-independence Africa was in many cases a far from simple matter, however. The new states experienced all the pressures of cultural and economic under-development, as well as the friction of tribal and religious divisions. Governments drawn from a narrow black elite rapidly enriched by corruption soon lost the allegiance of disfavoured sectors of society. With a few notable exceptions – such as the Ivory Coast and Senegal – most of the new black African regimes were challenged or overthrown within the first decade of independence.

There were some tragic cases of outright breakdown and civil war – in the ex-Belgian Congo (now Zaire) between 1960 and 1965, where the southern province of Katanga (now Shaba) attempted to secede and the east of the country subsequently rose in revolt, in Nigeria between 1967 and 1970, where the Biafran independence movement threatened to split the state, and in Chad, where a civil war, initially between north and south but ever more complicated with time, smouldered and flared almost continually from independence in 1960.

In most countries, however, open warfare was avoided, but governments were threatened by or succumbed to military coups. In the three years from 1965 to 1967 alone there were 11 successful military coups in black Africa – three in Nigeria, two in Dahomey, and one each in the ex-Belgian Congo, the Central African Republic, Upper Volta, Ghana, Burundi, and Togo. The reasons for each coup were different, but there were general causes for the prevalence of the phenomenon.

Since the armed forces were basically the old colonial armies with white officers gradually replaced by promoted blacks, they had no ingrained political ideology, but they did have a strong sense of professional pride. Many coups were a direct result of grievances about the place occupied by the army in national life, often almost like strike action in defence of army interests, pay and conditions. A coup was inevitably followed by a diversion of resources to the army, in the form of new equipment, higher salaries and the profits of high public office.

The political motivation behind the coups was most likely to be disgust with civilian politicians and their corruption or mishandling of affairs. Also, the military were in most countries drawn predominantly

from one or two ethnic groups – such as northern Hausa in the Nigerian Army – and by taking over the state they could promote or defend the interests of their own group.

Although some military governments proved beneficial, reducing corruption and increasing efficiency, military coups also threw up a number of sinister despots whose tenure of power was characterised by brutality, corruption and megalomania. Such were the regimes of Idi Amin Dada in Uganda, Jean-Bédel Bokassa in the Central African Republic and Mobutu Sese Seko in Zaire.

Search for stability

The relationship of the ex-colonial powers to military rulers and internal conflicts in the new African states followed practical self-interest. In general, they supported any government in place if it seemed to ensure stability, using their considerable influence – in the form of financial and technical aid – to keep rulers of whatever kind in line with Western economic interests. In some cases – such as that of Idi Amin in Uganda – the seizure of power by a military ruler was welcomed as an alternative to a regime viewed as dangerously left-wing, but almost all instances of direct military intervention by ex-colonial powers were in defence of an existing government.

Britain was keen to avoid military involvement if at all possible. In January 1964 British troops were sent in to quash army mutinies in Tanganyika (now known, with Zanzibar, as Tanzania), Kenya and Uganda, an intervention without which at least one of the governments might have been expected to fall. But this was militarily on a very small scale, and was not to be repeated. The only subsequent British armed intervention was reportedly by the Special Air Ser-

Above: French president Valéry Giscard d'Estaing with Jean-Bédel Bokassa, the ruler of the Central African Republic. The French kept close links with this former colony; Giscard d'Estaing was personally on very good terms with Bokassa. The former colonialists did not feel totally committed to Bokassa himself, however, and when the megalomania of this self-styled 'emperor' threatened to get out of hand, they were instrumental in overthrowing him in 1979.

vice (SAS) Regiment in the Gambia. In June 1981 Gambia's Police Field Force attempted to seize power from the president, Sir Dawda Jawara. Troops from neighbouring Senegal were called in to put down the rising, but the rescue of the president's family was apparently entrusted to a unit of the SAS.

France, on the other hand, has proved ever ready to intervene with military force in Africa. The first occasion for intervention came only weeks after the British operation in East Africa. In mid-February 1964 the president of Gabon, Leon M'Ba, was overthrown in a military coup. Very swiftly the approximately 100 French troops stationed in Gabon under the country's treaty of cooperation with France were joined by a substantial force flown in from the French base at Dakar, Senegal. The coup was easily reversed and M'Ba restored.

The French garrison in Senegal numbered 2500 men up to 1974, and the base had advanced strike aircraft among its equipment. This presence, along with another substantial garrison in the Central African Republic, greatly facilitated military operations in the continent. The Dakar base was officially transferred to the Senegal government in 1974, but France continued to use it much as before, with a battalion of Marines stationed there. The permanent garrison in the Central African Republic was withdrawn in 1971, but reestablished in 1979 with a commitment of some 1000 men.

In the 1960s, much of France's Africa policy consisted not of direct intervention in its own ex-colonies, but rather of support for secessionary movements in Nigeria (backing Biafra) and the ex-Belgian Congo (encouraging Katanga). In August 1968, however, it was considered that the situation in the former French colony of Chad had reached danger point. The regime of François Tombalbaye was menaced by a rebellion in the north of the country, which French paratroops were sent in to repress. The following year, it was necessary to expand the troop presence to 2500 men. This proved the first of a series of French troop commitments which waxed and waned with the bewildering changes of fortune in the civil war. By the 1980s, the aim of French intervention in Chad had shifted from the desire to maintain a particular government in power to the wish to repel Libyan ambitions in the mineral-rich north of the country.

In this, it came to resemble the French involvement in Mauritania in 1977, which was less a question of the survival of a regime than of upholding a certain regional balance of power and retaining control of mineral resources. Mauritania had joined with Morocco in 1975 to occupy the former Spanish colony of the Western Sahara, but armed resistance from Polisario guerrillas, backed by Libya and Algeria, had proved so successful that Mauritania itself was threatened with collapse. Polisario operations had included attacks on French staff at Mauritanian iron-ore mines. Keen to limit the influence of Libya and Algeria, France drafted in military advisers to Mauritania in October 1977, and the following December Jaguar aircraft from the Dakar base began air strikes against Polisario units. These moves were coordinated with Morocco, which simultaneously moved some 10,000 troops into Mauritania. The effect of the

Below: A British soldier examines an injured mutineer after the suppression of a mutiny at Colito barracks near Dar Es Salaam in January 1964. During this period, British forces intervened in Kenya and Uganda as well as in Tanganyika (now Tanzania) to put down mutinies. As a result the governments survived.

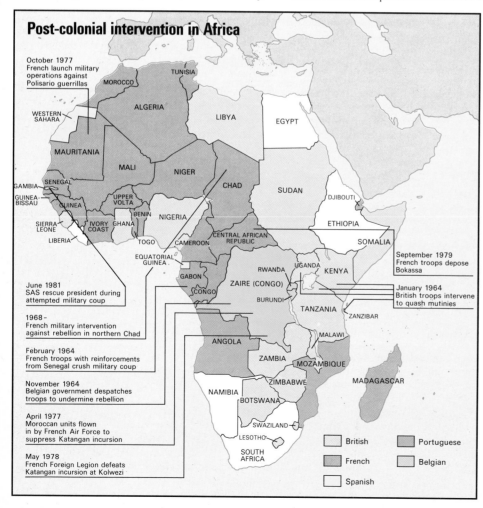

Post-colonial intervention in Africa

October 1977
French launch military operations against Polisario guerrillas

June 1981
SAS rescue president during attempted military coup

1968
French military intervention against rebellion in northern Chad

February 1964
French troops with reinforcements from Senegal crush military coup

November 1964
Belgian government despatches troops to undermine rebellion

April 1977
Moroccan units flown in by French Air Force to suppress Katangan incursion

May 1978
French Foreign Legion defeats Katangan incursion at Kolwezi

September 1979
French troops depose Bokassa

January 1964
British troops intervene to quash mutinies

TUNISIA, MOROCCO, WESTERN SAHARA, ALGERIA, LIBYA, EGYPT, MAURITANIA, MALI, NIGER, CHAD, SUDAN, DJIBOUTI, GAMBIA, SENEGAL, GUINEA-BISSAU, GUINEA, UPPER VOLTA, BENIN, NIGERIA, CENTRAL AFRICAN REPUBLIC, ETHIOPIA, SIERRA LEONE, IVORY COAST, GHANA, TOGO, CAMEROON, SOMALIA, LIBERIA, EQUATORIAL GUINEA, GABON, CONGO, ZAIRE (CONGO), RWANDA, UGANDA, KENYA, BURUNDI, TANZANIA, ZANZIBAR, ANGOLA, MALAWI, ZAMBIA, MOZAMBIQUE, MADAGASCAR, ZIMBABWE, NAMIBIA, BOTSWANA, SWAZILAND, LESOTHO, SOUTH AFRICA

British	Portuguese
French	Belgian
Spanish	

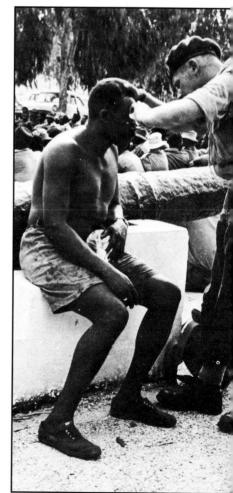

Above: French troops in the Central African Republic, during the intervention in 1979 that deposed the Emperor Bokassa. Bottom: A French marksman takes aim in Chad. The French gave constant military aid to the government of Chad during the 1970s and 1980s, latterly against Libyan forces.

intervention was not only to stop Polisario but also to make the Mauritanian government a virtual hostage of the Moroccans and their French allies, rendering ineffectual Mauritanian efforts to negotiate a settlement with the guerrillas.

France's close relationship with Morocco allowed her first intervention in a country that was *not* one of her former colonies to be largely conducted by proxy. The country in question was Zaire. The ex-colonial power, Belgium, had shown an ambivalent attitude towards its responsibility for this vast state ever since it became independent as the Congo in June 1960. The Belgians' precipitate departure at independence and their support for the Katangese secessionist movement in the south of the country – where valuable mineral reserves were located – helped initiate years of chaos from which the state never properly recovered. Although desiring to defend their interests in Katanga, the Belgians hesitated over their degree of commitment. In November 1964 Belgian paratroopers did go into Stanleyville (now Kisangani) against rebels holding white hostages; with American logistic support and the aid of white mercenary columns, the Belgians effectively undermined the rebellion. But they were far from happy with the denunciations for 'neo-colonialism' which flew in their direction after this event.

Backing Mobutu

The regime established by General Joseph-Désiré Mobutu (later renamed Mobutu Sese Seko) after a military coup in November 1965 was welcomed in the West as offering some hope of stability, and he continued to enjoy Western support even after his regime had revealed itself as appallingly corrupt and inefficient, marred by an extraordinary personality cult of the leader, and disturbed by an 'authenticity campaign' which involved not only an orgy of name-changing but also attacks on such 'relics of colonialism' as the Christian religion.

It was now in the Western interest to keep the mineral wealth of Shaba, as Katanga had been renamed, under the control of the central government of Zaire, whereas in the early 1960s such Western countries as France had backed the idea of an independent Katangese state under pro-Western control. In March 1977, when Katangese exiles invaded Shaba, the Western powers were agreed that they must be resisted. The Belgians were not eager to take the lead, so in April about 1500 Moroccan troops were flown into Shaba by the French. They swiftly dealt with the invaders – a feat that was far beyond Mobutu's army, despite the much-publicised efforts of pygmy troops operating under the cover of tall elephant grass.

The following year the Katangans returned, this time seizing the important mining town of Kolwezi. The Belgians once more held back, and so it was the paratroops of the French Foreign Legion who flew in to crush the invasion. Once they had succeeded, Belgians and Moroccans were among the force which relieved them. Both the Shaba invasions revealed France in the role of an international policeman in Africa, a role which had fallen to her for no other reason than her readiness to turn to military intervention, and proven ability to carry it off successfully.

But the principle of support for such regimes as Mobutu's, if they could guarantee a minimum level of stability, often put the moral and political credibility of the French government under strain. This was nowhere better demonstrated than in the Central African Republic (CAR), the only country in which the French intervened to unseat a government. The civilian regime established there at independence was overthrown in January 1966 by Colonel Jean-Bédel Bokassa, an officer who had seen service at lower rank in the French colonial army in Algeria and Indochina. France has important uranium interests in the CAR, and Bokassa was supported as liable to protect them. In the 1970s he developed a close relationship with French President Giscard d'Estaing, later leading to accusations of bribery against the French leader who had allegedly received extremely valuable gifts from Bokassa.

Bokassa's regime was characterised by spectacular acts of brutality, such as the public beating – to death in some cases – of prisoners in 1972, in which Bokassa personally participated. In 1976, Bokassa declared himself emperor, and his vastly expensive coronation in December 1977 was largely financed by France. In April 1979, however, the 'emperor' went too far; a massacre of schoolchildren on his orders revolted international opinion. For the French he had become a liability. In mid-September 1979 they cut off financial aid to Bokassa, with the predictable result that the 'emperor' went to Libya in search of financial backing. Once he was out of the country, on 20 September, the French flew in 1000 troops from Chad and Gabon, along with the man Bokassa had overthrown 13 years before, David Dacko, designated now to take his place. The takeover was a total success, but Dacko once more showed himself incapable of retaining power. In 1981 the chief of staff, General Kolingba, seized control, almost certainly with French encouragement.

Given the extreme weakness of most of the states which emerged from the decolonisation of black Africa – their vulnerability to regional revolts or military coups – continuing involvement of the ex-colonial powers in their internal affairs is inevitable, unless other major powers of the East or West take over that role. Whether the continuation of such an active style of intervention as that practised by the French is likely or desirable, however, remains to be seen.

Graham Brewer

In with the Legion

The Kolwezi rescue mission, 1978

In Kinshasa, on 13 May 1978, the ambassadors of Great Britain, the United States, the Soviet Union, France and Belgium were summoned to an emergency meeting by General Mobutu Sese Seko, president of Zaire (the former Belgian Congo), to hear an 'important statement'. There was no hint as to the subject of this statement, but André Ross, the French ambassador, suspected that it must be connected with news received that morning from his military attaché, and later confirmed by Colonel Yves Gras, head of the French military mission to Zaire, that Kolwezi had been occupied during the night by a large force of Katangese rebels. Kolwezi was the principal centre of the southern copper and diamond mining province of Shaba (formerly Katanga) and headquarters of the Gécamines mining company, employing locally some 3000 Europeans of various nationalities.

Ross was not mistaken in his supposition. When at 1645 hours General Mobutu finally appeared in full military regalia, it was to announce that: 'At dawn, mobile rebel Katangese forces attacked Kolwezi', but that the situation was 'well in hand' since the attack had been anticipated. This optimistic view was later repeated by the Zairean commander-in-chief, General Ba Bia, who told Colonel Gras, 'We are in complete control. No problems.'

This optimism, however, was far from justified. The invading force was a body of Katangese exiles who had fled from Zaire either in the 1960s, after the failure of the Katangese separatist movement led by Moise Tshombe and the subsequent establishment of Mobutu's autocratic regime, or more recently in March 1977 after a previous incursion into Shaba. The invaders were generally known as Katangese gendarmes, but relatively few had ever actually been

part of that force which had fought for Tshombe. During their exile in Angola the Katangans had participated in the colonial war there, on the side of the Portuguese, and in the post-independence civil war, on behalf of the Marxist Movimento Popular de Libertação de Angola (MPLA). Katangan support for the MPLA had been based on their hostility to Mobutu who was backing the other side in the civil war, the Frente Nacional de Libertação de Angola (FNLA). After the MPLA's victory, the Katangans were rewarded with training and arms from the MPLA's Cuban and Soviet backers. The Angolans gave them every facility to attack Mobutu's territory, hoping to discourage Zaire from backing continued guerrilla action by the FNLA.

Above: French paras of the 2nd REP landing in Zaire's Shaba Province. France reacted swiftly when Angolan-backed Katangese rebels seized the mining town of Kolwezi in May 1978.

Below: Two Katangan rebels, captured during an earlier invasion of Zaire in March 1977. Some of the rebels were former Katangese gendarmes, who were highly experienced soldiers.

Left: Zaire's president Mobutu Sese Seko, in the uniform of a Marshal of the Zairean Army. Mobutu seized power in 1965 after an army coup against Moise Tshombe. He was the target of many allegations of corruption and human rights violations but successful in his suppression of internal opposition.

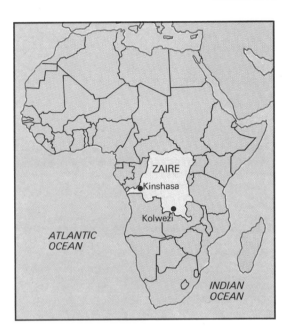

During their previous invasion in March 1977, the Katangans had shown themselves to be more than a match for the ill-disciplined and demoralised Zairean Army, although Moroccan troops had equally easily out-fought the Katangans. Once more, on this occasion, at the first sign of the invasion the small garrison of Kolwezi panicked and fled, or deserted to the other side. The Katangans were greeted with open arms by most of the local population, who were of the same tribal group and largely hostile to Mobutu's brutal and corrupt government. Showing discipline and efficiency, the Katangans quickly took the military situation in hand. They proved incapable, however, of maintaining order: by the evening of 14 May widespread looting had begun. There were also other disturbing developments. Several Europeans who refused to cooperate with the rebels were summarily executed, and whole families were incarcerated in the cellars of public buildings as 'hostages'.

When news of events in Kolwezi filtered through to Kinshasa and thence to the outside world, reactions were mixed. Some Western leaders interpreted the invasion as a Soviet-inspired attempt to wrest control of valuable mineral resources from Western companies and a pro-Western regime; there were even unconfirmed reports that Cuban troops were actively involved. Much of world opinion, however, saw the events as essentially a fully justified revolt against an unacceptable government. Even in the West, despite concern for the fate of the white hostages, doubts were expressed as to the advisability of continuing to prop up Mobutu's regime which seemed incapable of establishing political stability and which had demonstrated an economic incompetence and corruption that

Below: Zairean soldiers investigate a bow and arrow abandoned by a unit of Mobutu's pygmies during the 1977 fighting in Shaba. Though equipped with more modern weapons, the Zairean troops who faced the Katangans were ill-disciplined and demoralised. Only foreign intervention saved them from defeat.

was costing its Western backers dear. It was widely considered that it was up to Belgium, as the former colonial power, to take the initiative. Brussels, however, argued that 'European troop movements in Africa would only exasperate the rebels and thus goad them into further excesses'. This point of view seemed to be accepted even when it was learned that the elite corps of the Zairean Army, the 311th Parachute Regiment, flown in to retake Kolwezi, had been virtually annihilated.

Paradrop to disaster

The Katangans had been ready for the airborne operation which was launched on 16 May. As the Zairean paras floated down to earth many were killed in the air. Most of those who touched down fell to Katangese bullets or bayonets before they had time to free themselves of their parachutes. The few who managed to regroup were too demoralised to put up any effective resistance, let alone assume the offensive. By evening, the forlorn survivors had split up into scattered groups, and were trying to make good their escape under cover of the jungle.

In the meantime, Ambassador Ross had been in direct telephone contact with French President Giscard d'Estaing, urging a military intervention, and a decision to intervene was taken after the French had received an assurance of full American backing from President Jimmy Carter. The need to rescue the hostages and restore order provided an adequate public justification for the operation, and French intervention was, of course, welcomed by Mobutu.

The unit designated for the mission was the 2nd Régiment Etrangère Parachutiste (2nd REP), at that moment stationed at Raffali barracks on the outskirts of Calvi on the island of Corsica. Once the go-ahead had been given, it is doubtful whether any airborne operation has ever got under way so rapidly and with so little normal logistic support. The warning order was issued at 0430 hours on 17 May. By the evening

Above: French paras regroup after their almost unopposed landing near Kolwezi. Right: A rebel suspect is arrested during the operation to clear the captured town. Many of the local population had welcomed the rebels, and some of the massacres had been the result of local bitterness against the whites.

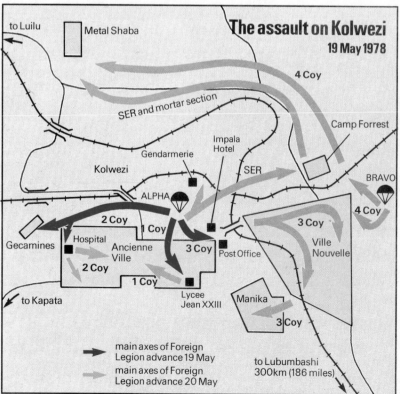

The assault on Kolwezi
19 May 1978

to Luilu
Metal Shaba
4 Coy
SER and mortar section
Camp Forrest
Gendarmerie
Impala Hotel
Kolwezi
SER
BRAVO
ALPHA
4 Coy
2 Coy
1 Coy
3 Coy
Gecamines
Hospital
Ancienne Ville
3 Coy
Ville Nouvelle
Post Office
2 Coy
1 Coy
to Kapata
Lycee Jean XXIII
Manika
3 Coy
to Lubumbashi 300km (186 miles)

→ main axes of Foreign Legion advance 19 May
→ main axes of Foreign Legion advance 20 May

Right: Colonel Erulin, commander of the 2nd REP which conducted the Kolwezi operation, briefs a group of his officers before the assault.

all men on leave, those on outlying duty on the island, or attending courses in France itself had reassembled, so that the move by truck to Solenzaro airport could be made during the night of 17/18 May.

Only five civilian DC8s had been brought together by the morning of the 18th, but the regimental commander, Colonel Philippe Erulin, mindful of the desperate urgency of his mission, decided that a first echelon consisting of the 1st, 2nd and 3rd Companies with a skeleton HQ company, must take off immediately. By 1130 hours all five DC8s were airborne, arriving the following day, 19 May, at Kinshasa. Then there occurred an infuriating delay before the legionnaires could be transferred to Zairean transport aircraft for the flight to Kolwezi itself. It was found that the release mechanism of the American T10 parachutes being issued from local stores did not fit standard French equipment. This meant that hours had to be spent while the legionnaires themselves made the necessary on the spot adjustments. However, no sooner had this problem been overcome than Colonel Erulin had to face two further obstacles. There was still no sign of the second echelon – the 4th Company, the SER (Section d'éclairage et de reconnaissance), the 81mm mortar platoon and the bulk of HQ company, and the fact that instead of the five Zairean C-130s and two Transall C-160s promised for the first echelon, only four C-130s and a single Transall could be mustered. Again Colonel Erulin did not hesitate. Reports were coming in of the worsening situation in Kolwezi. He decided that he would not wait for the second echelon, and that 80 men, instead of the regulation 64, would be packed into each aircraft. 'Enough', as Erulin himself said, 'to scare the wits out of the most hardened parachutist.' Take-off was at 1040 hours. At 1515 hours, the regiment began its first operational drop since the tragic battle of Dien Bien Phu 24 years previously.

The pre-selected dropping zone, code-named 'Alpha', was just to the north of what was known as the 'Ancienne Ville' and in the vicinity of the luxury Impala Hotel where, it was believed, a number of hostages were being held. It was, of course, broad daylight, but fortunately this time the Katangans were not expecting the attack. Furthermore, much of the dropping zone was covered by 3m (10 feet) tall elephant grass interspersed by 4m (13 feet) high ant-hills, which gave effective cover once the legionnaires had touched the ground. Colonel Erulin himself landed on an ant-hill heap and deemed himself lucky to have escaped with no more than a badly cut cheek.

Visibility was virtually nil in the elephant grass and there was an inevitable delay in regrouping. It was some hours before a number of legionnaires linked up with their units, but the majority was soon reassembled to begin an immediate move on the principal objectives. These were: for 1 Company, the Lycée Jean XXIII in the southern sector of the Ancienne Ville; for 2 Company, the town's western sector, in order to free hostages reported to be locked up in the hospital there, thence to seize the Gécamines offices and their huge garage just outside the walls, known to hold a vast stock of vehicles which Colonel Erulin hoped to use until the arrival of the regimental transport; and for 3 Company, to storm the Impala Hotel and the Post Office, and hold the bridge connecting the Ancienne Ville with the Ville Nouvelle.

Complete surprise

The few astonished Katangans in the vicinity of the dropping zone, taken completely by surprise, opened up a desultory fire which accounted for the first Legion death, that of Corporal Arnold, an Englishman. Opposition, however, was soon dispersed, but as the companies pressed on into the town they ran into stronger resistance and were subject to continual sniping.

The legionnaires were heavily outnumbered, but in addition to their determination to uphold regimental tradition, they were roused to what their war diary describes as 'superhuman efforts' by the awareness that the survival of the hostages depended on the speed with which the Katangans could be driven from their positions. They found plentiful evidence as they advanced that massacres had already taken place. One legionnaire remembered: 'our nostrils were filled by the stench of decomposing bodies on entering the maze of villa-bordered avenues. Corpses, many of which had been gnawed by stray dogs, were heaped in the gutters. There were pools of blood everywhere....' Undoubtedly, in their enthusiasm to advance as quickly as possible, the legionnaires themselves were none too discriminating over who they killed. Any blacks encountered were likely to be shot on sight with no questions asked. There was little time to sort out who was the enemy, especially since most of the local population were cooperating with the rebels.

Street fighting lasted all day. But the Katangese defence was so ill-organised that, despite frequent brief but savage encounters, by late afternoon all major objectives had been secured and a number of Europeans had been rescued, most of them in an advanced state of shock, as well as suffering severely from hunger and thirst. Legion casualties had been almost miraculously low, whereas the Katangese dead were estimated to number several hundreds. In addition, large stocks of modern arms, of Russian, Chinese and American origin, had been captured.

One of the last Katangese strongholds to fall was the Impala Hotel. There, the Katangans slaughtered their hostages before succumbing. The cellars were heaped with the mangled corpses of men, women and children.

At 1755 hours with the sudden tropical night about to fall, the C-130s carrying the regiment's second echelon appeared over the town, but by then Colonel Erulin was so satisfied with the results of the day's operations that he did not think it either wise, or necessary, to risk the possible confusion that might arise from a night drop in such close country. Orders were given, therefore, to continue the flight to the town of Lubumbashi (formerly Elisabethville), some 300 km (200 miles) to the southeast, occupied by the remnants of the ill-fated Zairean 311th Parachute Regiment. The reinforcements were to be back over target at first light the following morning.

Night skirmishes

For the legionnaires in Kolwezi, it was the third consecutive night without sleep. A double task confronted them. The first was to prevent infiltration by rebel forces from outside; the second to deal with Katangans who had shut themselves in deserted houses and who endeavoured to break through French posts and patrols under cover of darkness to rejoin their comrades in the open country. Fighting flared up, ending invariably to the legionnaires' advantage. By dawn the toll of Katangese dead had mounted sharply; six legionnaires had been wounded.

Dawn also saw the arrival of the second echelon from Lubumbashi. The SER, the mortar section and the bulk of HQ company dropped on zone Alpha. 4 Company fell on a new zone, designated 'Bravo', just to the east of the Ville Nouvelle.

The combined force then moved into action. 1 Company was to clear the last Katangans from the Ancienne Ville's southern sector, 2 Company performing a similar task in the west. The SER moved to the north of 'Alpha' to occupy the Gendarmerie and Camp Forrest, while 3 Company continued with the mopping up of the Ville Nouvelle prior to moving on

Below: While the rebels had massacred considerable numbers of the local white population, there were later reports of large-scale reprisals by the Zairean Army against Kolwezi mineworkers who were suspected of supporting the rebels.
Bottom: A mass is held for four legionnaires, killed during the fighting in Kolwezi.

to the little suburb of Manika where, it was reported, those Katangans who had escaped the Legion net were regrouping. From dropping zone 'Bravo' 4 Company took up positions to seal off any escape routes from the Ville Nouvelle to the east.

The morning saw surprisingly little action, but towards 1500 hours, as the Legion pushed out to comb the workmens' suburbs – a network of individual villages – 4 Company was heavily engaged in the neighbourhood of Metal Shaba, some 5km (3 miles) to the north. The leading platoon's *sergent-chef* (platoon sergeant), Daniel, was killed outright, a legionnaire mortally wounded, and the platoon momentarily pinned down. A call for support was promptly answered by the SER. Moving in confiscated vehicles with a section of the 81mm mortars, they opened up an accurate bombardment on the enemy positions. The Katangans were beginning to fall back when a newly-arrived lorry-borne Katangese column, supported by two light tanks of Soviet design, attempted to counter-attack. Engaged by the 89mm LRACs of the SER and the mortars, the counter-attack was broken up before it got under way, the tanks receiving direct hits and the lorries set ablaze. The survivors fled, leaving over 80 of their dead on the ground.

The 21st was a quiet day which saw the arrival of the parachutists' regimental vehicles. Mobile at last, three companies were despatched on the 22nd to the town of Kapata, well to the southwest of Kolwezi, where scattered Katangese groups were rounded up without the loss of a single legionnaire. The following day, the 23rd, a mobile column was sent to Luilu to the northwest. On the way a group of Europeans was picked up, mostly women and children who had seen their menfolk hacked to death before their eyes. Half starving and demented with fear, they had been wandering in the bush for eight days, brackish water their only means of subsistence.

Luilu was found to be deserted, but at 1630 hours a platoon of 1 Company was ambushed to the west of the town. Hidden by the elephant grass, the Katangans took the legionnaires by surprise. A legionnaire was killed and the senior corporal, Harte, seriously wounded. This minor action showed the rebels at their most determined. The ambushing party consisted of only five Katangans, prepared to die after inflicting maximum casualties on the enemy. It was not until night was falling that, after a confused skirmish in the tall grass, the party was finally cornered and the five men killed.

Final ambush

There was also another brief action that evening, during the return from the search of Kapata. One of the platoon commanders, Lieutenant Bourgain, was driving in a commandeered Mercedes, when two Katangans suddenly leaped from the bush and fired straight into the windscreen, shattering the glass. Reacting automatically, Bourgain's driver accelerated, running the two men down. At the same time a burst of fire from concealed enemy positions wounded Corporal Breton and Legionnaire Kruger. Fire was promptly returned, resulting in two more Katangans being killed.

By 24 May, it was obvious that what Mobutu had termed 'the second Shaba war' had been won. The Katangans withdrew to Angola; the last action, in fact, took place on 25 May when a large group of retreating Katangans was surprised, surrounded, and wiped out. Though Belgian and Zairean contingents were beginning to arrive, Mobutu was anxious to retain the REP. His request was refused by Giscard d'Estaing, who had no wish to hear France accused of neo-colonialism. The regiment moved into camp in Lubumbashi on 28 May and on 5 June the first batch of 2nd REP emplaned for the flight back to Solenzaro. The operation had brought great credit to the regiment. About 90 per cent of the men engaged had been without battle experience, yet, as Colonel Erulin stated, 'as soon as the first shot was fired, all acted like veterans'. They lost only five dead and 20 wounded.

In the aftermath of the invasion, a force of 3000 men from a number of African countries was drafted in to stabilise the situation, while the Belgians and French strove to improve the quality of the Zairean Army, which had further disgraced itself by acts of vengeance against the local population on reoccupying Kolwezi. But the crucial contribution to Zaire's security came from a new diplomatic agreement with Angola at the end of 1978, under which each country agreed to withdraw support from armed movements hostile to the other. Already weakened by defeats in 1977 and 1978, the Katangese exiles were now deprived of backing and bases.

Patrick Turnbull

Below: A Legion sergeant receiving orders during a lull in fighting. Note the red scarf worn around the right shoulder to identify French troops. Highly disciplined, well equipped and with a long tradition of colonial warfare, the Legion was the ideal instrument for French interventionist policy in Africa during the 1970s.

The fall

Tanzanian forces invade Uganda

It is ironical that the seizure of power by one of the modern world's most infamous rulers in Uganda in 1971 was greeted with enthusiasm by most of the Ugandan population and by much of world opinion. It was on the morning of 25 January, as President Milton Obote was returning from the Commonwealth Conference in Singapore, that elements of the Ugandan Army and police headed by the country's commander-in-chief Major-General Idi Amin Dada, a former sergeant in the King's African Rifles, seized control of the capital, Kampala. Key points in the capital and the international airport at Entebbe were occupied. Resistance to the coup was light and came from pro-Obote factions in the armed forces. In all, less than 100 casualties were reported.

Popular support for the coup was evidence of how, in the decade since independence in 1962, Obote's government had failed in its efforts to unite Uganda's 22 tribal groups and overcome the serious problems of the economy. Backing for Amin from the West was more a response to extreme measures – known as the 'Move to the Left' – adopted by Obote in 1970 to stem

the deteriorating political and economic situation. Most alarming to foreign interests were extensive proposals for nationalisation of foreign firms.

Yet plenty of evidence was already available to indicate the sort of regime Idi Amin might be expected to install. During his time in the British colonial force before independence, Amin had seen service against Mau Mau in Kenya and had been generally liked by his British officers, but his career in Uganda after 1962 was ominous. His rise to the top of the army had resulted from a readiness to serve willingly in the repression of opposition: in May 1966 he had led government troops in an assault on the palace of the Kubaka (King) of Buganda, Sir Edward Mutesa, who was the main focus of opposition to Obote. After some sharp fighting, with casualties on both sides, Mutesa had been driven into exile. As commander-in-chief, Amin had been widely suspected of embezzling government funds on a large scale; in January 1970 an officer who had accused Amin of embezzlement was murdered, along with his wife. It is almost certain that, had the coup not taken place, Amin

Above: A triumphant Tanzanian soldier being carried shoulder-high by Ugandan supporters of the anti-Amin Ugandan National Liberation Front during the capture of Kampala by Tanzanian and UNLF troops in April 1979. Right: Idi Amin, the feared and brutal dictator deposed by the Tanzanian invasion.

Left: The Kabaka of Buganda, Sir Edward Mutesa, who was deposed by a 1966 coup planned by Prime Minister Milton Obote and carried out by Idi Amin, then Obote's loyal commander-in-chief. Right: Obote (centre) with Daniel arap Moi of Kenya (left), Kenneth Kaunda of Zambia (second from left), and Julius Nyerere of Tanzania (far right). Obote assumed the leadership of Uganda in 1962, but soon became unpopular, relying more and more on his security forces, led by Amin.

f Idi Amin

would have been charged with these murders.

In the weeks following the coup, Amin moved to consolidate the support he had received, while covertly beginning to stifle opposition. Obote's secret police were disbanded and promises on the economy were freely bandied about, while within weeks Amin had established himself as head of the state and of the armed forces with no formal constraints on his power. He was unable to stifle external dissent from Tanzania, whose president, Julius Nyerere, had given refuge to Obote and was steadfastly refusing to recognise the new regime and promising aid to its opponents, but secret orders were given to purge the Ugandan Army of pro-Obote groups, drawn from the Lango and Acholi tribes based in the Karamoja region of northern Uganda. On 29 January the first victims of the purges, 1000 soldiers, many dead or badly beaten, were taken by covered convoy to Luzira prison in the suburbs of Kampala.

The Ugandan people's honeymoon with the new regime was short-lived as it failed to deliver on its early promises. A series of strikes by key workers between September and December 1971 prompted Amin to issue decrees suspending all political activities for two years 'as a temporary measure'. Coming from a small Muslim tribe in the west Nile region of northern Uganda, the Kakwa, he was well aware of the fragile nature of the national support he enjoyed and began to consolidate his position by establishing absolute personal control over the state and its machinery. The army and police were to become the instruments of his power.

Intimidation, torture and murder

Though Amin had abolished Obote's secret police he wasted no time in setting up his own. Two bodies, the State Research Bureau (SRB) and the Public Safety Unit (PSU) – supposedly operating to curb *magendo* (black-marketeering) – began to root out and silence dissent. Using intimidation, torture and murder the SRB's 2000 full-time agents, given a weekly allowance of up to £50 to pay informers, were likened to God, 'for they were found everywhere'. Both were given the power to detain indefinitely any person suspected of being dangerous or endeavouring to excite enmity between the people of Uganda and its government. An SRB identity card gave its owner the power of the state, allowing many to settle their own private scores. The secret police's victims were daily found dumped in Lake Victoria or Namanve forest outside Kampala.

To ensure the loyalty of the judiciary and civilian police Amin handed them over to the armed forces. In September 1972 the Ugandan chief justice was dragged out of the East African court of appeals and military tribunals were appointed to judge major violations of the law. The inspector-general of police was replaced by a Police Council whose members were drawn from the army. Military training became compulsory for the police.

The militarisation of Uganda was rapid and comprehensive. Between 1971 and 1972 the army's strength trebled and supplies were gathered to equip them. Initially, the supply of the Ugandan Army was carried out by Britain and Israel. In July 1971 Amin flew to both countries and received over £2 million worth of equipment, including armoured cars and smallarms. However, by 1972 his relations with the suppliers were deteriorating. In April 1972 Amin

The Tanzanian invasion
March 1979

SUDAN

NILE

Albert Nile

NORTHERN

KARAMOJA

Gulu

Moroto

Victoria Nile

UGANDA

Lake Albert

WESTERN

Lake Kyoga

EASTERN

ZAIRE

NORTH BUGANDA

BUSOGA

Fort Portal

Kampala

Jinja-Bugembe

Kilembe

Entebbe

KENYA

Lake Edward

Masaka

Mbarara

SOUTHERN

SOUTH BUGANDA

Lake Victoria

main axes of Tanzanian advance

Libyan military aid airlifted to Uganda

RWANDA

TANZANIA

Below: Amin relied totally on his control of the armed forces, purged and built up with members of his own Muslim tribe and Arab mercenaries. His secret police were responsible for many atrocities, and public executions became a feature of Ugandan life. Below right: Amin cultivated an image as a smiling paternal figure, loved by his people. Here he manages to combine it with the humiliation of a group of local white businessmen in July 1975.

expelled all Israelis and handed over their embassy to the Palestine Liberation Organisation. His expulsion of Ugandan Asians in the autumn of the same year and his proclaiming himself 'the conqueror of the British Empire' soured relations with Britain.

Amin turned to the Soviet Union and its satellites for aid. As early as July 1972 a delegation visited Russia, followed in April 1973 by a return visit from Moscow. At least four consignments of weapons, including T54/55s, armoured personnel carriers, bridgelaying equipment, MiG-17s and -21s and artillery, reached Uganda between 1973 and 1975. Ugandan troops were sent for training in the Eastern bloc and Soviet advisers gave instruction to the air force. Amin was able to boast to Tanzania that Soviet arms supplies would 'make the balance of power good in East Africa'.

After purging the armed forces Amin set about changing their character by drafting in Muslims from his own tribe or from Arab states, particularly Sudanese, Nubians and Palestinians. To reduce unemployment Uganda's urban poor were moved into the armed forces. In early 1973 6000 unemployed were gathered in City Square, Kampala and conscripted into the army after Amin had announced a nationwide programme in which military training facilities were to be reserved for jobless volunteers.

While establishing control over Uganda's armed forces, Amin strove to fulfil his promises to develop the economy. In 1972 he declared an 'economic war' against corruption and inefficiency. Between September and November the 27,000 Ugandan Asians, who formed the country's professional class and ran most of Kampala's small businesses, were expelled to 'Ugandanise' the economy. In response to Britain's subsequent ending of economic aid Amin nationalised 41 foreign-owned companies that were allegedly 'still milking the country's economy'. The expulsions and accusations were used to direct internal dissent against outsiders rather than the regime.

Thirty army and air force officers worked at distributing to Ugandans businesses which were left by the British Asians. Officers such as Major Malijawungu, commander-in-chief of the 2nd Infantry Brigade at Masaka, were put in charge of abandoned shops to ensure 'the fair allocation of business'. Amin himself took personal control of the Kilembe copper mines.

Under this inept and self-serving management the Ugandan economy began to collapse. Inflation rocketed and the output of raw materials plummeted. While publicly raving against black-marketeers and declaring that 'overcharging, hoarding and cheating would be treated as treason' with those found guilty likely to face the firing-squad, Amin and his closest advisers amassed massive personal fortunes. By mid-1977 he had given up all pretence of trying to control the economy.

As the regime's attempts to revitalise the economy failed Amin moved to secure his own future and curry favour with some Islamic states by building up a personal retinue of fellow Muslims whose allegiance would be beyond question. From 1976, in a programme of Islamisation, Arabic broadcasts were made on television and radio, the Islamic Friday became a

public holiday and conversion to Islam semi-official policy. A *mauledi* (mass conversion) was held for the Simba (Lion) Battalion and the 'Suicide Mechanised Revolutionary Reconnaissance Regiment' held its own grand conversion.

Already isolated from most Ugandans, Amin's attempts to create an Islamic state cut him off from elements of the armed forces. In September 1978 rumours of an assassination attempt prompted him to send units of the SRB and Marines to Gulu Barracks to kill soldiers of the Chui (Leopard) Battalion suspected of disloyalty. A month later a plot by members of the Simba Battalion was uncovered. Loyal troops compiled a death list of 7000 names drawn from the Lango and Acholi tribes, suspected of complicity.

In the early years of his regime Amin successfully manipulated the international political order to his own advantage; the Eastern bloc was played off against the West. After the cutting of the old colonial ties with Britain, the United States became the major market for Ugandan exports and, in return, American companies provided equipment for his security forces. The Soviet Union, eager to gain further bases in the area, was more than willing to supply the armed forces. Amin was also able to establish himself as a major figure in African politics during his chairmanship of the Organization of African Unity (OAU) between 1975 and 1976.

As stories of atrocities trickled out of Uganda and Amin's actions and pronouncements became more extreme, however, his regime was increasingly ostracised by the international community. Relations were worsened by some highly-publicised incidents: for example in July 1976, the disappearance of Dora Bloch, a hostage during the raid on Entebbe, believed murdered in hospital; and early in 1977, the murder of the Anglican Archbishop of Uganda. Thirty-three heads of state at the 1977 Commonwealth Conference condemned Amin's regime.

Sometime in October 1978 Amin took the decision to invade Tanzania. Aware of the growing unrest in Uganda he hoped to redirect internal opposition against a foreign state, to unite the army whose loyalty had been called into question by a series of recent mutinies and to exact some revenge for Nyerere's continuing support for Obote. By early November 3000 Ugandan soldiers had occupied the 950 square km (400 square miles) of the isolated Kagera salient in northern Tanzania.

Six years earlier, in September 1972, a force of Ugandan exiles had tried an invasion in the opposite direction, but their ill-equipped force had been easily defeated by the Ugandan Army. On that occasion Tanzania had not become actively involved in the fighting, although Amin's air force had bombed some Tanzanian border villages in retaliation for the exiles' action. With a substantial part of his territory occupied by the Ugandans, however, on this occasion President Nyerere decided to call Amin's bluff and began to move the Tanzanian Army up to the war zone. Nyerere was aware firstly that international opinion was by this time extremely hostile to Amin, and secondly that the Ugandan leader had now himself broken the OAU's founding charter by violating a neighbouring country's territory, thus justifying a Tanzanian riposte.

Pursuit across the border

At first the Tanzanian Army restricted itself to regaining its lost territory in the Kagera during November and December. By the start of 1979 this had been achieved, although Amin's troops had had time to massacre some 8000 of the inhabitants of the region. There was then a pause as Tanzania considered pursuit across the border. An intense political effort concentrated on the much-divided Ugandan exile groups succeeded in March in uniting them as the Ugandan National Liberation Front (UNLF), although at the cost of excluding Obote, Tanzania's own favourite to replace Amin. A force of some 10,000 Tanzanian troops and about 1000 exiles was assembled, and in March they embarked on an invasion to overthrow Amin.

Progress was cautious and slow. The Tanzanians chose to advance at infantry marching pace along two axes, one following the edge of Lake Victoria and the other pushing north to Fort Portal and then turning east against Kampala. The response of the Ugandan forces showed the depredations of Amin's rule. Although there was no mutiny or popular uprising, as Nyerere may have hoped, morale was clearly low.

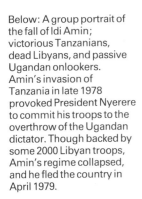

Below: A group portrait of the fall of Idi Amin; victorious Tanzanians, dead Libyans, and passive Ugandan onlookers. Amin's invasion of Tanzania in late 1978 provoked President Nyerere to commit his troops to the overthrow of the Ugandan dictator. Though backed by some 2000 Libyan troops, Amin's regime collapsed, and he fled the country in April 1979.

Uganda found arms supplies hard to obtain, as both Western and Eastern bloc suppliers shunned Amin. Colonel Gaddafi of Libya, however, came to his fellow Muslim's aid. About 2000 Libyan troops were airlifted in to defend Kampala.

After advancing for five weeks, fighting a number of scattered engagements, the Tanzanians assaulted Entebbe airport on 7 April. They then laid siege to Kampala, bombarding the defensive positions largely manned by Libyans. A counter-offensive was easily halted, with considerable damage inflicted on a Libyan column, and on 10 April Ugandan exiles, soon followed by Tanzanian forces, entered the capital virtually unopposed as the remnants of Amin's supporters retreated northwards. At the end of April, Amin fled the country, eventually to settle in Saudi Arabia. By the end of May most organised resistance had ceased.

Despite the possession of quite modern aircraft and armoured vehicles by both sides – largely Soviet-supplied in both cases – the war was chiefly fought at infantry level. Indisciplined Ugandan troops created mayhem in their retreat, causing considerable civilian casualties. Amongst the soldiers, the Libyans suffered proportionally the heaviest losses, with some 400 dead, a large number in a troop carrier which unfortunately tried to land at Entebbe after the airport had fallen to the Tanzanians.

After maladministration, terror and war, Uganda was in desperate need of peace and reconstruction, but its sorry plight continued. The first government, set up by Dr Yusuf Lule, lasted two months; in May 1980 his successor, Godfrey Binaisa, was deposed by pro-Obote elements in the UNLF's military commission. The following December, in extremely dubious elections held under military surveillance, with a force of 25,000 Tanzanian troops still occupying the country, Obote was finally returned to power. A quite unacceptable ruler to much of the population, he presided over a further slide of Uganda into chaos.

Already, by the time Obote took over, Tanzanian and Ugandan government forces had been accused of widespread massacres in Amin's home area of the west Nile, during operations in October 1980 official-ly designed to foil a supposed invasion by pro-Amin exiles from neighbouring Zaire. In Karamoja, also in 1980, famine took some 30,000 lives, as bureaucratic incompetence, corruption and the breakdown of law and order made relief operations ineffectual. After Obote's rise to power, the main opposition groups turned to armed resistance, adding various guerrilla groups to the already considerable number of armed bands of various descriptions roaming the country.

In January 1982 some of the guerrilla groups formed a Ugandan Popular Front, and declared themselves in control of much of the country. With the final withdrawal of Tanzanian forces in 1982, Obote's regime was very exposed. There were frequent ambushes, attacks on police posts and army barracks, and terrorist acts in Kampala itself. In February 1982 several hundred guerrillas raided the capital in a show of strength, and in March 1983 a general guerrilla offensive was announced by the most active movement, the National Resistance Army.

Government forces responded to the deteriorating security situation with mass arrests, torture and massacres. In 1982 some 20,000 refugees were reckoned to have fled to neighbouring countries since the government began operations against the rebels, and by 1984 no end to the chaotic warfare was in sight.

Ian Westwell

Above: Tanzanian soldiers arrest two Ugandans suspected of belonging to Amin's army. Though organised resistance had ended by May 1979, groups of undisciplined former Ugandan Army soldiers still loyal to Amin remained a serious security problem for the new government of Yusuf Lule and his successor Milton Obote, the man Amin had overthrown on his way to power.

Below: Ugandan refugees flee across the White Nile into the Sudan. Members of Amin's own tribe who feared reprisals, as well as victims of the armed bands which roamed the Ugandan countryside, swelled the numbers in Sudanese refugee camps.

NATO CRUISERS

The cruiser had its origins in the need for a ship to fulfil two roles in naval warfare: to defend against destroyers and other light ships making torpedo attacks on the main battle fleet, and to scout or to raid enemy commercial and military shipping. In the modern era the decline of the battleship has meant that cruisers are chiefly used to screen aircraft carriers against air and submarine attack, although they may still be used against, or in defence of, merchant and troop convoys.

The oldest cruisers currently serving in the West are those belonging to France and Italy. The French cruiser *Colbert* was laid down in December 1953 and commissioned in 1959, having been designed originally as an anti-aircraft cruiser. Displacing 11,500 tonnes fully loaded *Colbert* has been refitted several times, most recently in 1981-82, when it was provided with satellite communications. Perhaps the most important feature of this ship, now used for radar control of air strikes, is the electronics. *Colbert* is provided with a SENIT data automation system, radar intercept equipment, wireless intercept equipment, a DRBV 50 surveillance radar, a DRBV 23C air surveillance radar, DRBV warning radar, DRBI 10D height-finder radar and a Decca RM416 navigation radar. The armament consists of four Exocet MM38 launchers, two 100mm single automatic guns, and 12 57mm AA in twin mounts; fire control is provided by two DRBR 51 radars, one DRBR 32C and one DRBC 31. *Colbert* has an armoured belt of 50-80mm (2-3in) thickness and a 50mm (2in) thick armoured deck. Forty-eight Masucra (Mk 2 Mod 3) missiles provide the main anti-aircraft defence. Two propeller shafts connected to two sets of CEM-Parsons geared turbines giving 86,000 shp produce a top speed of 31.5 knots.

Also serving in the Mediterranean are the two Italian cruisers *Andrea Doria* and *Caio Duilio* (the latter named after the Roman admiral Caius Duilius). These are smaller cruisers, weighing 5000 tonnes standard and 6500 tonnes full load (only the American Leahy class is lighter). They carry four AB-212 helicopters for anti-submarine warfare (ASW), and are armed with Terrier surface-to-air missiles (SAMs) updated for Standard-ER missiles. They were designed as escort cruisers, and possess long-range search radar (*Duilio* has SPS 40, *Doria* SPS 768). Both ships have 3in dual-purpose, fully-automatic guns (eight in *Andrea Doria* and six in *Caio Duilio*), and Gyrofin-Salmoiraghi roll-damping stabilisers. Propulsion is provided by two Italian-built double-reduction geared turbines propelling two shafts with 60,000 shp. Though the horsepower is less than in *Colbert*, being lighter these two ships attain a similar speed of 31 knots.

The main cruiser force in Nato is provided by the United States Navy (USN); however, the majority of the current cruiser fleet did not officially become cruisers until 1975. Prior to that date, they were termed destroyer leaders. In this way the 35 ships rated cruisers either in service or reserve at the height of the Vietnam War have been replaced with a fleet of 32, although only five vessels are present on both lists and only seven ships are of new construction

The oldest ships in the present active cruiser fleet are the nine members of the Leahy class, rated as guided-missile cruisers. In keeping with the Task Force doctrine emerging from the carrier battle groups of World War II, these ships were intended to

Previous page: The USS *Mississippi* executing a turn at speed; the Mark 26 Asroc-Standard MR launcher is prominent on the bow. Above: The French cruiser *Colbert*. The 100mm turrets occupy the forward positions and the launcher aft is for the Masucra missiles.

Left: The *Caio Duilio* underway in the Mediterranean Sea. Below: The USS *Leahy* at anchor; the SPS 48 radar is the large square antenna atop the forward mack.

screen fast carrier forces. They were authorised in 1958 and 1959, and the last entered service in 1964 (USS *Richmond K. Turner*).

The Leahy class was followed by the nine-ship Belknap class. These were also originally rated as large destroyers, and were authorised in 1961 and 1962. Both of these classes were built after the world's first nuclear-powered warship, the USS *Long Beach*, which was also the first warship with a guided-missile main battery. Two other single-ship classes, the USS *Bainbridge* and the USS *Truxtun*, both of which were nuclear-powered, complete the generation of US cruisers authorised between World War II and the Vietnam War.

After that there was a pause in cruiser building by the USN until the early 1970s when two ships of the California class were laid down, entering service in 1974 and 1975. These were followed by the Virginia class of four ships, and the Ticonderoga class, projected of 10 ships (two were in service in 1984). At the time these ships were under consideration, a debate over the direction of US ship construction was occurring in the American military establishment. The argument was between supporters of expensive, high-technology ships and those who saw the future in larger numbers of cheaper ships with more emphasis on actual ordnance at the expense of high-cost electronic warfare equipment. By the mid-1970s a compromise had been reached in the concept of a 'high-low mix'. This envisaged a fleet of cheap, simple and robust ships built round a smaller group of expensive, high-technology vessels. These philosophies are meant to be embodied in the Ticonderoga and Virginia classes respectively. The high costs have not been entirely suppressed, as can be seen by the price tag for the *Ticonderoga* of $930 million.

Certain similarities can be seen running through all these classes, with two SAM launchers (single or twin) on all except the Belknap class and the *Truxtun* (the latter was built on a modified Belknap hull). The earlier ships are all equipped with the Mark 101 launcher firing Standard missiles; in the Belknap class and the *Truxtun* the launchers are dual purpose, also capable

Above: The USS *Belknap* anchoring in Agusta Bay, Sicily, with its SH-2F Seasprite on the flight deck. Right: The USS *Bainbridge* serves in the Pacific Ocean; above the bridge are two SPS-55B fire-control radar.

Below: This waterline photograph of the USS *Long Beach* shows the prominent clipper bow. This ship was the US Navy's first all-missile armed warship.

of firing Asroc anti-submarine rockets. The *Long Beach*, the *Bainbridge* and the Leahy class have a separate Asroc launcher. These ships are presently being fitted with the Phalanx CIWS (close-in weapons system) for protection against sea-skimming missiles like the Exocet, as well as low-flying aircraft. The Belknap class, *Long Beach* and *Truxtun* are all armed with 5in guns. The *Long Beach* has two 5in guns in the Mark 30 mount, while the *Truxtun* and the Belknap class have the 5in in the Mark 42 mount. All of these ships have been fitted since building with the Harpoon surface-to-surface missile, eight missiles to a ship in two quad-launchers. They also all carry the Mark 32 ASW torpedo – the *Long Beach* has two triple sets, as does the Leahy class, the *Bainbridge* and the Belknap class. The *Truxtun* only carries four tubes. The Belknap class and the *Truxtun* carry an SH-2F helicopter.

All of these ships have comprehensive radar, being provided with three-dimensional search radar (SPS 48 in all except the *Bainbridge*, which has the older SPS 52), air-search (SPS 49 in part of the Belknap class and the *Long Beach*, SPS 40 in the rest of the Belknap class and the *Truxtun*, SPS 37 in the Leahy class and the *Bainbridge*), and surface-search (SPS 10 in all ships). The classes have different fire-control radar. The Belknaps, and the Leahys and the *Truxtun*, are equipped with an SPG 35F and SPG 55B. The

Above: The USS *Truxtun's* nuclear propulsion gives it great endurance, very useful for the Pacific Ocean.

Below: The USS *Ticonderoga* launches a Standard-MR missile from its Mark 26 launcher while on sea trials.

Bainbridge has four SPG 55A, while the *Long Beach* has four SPG 55A, two SPG 49 and an SPW 2. All ships have bow-mounted sonar: SQS 23 series in *Long Beach*, the Leahys and *Bainbridge*; SQS 26 in *Truxtun* and the Belknaps (except for the *Belknap* itself which carries an SQS 53C).

The propulsion of these ships is similar. The Belknap and the Leahy classes are both propelled by two geared turbines with four boilers and two shafts. The turbines are either General Electric or De Laval, except in the USS *Halsey* and USS *Reeves* in the Leahy class, which were built by Allis-Chalmers. All these ships have two shafts and propellers, and 85,000 shp, producing top speeds which are almost identical (32.7 knots in the Leahy class and 32.5 knots in the Belknaps).

The *Long Beach*, *Bainbridge* and *Truxtun* are all nuclear-powered. The *Truxtun* was authorised as nuclear-powered although originally it was meant to have been the tenth member of the Belknap class; Congress attached the condition that one ship must be nuclear-powered. All these ships have pressurised water-cooled reactors, built by General Electric in the case of *Bainbridge* and *Truxtun*, while the *Long Beach* has a Westinghouse reactor. All have two geared turbines propelling two shafts and all achieve a speed of 30 knots.

There were no American cruisers built between 1967, when the *Truxtun* was commissioned, and the laying down of the USS *California* in January 1970. The two-ship California class and the four-ship Virginia class are similar, the former being slightly longer and narrower than the latter; weights are similar and both are nuclear-propelled. The California class and the Virginia class differ mainly in minor details. All six of these ships are armed with eight Harpoon SSMs in four quad-launchers. They are armed with Standard-MR SAM (the California class uses the single Mark 13 launchers while the Virginia class has the twin Mark 26 launcher) and the missiles can be Asroc

Top left: The octagonal shapes are SPY 1A paired arrays. Above left: The information centre of Aegis.

Above: The 20mm Phalanx CIWS (close-in weapons system) now being retrofitted to many ships of the US Navy. Above right: Three ships of the Virginia class in line abreast: USS *Texas* (top), USS *Mississippi* (centre) and USS *Arkansas* (front).

Below: The USS *California* was named in honour of President Nixon's home state. It serves in the Atlantic Ocean as an escort to the Nimitz-class carriers.

in the Virginias (the California class has a separate Mark 16 Asroc eight-tube launcher) and two 5in guns in single Mark 45 mountings. They both have two triple Mark 32 torpedo tube mounts.

The reactor in both these ships is identical – pressurised water-cooled General Electric D2G driving two geared turbines. The Californias have 60,000 shp propelling two shafts while the Virginias have 100,000 shp. Both classes travel in excess of 30 knots.

The radar in both classes is almost identical. For 3D search they have the SPS 48, for air-search the Californias have the SPS 40 while the Virginias have the SPS 40 and the SPS 55. SPS 10 radar is used for surface-searching, while fire-control is provided by the SPG 51, the SPG 60 and SPQ 9a. The Californias use the SQS 26CX bow-mounted sonar, while the Virginias are equipped with the SQS 53A. The Mark 74 missile fire-control system is in all ships, as is the Mark 86 gun and forward missile channel system. The digital Mark 116 ASW fire-control system is used in the Virginias. The Virginias have a helicopter hanger aft beneath the fan-tail flight deck. A telescoping hatch cover and an electro-mechanical elevator is also provided. Two LAMPS (light airborne multipurpose system) SH-2 helicopters are carried.

The most modern cruisers in the US fleet are the Ticonderoga class; originally designed as guided-missile destroyers, they were uprated to guided missile cruisers in January 1983. There are two ships

currently in service: *Ticonderoga* and *Yorktown*, and a further eight are presently authorised. They have been built on a Spruance-class hull, with a bow bulwark added. They weigh 9600 tonnes fully loaded. Armed with two four-tube Harpoon launchers and 88 Standard ER/Asroc missiles launched from two twin Mark 26 launchers, future ships after the first five will also have cruise-missile launchers and the improved Mark 41 mount for the SAMs. They also carry two 5in guns in the Mark 45 mount, two 20mm/76 Phalanx CIWS and two triple Mark 32 torpedo tubes, for ASW. Ticonderogas carry the SPY 1A radar in paired arrays, one forward and one aft, as a part of the Aegis system of air search and control. This is supplemented by an SPS 49 air-search radar, SPS 10 surface-search radar, SPQ 9 fire-control radar and an SQS 53 bow sonar. Four General Electric LM2500 gas turbines provide 80,000 shp propelling two shafts and giving a speed in excess of 30 knots. Two LAMPS helicopters are carried and also an SQR 10 towed sonar.

All these US cruisers are equipped with satellite communications equipment and the Naval Tactical Data System. The latter is a combination of digital computers, with displays and transmission links which assess tactical data from various sensors and provide a display of the tactical situation to the ship commander along with the defensive and offensive options. This data can be transmitted among similarly equipped ships and also linked with the AWACS carried in the E-2 Hawkeye aircraft.

The peacemakers

After the end of the October War in 1973 US Secretary of State Henry Kissinger embarked on a round of 'shuttle diplomacy' designed to achieve, on a step by step basis, a comprehensive Middle East settlement. A short-lived United Nations-backed conference on the Middle East in Geneva collapsed in December and from then on, Kissinger managed to exclude the Soviet Union entirely from the peace process, making the USA the central pivot of Middle Eastern diplomacy. In January 1974 he persuaded Egypt and Israel to sign a disengagement agreement whereby Israel withdrew from the west bank of the Suez Canal (the Canal itself was reopened in 1975) and from the east bank to a distance of 20km (13 miles), with accompanying force reductions on both sides. He also promoted a similar agreement between Syria and Israel on the Golan Heights. The prestige of the United States in the Middle East was high, with Kissinger accepted as a mediator by all the Arab states involved, and US ascendancy appeared to be confirmed by President Nixon's triumphal tour of the region in June 1974.

Kissinger's efforts to secure a further disengagement in Sinai were rather more time-consuming. Israel refused to abandon the whole of the peninsula and insisted on occupying an important oilfield and two passes in the area. She also demanded the right to keep Jewish settlements in the Sinai – these settlers had moved in after 1967. These proposals were rejected by Egypt as inadequate. Despite his anger at Israel's intransigence Kissinger embarked on a fresh round of shuttle diplomacy in August 1975. Accompanied by threats from US President Ford to reduce American support for Israel unless she agreed to concessions – he actually suspended weapons deliveries to her for a time – his efforts resulted in a package of agreements between Israel, Egypt and the United States on 1 September providing for a further Israeli withdrawal from part of the Sinai. The package also provided for American civilian personnel, as well as United Nations forces, to man early warning

systems in the two crucial passes. Large sums of American aid were promised to both Israel and Egypt, and the US was now closely involved with the security of both countries.

The Republican president and his secretary of state had been preoccupied with the aftermath of both the Watergate affair and of the Vietnam War; and although Kissinger's diplomacy had been very effective, a change of regime in Washington and Tel Aviv was to produce far more spectacular results. In January 1977, a new president, the Democrat Jimmy Carter, came to power in the US, while in May 1977, the ailing Labour government was replaced by Menachem Begin's right-wing Likud coalition in Israel. The combination of new men and new policies was to lead to profound changes in the Middle East.

Begin's initial hawkish statements about the inviolability of the territories occupied in 1967 seemed to bode ill for any future negotiations, but the new Israeli prime minister possessed both the prestige and the political skills to force a settlement on his divided and reluctant cabinet. He recognised that Israel's future security depended on the conclusion of peace with Egypt and that Egypt might be so anxious for a settlement herself that she might be prepared, in the last resort, to ignore the demands of the Palestine Liberation Organisation (PLO) for an independent Palestine. In this conjecture Begin was correct: Egyptian President Anwar Sadat wanted to secure the re-establishment of full Egyptian sovereignty over the Sinai. He believed that Kissinger's step by step approach was too cumbersome and that effecting a peace treaty with Israel would enable Egypt to reduce the size of her inflated armed forces, thus enabling Cairo to concentrate Egypt's resources on her rapidly deteriorating economy.

Sadat recognised that he had to ensure that such a peace treaty would open the way for the participation of the other Arab states in the negotiations. Otherwise Egypt would be left isolated in the Arab world; and

Above: The two national leaders whose unlikely agreement paved the way for peace between Israel and its most important Arab foe, Egypt, in 1979 – Menachem Begin (on left), who became prime minister of Israel in May 1977, and Anwar Sadat, effective ruler of Egypt since Gamal Abdel Nasser's death in 1970.

connected to this was his realisation that an agreement with Israel over the Sinai would have to be linked to an Israeli agreement to satisfy at least some of the aspirations of the Palestinian Arabs on the West Bank of the Jordan and in the Gaza Strip. Here lay the sticking point, for most Israelis were united in their opposition to any settlement which conceded the possibility of an independent Palestinian state. Such a state would, they felt, menace Israel's very existence, and would be dominated by the detested Palestine Liberation Organisation. Begin stated categorically in November 1977 that no Israeli delegation would 'ever negotiate in any way with the so-called Palestine Liberation Organisation, whether it is in Geneva, or Cairo or the moon.' It was on this rock that the Carter-Sadat hope for a comprehensive Middle Eastern settlement was to founder.

In 1977 Carter and his aides were intent on reviving multilateral negotiations rather than on returning to Kissinger's personal diplomacy which had failed to register any further progress after September 1975. Carter therefore adopted a Soviet suggestion for a joint Soviet-United States statement designed to pave the way for the reconvening of the Geneva Conference and which called for a 'comprehensive' settlement of the Israel-Arab dispute, including an eventual Israeli military withdrawal from the 1967 occupied territories and the satisfaction of the 'legitimate rights of the Palestinian people'. This statement caused an uproar in Israel and in the influential Jewish-American lobby in the United States. Carter was forced to climb down: in a speech at the United Nations General Assembly on 4 October 1977 and in private discussions with Israeli Foreign Minister Moshe Dayan in New York, he denied that he intended to impose a Palestine settlement on Israel and insisted that the future of the Palestinian people was a matter for negotiation between all the interested parties. This effectively ended Soviet-US collaboration to reopen the Geneva Conference and resulted in the

Shuttle diplomacy, Henry Kissinger style. Above left: Kissinger and President Assad of Syria. Kissinger made the US the arbiter of Middle East politics in 1974 and 1975.

Above: Kissinger looks on as Israeli Premier Yitzhak Rabin signs an agreement concerning partial withdrawal from Sinai in September 1975. Above right: Israeli M60 tanks prepare to pull back as part of the agreed withdrawal of Israeli forces. Below: Egyptian troops line the banks of the Suez Canal as it is reopened to shipping.

revival of high level US mediation to secure a direct settlement of outstanding Israeli-Egyptian issues. Thereafter the Soviet Union moved closer to the more radical Arab states – the fissures now opening in the Middle East offered her the opportunity of regaining her lost influence there.

The collapse of the multilateral approach to the Middle East paved the way for Sadat's dramatic visit to Jerusalem in November 1977. He hoped that his visit would remove the 'psychological barrier' which, he believed, impeded a settlement. On arrival he demanded the withdrawal of Israel from all the territories she had occupied in 1967 and Israeli recognition of the right of the Palestinians to self-determination in return for Egyptian recognition of Israel and her removal from the ranks of Israel's enemies. While the visit caused a sensation at the time – Sadat addressed the Knesset, the Israeli parliament – little that was concrete emerged from the private talks. Begin had no intention of acceding to Egypt's far-reaching demands, and he envisaged Sadat's visit as the first stage in a long process of bargaining, whereas Sadat wanted a quick settlement. The two leaders agreed to meet at Ismailiya on 25 December, where the atmosphere was less cordial than it had been at Jerusalem. Begin rejected any notion of a Palestinian state based on the West Bank and Gaza, bitterly attacked the PLO and would agree only to some form

of limited home rule for the Palestinians. The two leaders agreed to set up two committees – a political committee in Jerusalem and a military committee in Cairo. Two days later Begin issued a memorandum which set out the maximum concessions any Israeli leader could offer the Palestinians and remain in power – 'administrative autonomy' for the West Bank and Gaza Arabs in the form of an elected municipal-type council based in Bethlehem, while Israeli troops, although reduced in number, would remain in the West Bank and Gaza to maintain public order and security.

Carter steps in

The proposal was a long way from meeting the more ambitious plans for the area envisaged by Sadat and certainly stood no chance of acceptance by other Arab states. Then in January 1978 Carter intervened. He met Sadat at Aswan on the 4th and both men agreed on a formula which they hoped would satisfy Israeli fears by avoiding the use of the words 'self-determination' and 'independence' for the Palestinians and offered them instead their right 'to participate in the determination of their own future.' Even this was too much for Begin.

In another attempt to resolve the deadlock Sadat sent his Foreign Minister Mohammed Kamel to Jerusalem on 15 January. The visit was a disaster. Begin

patronised the youthful Kamel and rejected outright his call for Israeli withdrawal from the occcupied territories and for the acceptance of the 'national rights' of the Palestinians. Thereupon Sadat recalled the Egyptian delegation on the political committee. Fruitless negotiations continued during the spring and summer in private between the Israeli minister of defence and Sadat and more publicly at a US-sponsored conference of Israeli, Egyptian and United States foreign ministers in England in July.

Increasingly impatient with Israel's unwillingness to compromise and desperate to avoid renewed warfare in the Middle East, Carter summoned Sadat and Begin to meet him at the presidential retreat at Camp David on 5 September 1978. After much haggling and angry exchanges Carter, using a mixture of threats (he claimed he would cut all aid to Israel) and blandishments (increased aid to Israel), forced Begin to agree to a 'Framework for Peace'. This consisted of two agreements. The first was a draft Egyptian-Israeli peace treaty which provided for a phased withdrawal of Israeli troops and settlers from the Sinai over three years and full restoration of the peninsula to Egypt, together with various clauses detailing troop reductions and United Nations surveillance to satisfy the security requirements of both sides. The second agreement called for negotiations between Israel, Jordan and 'representatives of the Palestinian people' to settle the vexed question of the Arabs on the West Bank and Gaza. While these negotiations were proceeding a self-governing Arab authority would be set up for five years, which would replace the Israeli military government. Israeli forces were to be reduced in number and redeployed in security zones on the borders (Begin insisted that they would stay there even after a final settlement.)

During the negotiations – which Carter subsequently described as 'one of the most frustrating experiences I have ever had in my life' – both sides made significant concessions to the other. Begin agreed to remove all Israeli settlements from the Sinai and Sadat agreed to postpone the West Bank-Gaza settlement to an indefinite future. Predictably, the latter aspect was bitterly opposed by the Palestine Liberation Organisation which rejected any solution short of a fully independent state. Worse from the American point of view was the refusal of Jordan and Saudi Arabia to accept the agreement. They joined with the PLO and the more radical Arab states in denouncing it. Egypt was isolated in the Arab world faced by a solid bloc of rejectionist Arab states, backed in their intransigence by the Soviet Union.

Increasing strife in the Lebanon had also made the prospect of stability in the Middle East problematical in 1978. Since September 1970, the Palestinian activists expelled from Jordan had settled in the Lebanon. From there, guerrillas launched frequent terrorist raids into Israel. These prompted heavy Israeli retaliatory air raids on the guerrilla bases. The situation became even more confused when civil war broke out in the Lebanon in 1975 and Syrian forces entered the country ostensibly to restore order. Israel was drawn into the war initially in support of her Christian allies in southern Lebanon, and eventually Israeli forces invaded the country to establish a 10km (six-mile) wide 'security zone'. However, the situation remained unstable: Israel handed the security zone over to her Christian militia allies as a base for her re-entry into the Lebanon should the occasion arise.

In spite of all these complications, and in spite of the fact that the Camp David accords left major differences unresolved, an Israeli-Egyptian peace treaty was signed in 1979. Egypt had secured the return of the Sinai and acquired a breathing space to enable her government to devote resources to the appalling level of poverty and to the modernisation of her economy; while Israel had managed to dispel the nightmare of a war on two fronts that had dominated Israeli military thinking since the creation of the state. In effect, the peace treaty set the seal on Israel's rise to regional dominance, for with Egypt out of the reckoning, Syria alone hardly presented a realistic threat. Peace with Egypt was the successful outcome of four decades of military victory. . **Michael Dockrill**

Above: An afternoon visit to Gettysburg for the assembled politicians and advisers at the Camp David talks, September 1978. US President Jimmy Carter makes a point to Egyptian leader Anwar Sadat while Menachem Begin (left foreground) and Moshe Dayan (with eyepatch) look on.

Right: Gunmen on the streets of Beirut, armed with the Soviet AK series smallarms that became ubiquitous during the civil wars in the Lebanon. Private armies were formed by many of the religious and political groupings, the forces of the PLO were constantly present, while both Syria and Israel intervened from outside.

A shattered state

Lebanon's civil war, 1975-78

On 26 February 1975, a large demonstration took place in the Lebanese port of Sidon as local fishermen, backed by Muslim leftists, protested against the planned creation of a Christian-dominated fishing monopoly under the control of right-wing Maronite leader Camille Chamoun. It was a typically Lebanese conflict, containing all the complex ingredients of social, economic and religious antagonism which characterised Lebanese politics. As the demonstrators marched through the town, they were met by a unit of the Lebanese Army which fired on them, fatally wounding the mayor of Sidon.

Tension between the dominant right-wing Maronite Christians and the predominantly Muslim leftist opposition had been growing steadily, particularly since the issue of Palestinian military activity against Israel from Lebanese bases had been added to underlying, essentially Lebanese quarrels during the 1960s. The Sidon incident, therefore, escalated immediately, and on 29 February a second demonstration ended in a pitched battle between Lebanese Army troops and left-wing militia groups, backed by guerrillas of some of the more extreme Palestinian resistance organisations. The army, alarmed by the effectiveness of the opposition, subjected Sidon to a brief artillery bombardment before concluding a ceasefire and withdrawing its troops.

The Sidon incident provoked protests and demonstrations throughout Lebanon, with both moderate and radical Muslim leaders demanding reform of the army command, which they accused of acting as an instrument of the Maronites. The right-wing Maronites of the Phalange and other groups demonstrated enthusiastically in support of the army, further con-

vincing the Muslims that it could no longer be regarded as neutral.

The extent to which the fragile Lebanese constitutional balance had been undermined was soon revealed. On Sunday 13 April 1975, Phalangist gunmen ambushed a busload of Palestinians who had strayed into the Christian suburb of Ain el-Roumaneh in Beirut. Twenty-seven Palestinians, including women and children, were killed and 19 wounded. Within hours, barricades had been erected throughout Beirut and the first shots were being exchanged. By the following morning the first battles of the Lebanese civil war were under way.

At first the fighting was limited to more or less static positional battles between gunmen of the left-wing

Lebanon's tangled web

The foundation of the Lebanese state was based on an unwritten National Pact, agreed in 1943, which established a fixed political balance between the Lebanon's diverse communities. These groups, defined on religious lines and led by powerful patriarchal families, greatly complicate Lebanon's fundamental division between Muslims (some 60 per cent of the population by 1975) and Christians.

The Maronites, adherents of a Catholic sect, are by far the largest and most powerful of the Christian communities, with around 25 per cent of the Lebanon's total population. They are the traditionally dominant group, both commercially and politically, a fact recognised under the 1943 National Pact which allotted them the presidency. The Maronites traditionally look to the West, rather than the Arab world, for example and support. Since the 1930s, a prominent element in the Maronite community has been the Phalangist Party, originally set up in imitation of European Fascist movements, and closely associated with the Gemayel family. The geographical centre of Maronite influence is in East Beirut and the northern mountains.

The Sunni Muslims are traditionally the dominant element of the Muslim population, but not the most numerous, with perhaps 20 per cent of the country's population. Under the National Pact they were accorded the post of prime minster for one of their traditional leaders. From the late 1960s, the conservative community leaders lost much of their influ-

ence as radical sentiments spread among the Sunnis, so that attempts at a political compromise with the Maronites by Sunni leader Rashid Karami failed to win support in his community.

The Shi'ites form the majority Muslim group, with about 30 per cent of Lebanon's population. As the poorest element in the country, they have supported radical action, originally through Imam Musa Sadr's Movement of the Deprived, and later through the Amal armed organisation.

The Druze are a tight-knit community living in the Chouf mountains. Their numbers are small – around seven per cent of the population – but their influence has been great. Belonging to a small, enclosed Muslim sect, they are regarded as heretics by most of their co-religionists. Their relations with other Muslims have not been close, and in Israel they have cooperated with the Jewish state, being the only Muslim group to participate in military service. Nevertheless, under the leadership of the Jumblatt family, they became engaged in the forefront of the struggle against the Christians in the Lebanon – while always emphasising that their action was purely designed to promote their own Druze interests, as opposed to any wider Arab or Palestinian cause.

Other elements in the population include Greek Orthodox Christians (who took the Muslim side in the civil war), Christian Armenians, and of course the Palestinians, who at the height of their presence in the 1970s may have totalled almost 10 per cent of the Lebanese population.

Above: A Christian priest armed with an old Winchester in Zghorta, northern Lebanon. Zghorta was the base of President Frangieh's private force, the 'Zghorta Liberation Army'. Top: Frangieh's openly partisan approach led to calls for his resignation. Here, bodyguards of Phalangist leader Pierre Gemayel wait outside the Chamber of Deputies during a vote of no confidence in Frangieh.

Right: Progressive Socialist Party chief Kamal Jumblatt. Far right: Sheikh Mohammed Yaacoub, one of the founders of the Movement of the Deprived, the major Shi'ite political organisation. Jumblatt's Druze community and the Shi'ites were combined in the National Movement which opposed the continued Christian dominance of Lebanese politics. Below centre right: Rashid Karami, a Sunni Muslim; the conservative Sunni leadership supported the status quo and was prepared to liaise with the Maronites.

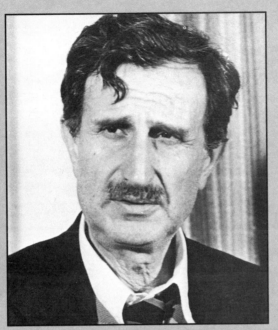

Above centre left: Sulieman Frangieh, president of Lebanon in 1975. Right: Bashir Gemayel, the commander of the Phalangist militia in the field. Far right: Pierre Gemayel, founder and chief of the Phalangist Party, the most important Maronite armed grouping. The Christians in Lebanon are divided more by individual personalities than political ideals or class conflicts.

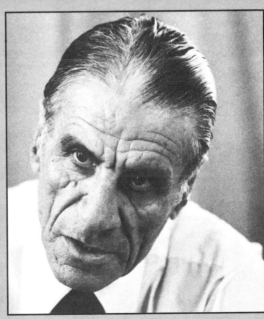

Lebanese parties, Maronite Phalangists and Palestinian commandos, each entrenched within its own suburb or refugee camp. Fighting was heaviest around the Palestinian camps of Tal Zaatar and Borj al-Barajneh, which were situated in predominantly Christian areas of the capital. Heavy fighting also broke out around the northern port of Tripoli, and minor clashes took place throughout the country. It was widely suspected that the Phalangists, who admitted responsibility for the Ain el-Roumaneh massacre, were intent upon a deliberate military confrontation with the Palestinians and their left-wing supporters.

Under Yassir Arafat, the bulk of the Palestinian forces of the various groupings within the PLO had so far stayed out of the fighting, in accord with Arafat's explicit policy of avoiding entanglement in the affairs of a host nation. The Ain el-Roumaneh massacre bore all the hallmarks of a deliberate attempt to draw the PLO into direct confrontation with the Lebanese Christians, and, therefore, forcing the army, which although it had a slight Muslim majority was officered predominantly by Maronites, to intervene directly against the Palestinians. The Maronite right would then be in a position, it imagined, to expel the Palestinians from Lebanon and impose its own domination over the Muslim opposition.

The Muslims organise

That opposition came largely from the National Movement, an alliance of the Druze Progressive Socialist Party, whose leader, Kamal Jumblatt was the Movement's main spokesman, a number of Nasserite, Arab nationalist and Islamic groups, the two Lebanese communist parties, the Parti Populaire Syrien and the Shi'ite Movement of the Deprived, led by Imam Musa Sadr. Closely allied to the more militant Palestinian resistance groups of the Rejection Front, the National Movement was outraged by the Ain el-Roumaneh massacre, and demanded the sacking of two cabinet ministers who were members of the Phalangist grouping. Jumblatt soon went further, declaring that he would back no government which included any Phalangist. Tantamount to an open declaration of war, this was a direct repudiation of the 1943 National Pact upon which the Lebanese constitution was based and persuaded the Maronites that their whole position was under attack, helping to rally support for the more extreme Phalangists.

While the Maronite community as a whole prepared to defend its interests, the Phalangists retained the hope of extracting some advantage from the crisis, and used the National Movement's demands as a pretext for precipitating a prolonged government crisis by withdrawing their ministers. After a brief lull, fighting was renewed in mid-May, this time with the Phalangist militia receiving support from the 'Tigers' of former President Camille Chamoun's National Liberal Party and from followers of the then President Sulieman Frangieh around the northern Lebanese town of Zghorta, while the Palestinians now had more organised backing from the smaller Lebanese leftist groups. On 23 May, President Frangieh announced the formation of a military government, but this was merely an example of Maronite wishful thinking, and three days later it was forced to resign. The situation was deteriorating swiftly, and fighting was spreading throughout the country, raising fears in Lebanon's neighbour Syria that the

Right: Christian militiamen round up Muslim non-combatants in the Karantina district of Beirut. Civilians have suffered heavily in fighting in Beirut, whether Christian, Muslim or Palestinian; both sides have indulged in mass murder for the purposes of revenge or terrorisation.

Below right: A member of a Nasserite militia with an AK-47 taking cover in Beirut. Below far right: A Muslim checkpoint in Beirut with children at play. The militias on both sides were numerous but many were small and insignificant.

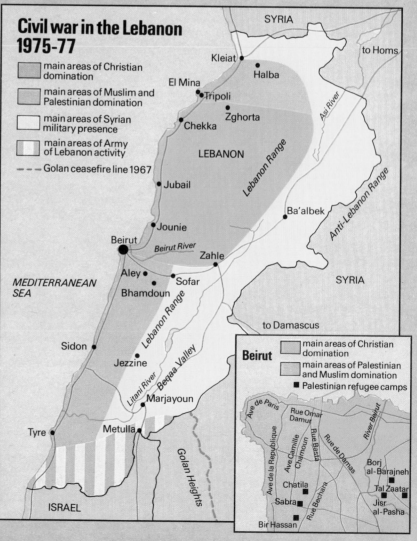

Civil war in the Lebanon 1975-77

■ main areas of Christian domination

■ main areas of Muslim and Palestinian domination

□ main areas of Syrian military presence

▨ main areas of Army of Lebanon activity

– – – Golan ceasefire line 1967

SYRIA

to Homs

Kleiat

Halba

El Mina

Tripoli

Zghorta

Chekka

Asi River

LEBANON

Lebanon Range

Anti-Lebanon Range

Jubail

Ba'albek

Jounie

Beirut

Beirut River

Zahle

MEDITERRANEAN SEA

Aley

Sofar

Bhamdoun

SYRIA

Lebanon Range

to Damascus

Sidon

Jezzine

Beqaa Valley

Litani River

Marjayoun

Tyre

Metulla

Golan Heights

ISRAEL

Beirut

■ main areas of Christian domination

■ main areas of Palestinian and Muslim domination

■ Palestinian refugee camps

Ave de Paris

Rue Omar Damur

River Beirut

Ave de la Republique

Ave Camille Chamoun

Rue Basta

Rue de Damas

Borj al-Barajneh

Chatila

Rue Bechara

Tal Zaatar

Sabra

Jisr al-Pasha

Bir Hassan

country might be torn apart, in the process provoking direct Israeli intervention on Syria's western flank.

Syrian pressure, already exerted against the military government experiment, resulted in President Frangieh calling on Sunni Muslim politician Rashid Karami to form a new government, which contained neither Phalangists nor representatives of Kamal Jumblatt, but had the support of Chamoun, who was appointed minister of the interior; the government, therefore, retained the confidence of the Maronites. It also represented the possibility of a political solution, as Prime Minister Karami also held the defence portfolio, in order to prevent the use of the army by the Maronite right.

The new initiative seemed successful at first, and a degree of calm returned to the Lebanon during the early summer of 1975, but beneath the veneer of peace the militias were arming and organising, convinced that the last word had not been said, nor the last shot fired.

By autumn, the Maronite forces had grouped themselves into the Lebanese Front, which included the 10,000-strong Phalangist militia, and the smaller Tigers and Zghorta Liberation Army, which together mustered a further 5000 men. The Zghorta Liberation Army was in fact the private army of President Frangieh, commanded by his son Tony. This open partisanship by the theoretically impartial head of state contributed to the increase in tension, which resulted in renewed fighting from the middle of September 1975. On 17 September, the Phalangist militia began an artillery bombardment of the predominantly Muslim districts of West Beirut, which in turn provoked the well organised Nasserite Mourabitoun militia, cooperating with the Palestinian PFLP-General Command, to escalate the war, taking the battle to the Phalangists and clearing them from most of West Beirut and the hotel district. The capture of several of the largest hotel tower blocks was particularly significant, as it gave the leftists command of large areas of central Beirut.

This setback seems to have convinced the Lebanese Front of the need to consolidate the territory it still held; in plain language this meant the elimination of all Muslim and Palestinian enclaves and refugee camps in the Christian-held area north of the Beirut-Damascus road. By January 1976, the Palestinian refugee camps of Tal Zataar and Jisr al-Pasha were under siege, while the camp at Dbayyah fell to the Lebanese Front on 14 January. Four days later Phalangist gunmen captured the Muslim Beirut suburbs of Qarantina, Maslakh and Naba'a, massacring or expelling their inhabitants. In attacking the Palestinian camps the Maronites had ignored direct and repeated warnings from the PLO leadership of Yassir Arafat. The bulk of the PLO forces had thus far kept out of what they regarded as a purely Lebanese dispute in which intervention could have only negative consequences for the Palestinians. The Maronite attacks forced the PLO to act, however, and in doing so swung the military balance decisively in favour of the Muslim-leftist coalition.

The PLO had held its forces largely in the south to avoid involvement in the civil war, but now they swung north along the coast towards Beirut. The advancing Palestinians joined the National Movement's assault on Chamoun's Tigers in Damour. The town fell on 20 January, and much of the population was massacred.

The fall of Damour, the last Maronite base outside their mountain stronghold in northern Lebanon, and the intervention of the PLO suggested that the war would end with either a limited Maronite defeat, allowing them to set up a separate Christian state in the north, or a total Maronite defeat, and the establishment of a leftist/Palestinian-dominated Lebanese state. Either result would invite Israeli intervention, and therefore both provoked Syrian anxieties.

On the day before the fall of Damour, Syria's President Hafez Assad had signalled his disquiet by despatching units of the Syrian-officered Palestinian Liberation Army to Lebanon, and on 21 January the Syrian foreign minister arrived in Beirut to arrange a ceasefire. This was to be founded on a number of reforms, which the Syrians hoped would defuse the crisis. Muslims and Christians were to have equal parliamentary representation, and there was to be a reform of the civil service. More importantly perhaps, Lebanon was to be confirmed as an Arab country. All this was regarded as no more than a sop by the National Movement, but the reference to the Arab character of the Lebanon inflamed Maronite sensibilities. The Druze leader, Kamal Jumblatt, was also hesitant in accepting the Syrian compromise, and while he vacillated the Lebanese Army, upon which the Maronites had originally placed such extravagant hopes, and which in spite of, or more accurately because of, its inactivity remained a vital factor in any plan for a new Lebanese political balance, dissolved into its constituent, hostile parts.

A young Sunni lieutenant, Ahmed Khatib, led a mutiny, setting up his own Army of Lebanon in the Beqaa Valley. By March, the process was well advanced, and Muslim units were ridding themselves of their Maronite officers and going over to Khatib. The reforms proposed by Syria were now a dead letter and Khatib, demanding the outright resignation of President Frangieh, marched on the presidential palace at Ba'abda. Finding his way barred by pro-Syrian PLA troops, he nevertheless forced Frangieh to flee, training his artillery upon the palace.

The peace plan had been shattered, and the army had disintegrated; fighting again became heavy, with Jumblatt calling for a total military victory over the Maronites. For the Syrians, Jumblatt, rather than the Lebanese Front, was now seen as the main stumbling block to an acceptable settlement. They therefore exerted increasing pressure upon him, while at the same time attempting to find a compromise candidate to replace the discredited President Frangieh. The Maronites, unable to stem the advance of Palestinian/ leftist forces that had captured the last Christian positions in West Beirut and were moving into the Maronite mountain strongholds, in their turn saw the Syrians as potential saviours. While the Maronites mobilised for a last-ditch struggle Pierre Gemayel, the Phalangist leader, called for direct Syrian intervention. The leftists, blind to Syria's likely reaction, continued to press for total military victory.

Yassir Arafat and the more moderate PLO leaders understood Syrian fears and attempted to restrain Jumblatt and his allies, but by now the Palestinians were being dragged along by forces beyond their control toward a confrontation with their most important Arab ally. On 1 June 1976, Syrian troops entered Lebanon and began to move on Beirut and Sidon. The Syrian advance was slow and hesitant, however, and came up against unexpectedly effective Palestinian resistance, especially around Sidon. Assad opted for a ceasefire rather than risk large-scale fighting that would have created immense domestic and international political problems for him. Yet despite the Syrian presence (which was soon supplemented by an Arab peacekeeping force of Sudanese and Libyan troops) the civil war continued.

Massacre at Tal Zaatar

The diversion of Palestinian forces to face the Syrians had given the Maronites an opportunity to return to their aim of eliminating the Palestinian refugee camps in Christian areas, and pressure on Tal Zaatar and Jisr al-Pasha was stepped up. Towards the end of June, a joint force of Phalangists, Chamoun's Tigers and former Maronite soldiers of the Lebanese Army took Jisr al-Pasha, and on 12 August Tal Zaatar fell after a 53-day siege. Many inhabitants of Tal Zaatar were slaughtered by the Maronite gunmen, and survivors were expelled from Christian territory.

Between July and September the Syrians fought to clear the Maronite heartland north of the Beirut-Damascus road of Palestinian/leftist forces, and early in October Syrian troops began to advance from Sofar on Beirut. Heavy fighting took place at Bhamdoun on 13 October, prompting Saudi Arabia to propose a peace initiative in order to preserve Arab unity. The resulting agreement, reached at a summit in Riyadh on 16 October and ratified by the Arab League, apart from Iraq and Libya, at a conference in Cairo on 25 October provided for a predominantly Syrian peacekeeping force to be stationed in Lebanon, whose existence was to be preserved under the new president Elias Sarkis. The Palestinians were to observe the 1969 Cairo Agreement, by which they had received legitimation for their military presence in Lebanon in return for observance of Lebanese sovereignty and authority. On 14 November Syrian troops entered Beirut as the guarantors of the new agreement.

Bitterness and tensions remained, however, and terrorist activity continued to be a threat to stability. Accounts remained to be settled, and in March 1977 Druze leader Kamal Jumblatt was assassinated in the Chouf mountains, the traditional Druze stronghold. His enraged supporters retaliated by massacring local Christian villagers, though it was widely suspected that Syria had been responsible for his death.

Syrian policy in the Lebanon was essentially a failure, however, and the country remained not only politically, but also geographically divided, with the Maronite mountains a virtually independent state within a state, and the south still largely controlled by the Lebanese Druze and Muslim leftists and their Palestinian allies.

Robin Corbett

Main picture: Beirut was devastated by the factional conflict; the Syrian intervention led to the creation of an Arab League peacekeeping force.

Left: Kamal Jumblatt, assassinated in March 1977, lies in state surrounded by his mourning Druze followers.

Operation Litani

The Israelis go into the Lebanon

When, in April 1975, the ancient hatreds between Muslim and Maronite Christian finally plunged Lebanon into the bloody cauldron of civil war, for those living in the southern half of the country this was merely an extension of troubles which had begun with the arrival of armed units of the Palestine Liberation Organisation (PLO) in the wake of their ejection from Jordan during the battles of 'Black September' 1970. From the PLO's viewpoint the enforced move to Lebanon was not without its advantages. Whereas other Arab states, including Syria, were able to keep its activities under strict control, the weak government of Lebanon, unable to stop the growing violence within its own frontiers, could impose few restraints on its activities. Moreover, the avowed purpose of the PLO was war against Israel and from Lebanon it was well placed to mount attacks against Jewish settlements in northern Galilee.

Lebanon had taken part in the 1948 war against Israel, and despite the fact that she was not involved in either the Six-Day War or the Yom Kippur War, there had always been Palestinian groups present who had carried out cross-border raids. Israel had protested repeatedly to no avail and in the end had resorted to a series of punitive raids of varying weight and type, of which the heaviest, carried out on 28 December 1968, resulted in the destruction of 13 Arab-owned airliners at Beirut International Airport by a squad of helicopter-borne commandos.

After 1970, however, the PLO presence in south-

ern Lebanon led to an extension of the guerrilla raids, and to further Israeli retaliation. The Lebanese government was forced to agree to the PLO deploying heavy weapons in defence of its refugee camps from 1973 onwards, and increasingly close relations between the PLO and leftist groups within Lebanon (notably various Shi'ite parties and the Druze Progressive Socialist Party under Kamal Jumblatt) dragged the PLO into the complex politics of the country. In spite of Yassir Arafat's avowed policy of avoiding entanglement in the internal affairs of a host nation, when full-scale civil war broke out in 1975, the PLO

Below: The bodies of the victims are carried from the wreckage of the bus in which 35 Israeli civilians died on 11 March 1978 during the PLO terrorist raid that precipitated the Israeli invasion of southern Lebanon.

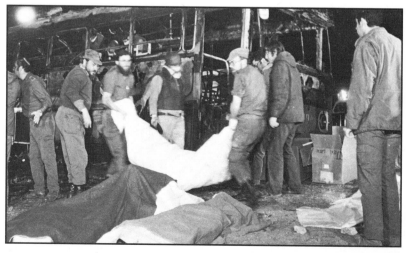

Left: Israeli armour roars into Lebanon during Operation Litani. Using effective modern tanks such as the Centurions shown here the Israelis were able to sweep their way to the Litani River, but the PLO forces retreated northwards or into the defensible enclaves of their major camps, avoiding decisive engagement.

Below: The town of Nabathieh in southern Lebanon, wrecked by Israeli air and naval bombardment on 18 March 1978. If PLO terrorist attacks enraged Israeli public opinion, then the Israeli attacks on Palestinian enclaves in Lebanon (attacks in which the innocent suffered far more than the guilty) were at best an indiscriminate revenge, that in their turn hardened Palestinian opinion against the state of Israel.

was inevitably caught up in the fighting.

For Lebanon's neighbours, Syria and Israel, the Lebanese civil war provided both a problem and an opportunity. Neither country wished to see a regime unfavourable to itself established in Lebanon, but at the same time, each could see that the collapse of central control might enable it to achieve some of its long-term aims. In the tortuous course of the civil war, Syria eventually intervened (with tacit approval from Israel) against the Muslim leftists and in support of the Maronite Christians; but while Palestinian forces were engaged in the more northern fighting, Israel took the opportunity to help Christian militias in the south, under a cashiered former major in the Lebanese Army, Saad Haddad. Haddad's forces, with Israeli help, established control over the predominantly Shi'ite Muslim population around and to the south of the Litani River.

Raids and retaliation

By 1977, with a substantial Syrian-run force keeping some form of peace in the north and centre of Lebanon, PLO units began to contest Haddad's position in the south; in this, they probably had some Syrian assistance. Israel, in its turn, kept up support for its client, and in September the Lebanese president, Elias Sarkis, accused Israel of deploying tanks on Lebanese soil. In that month, a ceasefire was negotiated by the USA, but the break in the fighting did not last. PLO raids into Israel, and the bombardment of settlements in Galilee, continued – as did Israeli retaliation – while the fighting between the PLO and Haddad's militia soon restarted.

A major clash was bound to occur sooner or later and the incident which provoked this took place on 11 March 1978, when a PLO terrorist group hijacked a bus on the Tel Aviv-Haifa coast road; only two of the terrorists survived the resulting gun battle as Israeli security forces stormed the bus, but 35 civilians were killed and 82 more were wounded.

Under pressure to mount a punitive operation into Lebanon without delay, the Israeli General Staff was faced with a number of difficult considerations, of which geography was the most obvious. From north to south, Lebanon is divided lengthwise into four zones: the coastal plain, which is comparatively narrow; the Lebanon Range, with peaks rising to 2000m (6500ft); the Beqaa Valley, which is a northern continuation of the Jordan Valley; and the Anti-Lebanon Range, which includes Mount Hermon and forms the frontier with Syria. Reasonable roads running from north to south exist only on the coastal plain and in the Beqaa Valley, but the sole good lateral route is the Beirut-Damascus road, which crosses both ranges on the bed of an old railway. Thus, the path of an invader entering Lebanon from the south is a difficult one, further complicated by the steep-banked Litani River, which flows into the sea some distance north of Tyre.

The second consideration was that since its unfortunate experience in Suez City during the Yom Kippur War, the Israeli Defence Forces' (IDF) policy had been to avoid costly street fighting if at all possible, since it lacked the manpower resources to sustain this type of warfare. Therefore, while the operation was to take the form of a large-scale sweep from the border to the Litani River, it would by-pass Tyre and the Rachidiye refugee camp, both of which had been heavily fortified by the Palestinians. There was to be no pursuit beyond the river, and the raid would be of limited duration.

Operation Litani, as the raid was code-named, commenced during the night of 14/15 March and lasted for seven days. Over 20,000 Israeli troops, supported by tanks, artillery and aircraft, crossed the border, but there were no major engagements and

Left: Major Saad Haddad, leader of the Christian forces that the Israelis used to try to establish a buffer zone in southern Lebanon. Haddad's men refused to allow the UNIFIL peacekeeping force to enter their enclaves, even after the ceasefire.

those PLO units which did not retreat into their strongholds found safety beyond the Litani, having followed the guerrilla principle of disengaging in the face of superior strength. On 15 March, an IDF spokesman had claimed that the intention was to establish a 'security zone' some 10km (6 miles) wide, but the attack into Lebanon by ground forces was accompanied by heavy bombing of Palestinian camps further north. The use of cluster bombs in these air attacks, in defiance of an understanding with Israel's US suppliers that these weapons should not be employed against civilian targets, lost the Israelis much international sympathy. The UN Security Council passed a resolution on 19 March calling for an end to the fighting, and on 22 March, the first unit of the United Nations Interim Force In the Lebanon (UNI-FIL) arrived to take up position between the IDF and Lebanese forces. The IDF eventually withdrew completely in mid-April, but continued to give support to Haddad's militiamen, who refused to let UNIFIL units enter their enclaves; in effect, therefore, the

Below: Palestinian fighters, from a Nasserite group that attacked the Israeli forces from their base at Tyre. Here the Palestinians are celebrating the withdrawal of the Israelis in April 1978.

Israelis had achieved their security zone, in that a Christian-dominated corridor, stretching from Naqoura on the coast to the Syrian border southeast of Marjayoun, separated the Israeli forces from UNIFIL and the PLO forces to the north.

In the final analysis, Operation Litani probably did Israel more harm than good, however. For in spite of the presence of UNIFIL and the buffer zone of Christian forces (in 1979, Haddad named his region 'independent free Lebanon'), PLO activities had not ceased. The Palestinians simply returned to their camps, jubilant not only because they had survived an encounter with the IDF, but also because the latter was demonstrably fallible. Soon the Israeli settlements in northern Galilee were being hit regularly by artillery fire from inside the PLO bases. UNIFIL was powerless to stop this and once again it became inevitable that Israel would retaliate in strength; and when she did so, she would certainly take advantage of the lessons learned during Operation Litani.

Bryan Perrett

Key Weapons

F-5/F-20

The Northrop F-5A Freedom Fighter and its successors the F-5E and F-20A are lightweight, single-seat tactical fighters combining supersonic performance with a relatively low cost, ease of maintenance and good handling qualities. They are well suited to the needs of the air forces of Third World nations and the smaller member states of the Nato alliance. Much of the initial design and development work on the F-5A fighter was undertaken by the Northrop Corporation as a private venture, although the US Department of Defense belatedly funded the building of three prototypes in 1958; it was a parallel development with the T-38A Talon supersonic trainer which entered service with the USAF in 1961 as a replacement for the Lockheed T-33. In July 1959 the prototype Freedom Fighter (Northrop Model N-156F) first flew and in 1962 the F-5A was ordered into production for supply to nations allied to the United States under the Military Assistance Program.

The initial F-5 contract called for 71 single-seat F-5As and 15 F-5B two-seat conversion trainers. The two-seaters are generally similar in performance and capability to the F-5As, but lack the fighter's nose-mounted armament of two 20mm M39 cannon. A third variant, the RF-5A, carries four reconnaissance cameras in the nose in addition to the cannon armament. Powered by two General Electric J85-GE-13 turbojets, which each produce 1850kg (4080lb) of thrust with afterburning, the F-5A can reach a top speed of Mach 1·4 at 11,000m (36,000ft). In air-to-

air combat the F-5A is highly manoeuvrable at low and medium altitudes, but its weapons load is limited to the built-in cannon and two AIM-9 Sidewinder missiles mounted on the wingtips. Furthermore, it lacks radar and so cannot detect targets beyond visual range. Maximum ordnance load for ground attack missions is 2700kg (6000lb), but when operating over a 320km (200-mile) mission radius this load is halved. Yet within its limitations the F-5A is a very effective warplane, which is still widely used in the mid-1980s.

The first production deliveries of F-5As and Bs were made in 1964 to the USAF's 4441st Combat Crew Training Squadron at Williams AFB, Arizona

Previous page (top): F-5E Tiger IIs of the 57th Tactical Training Wing based at Nellis AFB in Nevada. Previous page (bottom): The first prototype F-20A Tigershark in a quasi-camouflage scheme with a General Electric logo on the engine air intake. Top: F-5A Freedom Fighters of the US Air Force; the projections from the fuselage are in-flight refuelling probes indicating that these aircraft were probably used in Project Skoshi Tiger. Above: An F-5B of the Republic of Korea Air Force.

Left: A Canadian Armed Forces Canadair CF-5D prototype landing; now designated the CF-116D, four of these are currently in service.

– this squadron was responsible for training foreign crews on the aircraft. Early in the following year the Imperial Iranian Air Force received its first F-5As; this service was eventually to operate a total of 104 F-5As and 23 F-5Bs, which were supplied under the Military Assistance Program or bought through the Foreign Military Sales Program. Other major operators of American-built F-5As included Taiwan, South Korea, the Philippines, Turkey and South Vietnam. The design was also manufactured by Canadair for the Canadian Armed Forces, the Royal Netherlands Air Force and the Royal Norwegian Air Force; CASA in Spain assembled Northrop-built aircraft for the Spanish Air Force. A number of the Nato F-5 operators introduced special modifications to the basic design. For example, the Canadian Armed Forces' CF-5As were powered by 1950kg (4300lb) thrust Orenda J85-CAN-15 engines, and had in-flight refuelling probes and gyro gunsights; Norway's F-5As had an arrester hook, provision for rocket-assisted take-off and engine anti-icing equipment to suit them to local conditions; and the Netherlands improved the F-5As already excellent manoeuvrability yet further by fitting manoeuvring flaps to their NF-5As.

Despite the F-5A's popularity with foreign air forces, the USAF was unconvinced of the value of the lightweight fighter concept. However, in the mid-1960s, as the United States became increasingly involved in the Southeast Asia conflict, the USAF decided to evaluate the F-5A under combat conditions in South Vietnam under Project Skoshi Tiger. Twelve F-5As, modified by fitting armour plate and in-flight refuelling probes, were despatched to Da Nang in October 1965. They carried out close air support, interdiction and armed reconnaissance missions over South Vietnam and Laos, together with combat air patrols over North Vietnam. Although the aircraft's payload/range characteristics were poor in comparison with other tactical fighter aircraft, the F-5A generally performed well in ground attack missions. It was found that because of the F-5A's small size and lack of conspicuous engine exhaust smoke it suffered less damage from ground fire than other USAF attack aircraft. However, as no enemy fighters were encountered during sorties over North Vietnam, the F-5As capabilities in air combat could not be put to the test. At the end of the combat evaluation, F-5s were assigned to a squadron of the USAF's 3rd Tactical Fighter Wing at Bien Hoa. No other F-5s were to serve with a frontline USAF unit and plans to build F-5C fighters and F-5D two-seaters for that service were dropped. Yet the Skoshi Tiger evaluation had not

Top: An F-5E Tiger II of the US Air Force carrying Sidewinder missiles and Paveway II laser-guided bombs. Above: An F-5A Freedom Fighter, part of the US 4503rd Tactical Fighter Squadron, drops ordnance on a suspected Viet Cong position. The F-5A lacked the more conspicuous engine exhaust smoke of the F-4 Phantom.

Below: A CF-5 of the Canadian Armed Forces Air Command; it is armed with rocket pods as well as its internal cannon.

Northrop F-5A

Type Single-seat, lightweight fighter
Dimensions Span 7·7m (25ft 3in); length 14·38m (47ft 2in); height 4·01m (13ft 2in)
Weight Empty 3667kg (8085lb); maximum take-off 9379kg (20,677lb)
Powerplant Two 1850kg (4080lb) General Electric J85-GE-13 turbojets with afterburning

Performance Maximum speed Mach 1·4 or 1488 km/h (924mph) at 11,000m (36,000ft)
Range Combat range in interceptor role 314km (195 miles)
Ceiling 15,390m (50,500ft)

Armament Two 20mm M39 cannon with 280 rounds of ammunition per gun, plus up to 2700kg (6000lb) of ordnance, including two wingtip mounted AIM-9 Sidewinder AAMs, four AGM-12 Bullpup ASMs and iron bombs

Northrop F-5E Tiger II

Type Single-seat, lightweight fighter
Dimensions Span 8·13m (26ft 8in); length 14·45m (47ft 4in); height 4·06m (13ft 4in)
Weight Empty 4410kg (9723lb); maximum loaded 11,214kg (24,722lb)
Powerplant Two 2270kg (5000lb) General Electric J85-GE-21 turbojets with afterburning

Performance Maximum speed Mach 1.56, or 1705 km/h (1060mph) at 11,000m (36,000ft)
Range Combat radius in interceptor role 1056km (656 miles)
Ceiling 15,790m (51,800ft)

Armament Two 20mm M39 cannon with 280 rounds per gun and up to 3175kg (7000lb) of ordnance, including rocket pods, iron bombs and cluster bomb units; two AIM-9 Sidewinder missiles on wing-tip launchers

been an entirely wasted effort, because the F-5A was subsequently operated in large numbers by the South Vietnamese Air Force.

The F-5's somewhat limited air-to-air combat capabilities were much improved by the new F-5E Tiger II version of the fighter which made its first flight in August 1972. It was fitted with two 2270kg (5000lb) thrust J85-GE-21 engines, which gave 20 per cent more power than the earlier powerplant. Manoeuvrability was enhanced by fitting automatic manoeuvre flaps (first used on the NF-5A) and by increasing the area of the F-5A's small wing leading-edge root extension to provide more lift. Internal fuel capacity was increased and the capacity of underwing drop tanks was also expanded. Target acquisition and fire control was greatly improved by the fitting of an APQ-153 lightweight search and tracking radar and a lead computing gunsight which uses data input from the airborne radar to aim. The F-5F is a two-seat conversion trainer variant of the F-5E, while the RF-5E reconnaissance aircraft carries various combinations of cameras and infra-red linescan in a modified nose section.

The F-5E has proved to be as popular as its predecessor with overseas air arms and has been supplied to 20 nations, as well as serving in the combat training role with the USAF and US Navy. In Asia, South Korea and Taiwan are both manufacturing the aircraft under licence, against requirements for 220 aircraft for the Republic of Korea Air Force and 248 for the Chinese Nationalist (Taiwan) Air Force. Pre-revolutionary Iran was another major customer for the F-5E/F and received a total of 166. However, following the Shah's overthrow and the breach of relations with the United States, spares shortages and the lack of technical expertise has reduced the Iranian operational inventory of F-5Es to less than 60 aircraft. These have been reported to equip eight under-strength squadrons, which have flown ground attack missions against Iraqi forces in the Gulf War. South Vietnam had also received a number of F-5Es before the ceasefire agreement of January 1973 cut off American supplies. After the defeat of South Vietnam in 1975, both F-5Es and F-5As were taken over by the Vietnamese People's Air Force. Although none of the Nato powers which operate F-5As have ordered the F-5E, Switzerland has produced 110 Tiger IIs to replace Hunters and Venoms in the air defence and ground attack roles.

In American service the F-5Es equip four 'Aggressor' squadrons of the USAF and the US Navy's Fighter Weapons School. Their role is to simulate Soviet fighters in air-to-air combat training, a task for which the F-5E is particularly suited because of its similarity in performance to late-model MiG-21s. The need for such training became apparent during the early years of the Vietnam War, when it was found that American fighter pilots, who were accustomed to flying against other American fighters in mock combat, had difficulty in dealing with the small and agile Soviet interceptors encountered over North Vietnam. The outcome was the US Navy's Top Gun programme, which provided realistically simulated Soviet-style fighter opposition during combat training. The idea spread to the USAF, and today Aggressor squadrons operate in the European and the Pacific theatres, as well as in the United States.

The latest fighter in the F-5 line is the F-20A Tigershark (originally designated F-5G). It is pow-

Left, top to bottom: A US Air Force RF-5E Tigereye; a Swiss Air Force F-5E Tiger II; a Brazilian Air Force F-5E Tiger II; a Saudi Air Force RF-5E Tigereye. The F-5 series of aircraft have been a highly successful product for the Northrop Corporation and served as the basis for their contribution to the F/A-18 programme, made in conjunction with McDonnell Douglas.

Right: Three F-5Es from 'Aggressor' squadrons; the Aggressors were set up to give US and allied nations experience in Soviet fighter tactics. In large scale combat simulation they have had many successes against the highly praised F-15.

Main picture: An F-20A Tigershark fires an AIM-9L missile. Right: The first prototype F-20A takes off. The F-20A was originally known as the F-5G and has almost twice as much engine thrust as the F-5E. Bahrain has provisionally ordered four of these aircraft.

ered by a single 7710kg (17,000lb) thrust General Electric F404-GE-100 afterburning turbofan, which gives the F-20A a maximum speed of Mach 2. Manoeuvrability is further increased by an enlarged wing leading-edge root extension and a reshaping of the nose undersurfaces to provide more lift. The result is an aircraft which is virtually unspinnable even when flown to the limits of its performance. A much improved radar, the APG-67(V), is a multi-mode sensor, which can be used for air-to-air 'track while scan' mode; for example, it can detect and track up to 10 different targets simultaneously.

The Tigershark prototype first flew in August 1982. Despite its impressive performance, which falls midway between the F-5E and the far more expensive F-16A, no production orders have yet been placed. Once the F-20A is being built in quantity, many Third World air forces are likely to buy the fighter in relatively small numbers; what is lacking is the large initial order which will justify the costs and risks of putting a new warplane into production. In the past Northrop could have looked to Iran, South Vietnam or Taiwan for a substantial production contract but for political reasons these markets are now closed. Other traditional customers in Europe and the Middle East are now more interested in technologically advanced – and expensive – warplanes in the class of the F-16, F-18 and even the F-15. Therefore the future of the low-cost, high-performance fighter is in doubt and the F-20A could remain nothing more than an interesting prototype.

Northrop F-20A

Type Single-seat, lightweight fighter
Dimensions Span 8·13m (26ft 8in); length 14·17m (46ft 6in); height 4·22m (13ft 10in)
Weight Empty 5089kg (11,220lb); maximum take-off 12,474kg (27,500lb)
Powerplant One 7710kg (17,000lb) General Electric F404-GE-100 turbofan with afterburning

Performance Mach 2 above 11,000m (36,000ft)
Range Combat radius with maximum internal fuel, two external tanks and typical weapons load 713km (443 miles)
Ceiling 16,765m (54,700ft)

Armament Two 20mm M39 cannon with 450 rounds per gun, plus up to 3765kg (8300lb) of ordnance, including up to six AIM-9 Sidewinder AAMs, laser, optical and radar guided ASMs, 30mm cannon pods and iron bombs

Above: The first F-20A Tigershark prototype dropping bombs during its trials. Right: The F-20A cockpit. Below left: The 20mm M39 cannon of an Aggressor's F-5E Tiger II undergoing maintenance. Below: The General Electric J85-21 engine, which powers the F-5E, being installed at the Northrop Corporation plant near Los Angeles.

Reds in rivalry

Indochina 1975-78

On 17 April 1975, the Cambodian capital, Phnom Penh, fell to the communist Khmer Rouge forces; 13 days later Saigon, the capital of South Vietnam, was in the hands of the North Vietnamese Army; while in Laos, the Pathet Lao had effectively asserted military supremacy by June of that year, and confirmed their success by establishing a communist regime in December. All of former French Indochina was now under communist control, and the efforts of both the French and US military establishments had proved unable to stem the tide. The other nations of Southeast Asia watched uneasily the formation of this seemingly monolithic bloc of revolutionary states – would Thailand and Malaysia feel an inevitable 'domino effect' in renewed communist insurgency fuelled and supported from the Indochinese states?

The perspectives of the rest of the world were very different four years later, however, for the triumphant communism of 1975 had revealed itself as deeply divided by 1979. The imposition of revolution upon the societies of South Vietnam, Laos and especially Cambodia proved to be a horrific business for many of the groups involved, while once the military victory had been won, traditional antagonisms in the region began to reassert themselves – national and racial problems led to international conflict. Instead of the aggressive group of allied states that had been feared in 1975, Indochina presented the spectacle of an inward-looking region, locked in its own feuds.

It was, perhaps, inevitable, that the transformation of society after communist victory would involve hardship, especially for those most closely associated with the former regimes. In Vietnam, all former government officials and soldiers were compelled to register with the authorities and prominent supporters of President Thieu were sent to re-education camps (Trai Cai Tao) where they were subject to a harsh regime of labour and indoctrination. It has been estimated that about 200,000 individuals were sent to these camps, although the government claimed that 90 per cent had been released by spring 1978. On other levels, the new regime imposed itself by making life more difficult for practising Catholics, Buddhists, and the members of the syncretic sects, the Hoa Hoa and Cao Dai.

In December 1976, a Five-Year Plan was announced which included the relocation of many city dwellers in the countryside. By early 1978, about 1,200,000 people had been moved (with considerable attendant distress), while in March of that year the government announced that it intended to stop 'bourgeois trade'. This measure affected, in particular, the country's population of ethnic Chinese, who numbered well over a million. These Chinese formed a great part of the refugees who began to leave Vietnam in large numbers from spring 1978 onwards. By the summer of 1979, it is estimated that 675,000 people had fled the country. About 250,000 of these were Chinese who moved back across the border into communist China, but the remainder tried to escape by sea, with the open encouragement of the Vietnamese authorities, and became known as the 'boat

Below: The crew of a merchant ship rescues a family of Vietnamese boat people in the South China Sea. The refugees were predominantly ethnic Chinese, whose position in Vietnam had sharply deteriorated after 1975. Enormous numbers were prepared to face pirates, typhoons and starvation in a fleet of tiny boats, in the hope of a better life elsewhere. The exodus increased tension between Hanoi and Peking, and worsened relations with Vietnam's Southeast Asian neighbours, who were fearful of the effects of accepting large numbers of ethnic Chinese, who might upset their own delicate racial balance.

Indochina

people'. Suffering the ravages of attack by pirates as well as the dangers of bad weather, and the frequently inhospitable attitude of the countries in which they landed, the boat people were an indicator of the continuing misfortunes of the population of Vietnam.

In Laos, too, there were difficulties in the adjustment to communist rule, particularly among the hill tribes who inhabited the mountainous areas in the east of the country. Many of these hill tribes, notably the Meo, had been employed by the Americans as a mercenary force deployed against the communists, and resistance to any centralised rule had always been traditional among them. The result was that the hill tribes found themselves in conflict with the communist government, and a small-scale guerrilla war was soon in progress.

The problems in Laos were as nothing, however, compared to those in Cambodia, or Kampuchea as it was renamed in December 1975. This country, which under the astute Prince Norodom Sihanouk, had managed to stay out of the wars of Indochina until the late 1960s, was the scene of a mass tragedy during the 1970s. Immediately after their takeover, Pol Pot's Khmer Rouge decided to embark on a policy of forcibly revolutionising the country by moving the population out of the towns, and especially by forcibly relocating the 2,500,000 inhabitants of Phnom Penh, many of whom were refugees from the fighting of the early 1970s. About four million people were made to set up 'new villages' during the autumn of 1975. Starvation and the rigorous new regime soon took their toll, accentuated by the brutal attitudes of the new rulers. Former members of the Lon Nol regime were systematically eliminated, and 're-education' was more intensive than even in Vietnam. Executions, starvation and disease led to hundreds of thousands of deaths. The barbaric regime in Kam-

Below: A victim of a massacre of left-wing students at Bangkok University in 1977 is rescued by Thai soldiers. Thailand's vulnerability to pressure from her communist neighbours after 1975 provoked a wave of anti-communist hysteria, and the setting up of private armies such as the 'Red Gaurs' (below left), who operated in the Thai jungle against communist gerrillas.

puchea was particularly severe on ethnic Vietnamese, of whom 170,000 had fled by the end of 1978, while tens of thousands of Khmers fled to Thailand.

The plight of the ethnic Chinese in Vietnam and of the ethnic Vietnamese in Kampuchea was indicative of problems in Indochina wider than those of adjustment to revolution within a particular society. For national antagonisms that had been masked during the war against the American-backed regimes of the area were now beginning to reveal themselves. The two most notable antagonisms concerned the Vietnamese – in their relations with Kampuchea and with China.

There was a long history of conflict between the Vietnamese and the Khmers: Vietnamese expansion southwards into Indochina had been at the expense of Khmer states, and the area of the Mekong Delta had been annexed as recently as the 18th century. Vietnamese attempts to eradicate Khmer culture in areas of Cambodia occupied during the 1830s left a legacy of suspicion. Indeed, as late as 1970, when Lon Nol took over from the deposed Sihanouk in Cambodia, there were spontaneous anti-Vietnamese demonstrations that caused disquiet to the South Vietnamese government of President Thieu, whom Lon Nol was ostensibly supporting.

After the triple communist success of 1975, the Vietnamese expected to be treated as the dominant force in Indochina. In Laos, the Pathet Lao, who had always been in a client position in relation to the North Vietnamese, were prepared to accept this. In July 1977 they signed a Treaty of Friendship and Cooperation that bound the two countries very closely together. But the Khmer Rouge, led by Pol Pot, would not subscribe to such a subordinate position. The Khmer Rouge claimed parts of Vietnam as Kam-

Above: Children clear waste ground at a Vietnamese orphanage. Hanoi faced staggering internal problems in the wake of decades of warfare. Below right: Khmer refugees, driven from their homes by fighting between the Khmer Rouge and Vietnamese after the 1978 invasion. Even in Thai refugee camps they remained victims of Khmer Rouge terror and pawns in the diplomatic game.

puchean territory, and accused the Vietnamese of plotting coups; on two occasions in 1977 (April and September) Khmer Rouge forces made assaults into Vietnam. In December of that year, Vietnamese forces carried out a retaliatory incursion, and then the Vietnamese offered to establish a buffer zone.

Vietnamese ambitions were almost certainly to establish themselves as undisputed power brokers in Indochina, but with the minimum of force necessary; the Hanoi politburo was also probably concerned at the fate of the ethnic Vietnamese and at what might come of the savage attempts to reorder Kampuchean society. The Khmer Rouge, on the other hand, were genuinely concerned to assert their independence of Vietnam, while the state of paranoia and fear that was rampant in Kampuchea no doubt contributed to the aggressive nature of their policy. However unbalanced the new rulers of Kampuchea might be, they could see that in any forthcoming major clash with Vietnam they would need powerful support; and so, during 1978, they began drawing even closer to communist China – a move that served to bring into sharper relief the other major national antagonism of the region, the tension between the Chinese and the Vietnamese.

Distrust and persecution

Most of the states in Southeast Asia have good reasons for mistrusting China, in that they all contain substantial Chinese minorities which tend to form close-knit cultures within the dominant society, and could form the basis of an insurgent movement, as the Chinese did in Malaya during the Emergency. This has led to the persecution of such Chinese minorities – in Indonesia during the 1960s and in Vietnam during the 1970s. In the Vietnamese case, there was an additional complication, however. Vietnam and China had been traditional enemies for hundreds of years, with Vietnamese rulers accepting titular Chinese sovereignty, but resisting fiercely any form of direct rule. The communist Chinese forces that took over in China in 1949 supplied the Viet Minh, who defeated the French in the First Indochina War, with weapons and support, but by the late 1960s the relationship between communist Chinese and communist Vietnamese was wearing thin. The underlying reason for this was the Sino-Soviet split, and the gradual readjustment of world alliances. China's rapprochement with the US during the early 1970s was a source of concern to the Vietnamese communists, and Vietnam inevitably became closer to the Soviet Union.

Frontier disputes, and common claims to the Paracel and Spratly Islands in the South China Sea were but the small change of a deteriorating relationship that became more obviously antagonistic during 1978. In June, the Chinese cut off all aid to Vietnam and removed their technicians and diplomatic staff, while in November came the most dramatic illustration of the extent of disunity among the communists of Southeast Asia: Vietnam signed a Treaty of Peace and Friendship with the Soviet Union. Such a treaty at once put Vietnam in the Soviet camp so far as world communism was concerned, and in effect rendered the split between itself and China irreconcilable. With border clashes between Vietnam and Kampuchea escalating, and with the ethnic Chinese of Vietnam coming under severe government controls, the stage was set for a further round of warfare in the region.

Ashley Brown

Kampuchea
Vietnamese invasion and Khmer resistance

The Khmer Rouge movement which controlled Kampuchea (formerly Cambodia) from April 1975 until January 1979 became a symbol of the modern subordination of humanity to ideology, and came to rank with the Nazi SS as a byword for the systematic commission of atrocities upon the innocent. This image, reinforced by photographs of pyramids of human skulls, and the eyewitness testimony of survivors, has been carefully and skilfully cultivated by the Vietnamese, who encouraged foreign journalists to visit the scene of Khmer Rouge atrocities in order to deflect international criticism of their own armed interference in the affairs of a sovereign state. In fact, the internal character of the Khmer Rouge regime played only a minor role in the Vietnamese decision to invade Kampuchea in December 1978. It was the rapid deterioration of Kampuchean-Vietnamese relations, posing an implicit threat to Vietnamese security, that persuaded Hanoi to resort to armed force.

Differences between the Vietnamese and Cambodian communists can be traced back to the period following the 1954 Geneva Conference, which formalised the division of the former French colony of Indochina into the independent states of Vietnam (North and South), Laos and Cambodia (renamed Kampuchea in 1975). The Indochinese Communist Party, founded by Ho Chi Minh in 1930, had been dissolved in 1951, and a separate Cambodian communist guerrilla movement formed, known as the Khmer Issarak. As part of the Geneva Agreement, the

Above: Khmer Rouge leader Pol Pot, strong-man of the post-1975 Khmer Rouge regime and leader of the military resistance to the Vietnamese occupation. Below: Khmer Rouge soldiers captured by the Vietnamese during border clashes in August 1978. The fighting, which had begun in 1975, became increasingly severe, and provoked Hanoi into the invasion of Kampuchea in December 1978. Right: Vietnamese troops parade in Phnom Penh.

bulk of the pro-Vietnamese Khmer Issarak forces regrouped in North Vietnam, with only a small underground organisation left behind in Cambodia. During the 1960s, many pro-Vietnamese veterans were eliminated by a faction of the Cambodian Communist Party led by Pol Pot, who became its general secretary in 1962. Under Pol Pot's leadership the Cambodian Communist Party adopted an increasingly hostile attitude to Prince Sihanouk, the Cambodian head of state, which brought it into conflict with the Vietnamese communists, who regarded the war against the Americans as paramount, and Sihanouk as a valuable, though covert, ally. Relations were further soured after Hanoi signed the 1973 Paris Agreements with the United States. The Khmer Rouge (as the Cambodian communists had been renamed by Sihanouk) rejected this compromise as a betrayal and stepped up the purge of pro-Vietnamese from its ranks.

The uncertain status of the Cambodian-Vietnamese border also supplied cause for conflict. The pro-American Saigon government had laid claim to a group of Cambodian islands in 1960, and there were disputes over the position of the land frontier at a

The Vietnamese invasion of Kampuchea Dec 1978-84

→ main axes of Vietnamese/United Front advance, December 1978
→ Khmer Rouge infiltration routes

number of points. Unable to reach a satisfactory agreement with Saigon, and realising the possibility of a communist victory in South Vietnam, Sihanouk attempted to negotiate a settlement of the border issue with the South Vietnamese communist National Liberation Front in June 1964 and August 1966. The NLF recognised Cambodian sovereignty over the disputed islands, but refused to make further concessions requested by Sihanouk.

Oil and water

The Lon Nol coup and the extension of American military operations to Cambodia in 1970 led to the fall of Sihanouk, but also resulted in closer military cooperation between the Khmer Rouge and the Vietnamese communists. Though this cooperation greatly diminished after 1973, it was an important factor in the Khmer Rouge victory of April 1975. Within weeks of their capture of Phnom Penh, however, Khmer Rouge troops were involved in border clashes with the Vietnamese, and they seized the Vietnamese island of Phu Quoc early in May 1975, being driven out a few weeks later by a vigorous Vietnamese counter-attack. Negotiations between Vietnam and Kampuchea, held in Phnom Penh during May 1976, led to agreement that the land border between the two countries should be that defined by the pre-1954 French colonial authorities, but no formula was found to resolve the problem of disputed territorial waters, which since the discovery of oil deposits in the area had taken on a new significance.

By 1977 the situation was deteriorating rapidly, and Khmer Rouge units were conducting raids in depth into Vietnam, seizing strategic positions, massacring Vietnamese villagers and attempting to create a depopulated buffer zone along the Vietnamese side of the border. By late 1977, several Kampuchean divisions were operating permanently in the border area, and Vietnamese territory was subject to regular shelling by Khmer Rouge artillery.

The confrontation seemed to be far from universally popular within the ranks of the Khmer Rouge, however, and there were rumours of an attempted coup against the Pol Pot leadership during April 1977. The revolt was ruthlessly suppressed and purges of suspected pro-Vietnamese intensified. Many of the survivors of these purges, along with large numbers of refugees fleeing Khmer Rouge-style communism, sought refuge in Vietnam, where an anti-Khmer Rouge movement was being formed with Vietnamese encouragement.

During the autumn of 1978, the Khmer Rouge stepped up their operations against Vietnam's border provinces, taking advantage of severe flooding, which hampered the Vietnamese Army, to advance deep into Vietnamese territory. Hanoi reacted by announcing the formation of a Khmer United Front for National Salvation, led by Heng Samrin, a 44 year-old former Khmer Rouge political officer. On 25 December 1978 the Vietnamese struck: their troops entered Kampuchea, engaging the bulk of the Khmer Rouge forces, which was concentrated along the border, mostly in the Parrot's Beak (Svay Rieng Province) and Fish Hook (Kompong Chom) salients. These concentrations were encircled and destroyed by the Vietnamese during the early stages of the fighting, and the subsequent advance along Routes 19 and 7, supported by troops of Heng Samrin's United Front, seems to have been largely unopposed.

By 30 December, the United Front 'Voice of the Cambodian People' radio station was claiming the capture of large areas of Ratanakiri Province, and two days later announced the fall of Kratie. Khmer Rouge casualties were heavy, and there were many defections to the United Front as Khmer Rouge control of the country disintegrated under the blows of the Vietnamese Army. Many Khmer Rouge simply withdrew into the countryside, however, and guerrilla attacks on Vietnamese forces began almost immediately. It was estimated by Western intelligence sources that some 100,000 Vietnamese troops, supported by 20,000 men of the United Front, advanced into Kampuchea along several axes, entering Phnom Penh on 7 January 1979.

The Vietnamese pursued the retreating Khmer Rouge eastwards along Routes 5 and 6, reaching the Thai border by mid-January. The Heng Samrin government, established in Phnom Penh on 8 January, still faced the enormous task of establishing its control over an almost derelict country which contained large pockets of Khmer Rouge resistance, bypassed by the rapid advance of the Vietnamese invasion.

Large areas along the frontier with Thailand remained under Khmer Rouge control, and a conference of Khmer Rouge leaders, held on 1-2 February 1979, decided on a strategy of guerrilla warfare and harassing attacks on the Vietnamese. The Khmer Rouge was able to sustain its guerrilla campaign, despite Vietnamese superiority, because of the international reaction to the 1978 invasion.

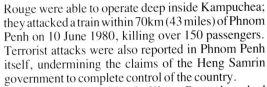

Although Vietnam, the Soviet Union and many pro-Moscow governments recognised the Heng Samrin regime, there was sufficient international opposition to the Vietnamese invasion, and the perceived threat of increased Soviet influence in the region, for the Khmer Rouge to retain its place at the United Nations as the recognised government of Kampuchea. The main diplomatic and material backing for the Khmer Rouge came from China, but fears of Vietnam among the governments of the Association of South East Asian Nations (Asean), and in particular in Thailand, provided China and the Khmer Rouge with a number of local allies.

Thailand, in particular, felt vulnerable to the threat of Vietnamese expansion, and gave tacit support to the Khmer Rouge in the hope of forcing a Vietnamese withdrawal from Kampuchea and a return to its traditional role as a buffer between Thailand and Vietnam. Supplies of Chinese equipment were transferred to Khmer Rouge bases through Thailand, and the Thai Army turned a blind eye to Khmer Rouge use of refugee camps as recruiting grounds and military bases. Fighting continued throughout 1979-80, and though the Vietnamese/Heng Samrin forces were able to consolidate their control of most of the country, the Khmer Rouge remained active, particularly in the western provinces.

The resistance to the Vietnamese now included right-wing Khmer Serei guerrillas as well as the Khmer Rouge. The Khmer Serei included many former supporters of the Lon Nol government, and though strongly anti-communist, operated an informal and fragile truce agreement with the Khmer Rouge. Pol Pot's forces were by far the strongest opposition to the Vietnamese, with an estimated 20,000-35,000 men, while the Khmer Serei had a maximum of 6000 men, split between a number of competing factions. Prince Sihanouk, virtually exiled to China by the Khmer Rouge, re-emerged as a unifying symbolic leader of the Khmer resistance accepted by both the Khmer Rouge and the Khmer Serei, but without his own military base, and dependent upon his undoubted diplomatic and political skills in his efforts to influence the course of events.

In spite of a number of Vietnamese offensives which had pushed large numbers of Khmer Rouge guerrillas across the border into Thailand, the Khmer Rouge were able to operate deep inside Kampuchea; they attacked a train within 70km (43 miles) of Phnom Penh on 10 June 1980, killing over 150 passengers. Terrorist attacks were also reported in Phnom Penh itself, undermining the claims of the Heng Samrin government to complete control of the country.

During February 1981, the Khmer Rouge launched an offensive aimed at disrupting elections being held to demonstrate support for the pro-Vietnamese government. The offensive forced the Vietnamese to employ helicopters to resupply their garrisons, isolated along the Thai frontier, and managed to close Routes 5 and 6 at several points.

The Vietnamese and Phnom Penh forces launched their counter-attack in October, with the beginning of the dry season which allowed the Vietnamese to maximise their advantage in heavy equipment and armour. The Khmer Rouge guerrillas were subjected to bombing by Vietnamese aircraft, and Vietnamese troops were airlifted into the battle zones. The heaviest fighting took place in the north, where the Khmer Rouge military headquarters was situated near the Thai and Laotian borders, and in the area south of Poipet. The Khmer Rouge headquarters fell to Vietnamese troops in December 1981 and though it was retaken the following month, it remained subject to heavy bombing from Vietnamese aircraft based at Siem Reap.

Thai support

While the Khmer Rouge were able to sustain a serious guerrilla threat to the stability of the Heng Samrin government, and a constant danger to the occupying Vietnamese, it was clear that they relied heavily upon safe bases and supply routes on Thai territory, without which they would have been unable to sustain their campaign inside Kampuchea. Relations between Thailand and Vietnam were strained almost to breaking point, and there were a number of serious border incidents. In June 1980, for example, after Thailand had repatriated large numbers of refugees to areas of Kampuchea controlled by the Khmer Rouge, the Vietnamese crossed into Thailand at a number of points, attacking Khmer Serei bases at Nong Makhoon and Nong Chan, before withdrawing in the face of a Thai counter-attack. Incidents involving Vietnamese shelling of Thai territory and hot pursuits of Khmer Rouge guerrillas across the border became commonplace, and seemed designed to persuade Thailand to recognise the Heng Samrin government and withdraw its support from the Khmer Rouge.

While the Khmer Rouge was reliant upon Chinese and Thai backing, Vietnam was forced to turn to the Soviet Union for military and economic assistance in order to sustain its expensive occupation of Kampuchea. In return for this aid, Moscow was able to extract the use of a number of military bases from Hanoi, which further convinced China that Vietnam was a tool of Soviet aggression, and strengthened the China-Asean-Khmer Rouge axis.

By 1984 the military situation had settled into a stalemate in which the Vietnamese were able to maintain control of the administrative centres of Kampuchea and remained in a position to mount offensives against Khmer Rouge concentrations wherever they posed a serious threat, but were unable to totally eliminate the Khmer Rouge resistance.

Robin Corbett

Above: Thai soldiers question Khmer Rouge seeking refuge in Thailand from a Vietnamese offensive. Left: Right-wing Khmer Serei guerrillas, armed with RPG-7 rocket launchers, at a camp in Thailand. Thai support for the Khmer resistance was vital to its survival against the Vietnamese. Below: The eternal victims of modern Indochinese history: peasant refugees driven from their homes.

The dragon strikes

China attacks Vietnam

On 17 February 1979 China launched an invasion of northern Vietnam, foreseeing a brief punitive action that would 'teach the Vietnamese a lesson'. But the Chinese People's Liberation Army (PLA) was to find its fellow communists a far tougher proposition than the Indian Army had been in 1962.

Hostility between China and Vietnam had built up over a long period before the 1979 invasion. Although China had provided Hanoi with extensive military aid during the Vietnam War, the rapprochement between China and the United States – US President Nixon paid an official visit to Peking in 1972 at the same time that the US Air Force was carrying out heavy raids on North Vietnam – led the Vietnamese to depend more and more exclusively on the Soviet Union for support. After the North Vietnamese victory in 1975 this trend was confirmed. Pro-Chinese elements in the Vietnamese politburo were ousted by their pro-Soviet opponents. The toughening of Vietnamese socialism, cracking down on private businesses, was by 1978 beginning to have a profound effect on the country's large Chinese community (known as the Hoa) who formed most of the small business class. An exodus of Hoa to China built up, some 160,000 crossing the border between April and July 1978. This further exacerbated relations, and all remaining Chinese advisers were withdrawn from Vietnam that summer.

In November 1978 the relationship between Vietnam and the Soviet Union was cemented by the signing of a Soviet-Vietnamese Friendship Treaty which was immediately followed by a movement of Soviet advisers into Hanoi and of Soviet naval vessels into Cam Ranh Bay. This was bound to appear threatening to the Chinese, who already felt menaced by Soviet forces along their long border in northern Asia.

The Chinese were also hostile to the spreading power of Vietnam throughout Indochina. Vietnamese advisers constituted a major presence in Laos, a situation China could do little about, but in Kampuchea the Chinese were able to back Pol Pot's Khmer Rouge regime in its confrontation with Vietnam. When the Vietnamese invaded Kampuchea in December 1978, driving Pol Pot out of Phnom Penh the following month, the Chinese held back from direct military intervention, but they were keen to take some action to help Khmer Rouge resistance.

It is likely, therefore, that the Chinese invasion was partly designed to relieve military pressure on Pol Pot's men, but it was officially concerned with a long-standing border dispute. The Vietnamese claimed that when the French had delineated the border between their Indochina empire and China, they had ceded territory which was rightfully part of Vietnam. Tension over the border line was exacerbated by territorial disputes elsewhere – over the Paracel Islands, seized by China from South Vietnam in January 1974, and the Spratly Island group held by Vietnam but claimed by China. During late 1978 and early 1979 local clashes between Vietnamese and Chinese forces along the border became a daily occurrence. The Chinese therefore explicitly justified their decision to invade as a punitive action, designed to discourage the Vietnamese from any further small-scale skirmishing. The Chinese gathered 85,000 men supported by 200,000 reserves along the border. These troops, backed by 1000 T62 tanks, K-63 armoured personnel carriers and a mixture of Soviet and Chinese artillery, were drawn from the Kumming and Guangzhou Military Districts. The 41st and 42nd

Left: A rally in Hanoi to protest at the Chinese invasion of Vietnam's northern border provinces in February 1979. Sino-Vietnamese relations deteriorated sharply during the 1970s, and border clashes escalated to full-scale war. Above: Ethnic Chinese refugees fleeing Vietnam wait near the border for permission to enter China.

Below: Chinese T59 tanks, closely supported by infantry, assault a hilltop position. Chinese tactics and equipment were badly outdated, and PLA casualties were severe during the 'punitive' expedition into Vietnam. Below right: A battery of Chinese 152mm howitzers shells Vietnamese positions.

the natural defensive positions with concrete bunkers. Built in groups of three to five, connected by trenches and protected by minefields, they were located on vantage points overlooking key strategic towns and highways linking the region with Hanoi, 125km (85 miles) to the south.

At 0500 hours on 17 February, under cover of artillery fire, the Chinese crossed the border at 26 points. Many crossings were purely diversionary attacks and it soon became clear that their main attention would focus on the provincial capitals of Lao Cai, Cao Bang and Lang Son. All were strategic access towns lying within easy grasp, and Lao Cai and Lang Son both lay on railway routes between the two countries. After recovering from their initial shock the Vietnamese were able to put up stiff resistance against Chinese attempts to seize villages dotted around the three towns. By the 20th the PLA advance was bogged down and contained within 10km (6 miles) of the border. The regional militia suffered heavily, but effectively halted the invaders, claiming to have inflicted 3500 casualties and destroyed 80 tanks.

Armies of the PLA under the overall command of Peking military headquarters provided the main elements of the attacking force. The army had, however, seen little action over the last 25 years and the morale of its officer corps had suffered after the widespread purges of the Cultural Revolution. For their part, the Vietnamese, commanded by Van Tien Dong, had to rely on local regional and militia units, 60,000 strong, as much of the regular army was engaged in Kampuchea or stationed in the south of Vietnam. Nevertheless, many of the available forces had recent combat experience.

To assure success in the campaign the PLA would have to find an effective answer to the difficult terrain of northern Vietnam. The prospective battlefield sprawled over three military districts that included the provinces of Lai Chau, Hoang Lien Son, Ha Tuyen, Cao Bang, Lang Son and Quang Ninh. Each consisted of inaccessible mountain ranges separated by narrow valleys filled with tributaries of the Clear, Black and Red Rivers. These provinces would be difficult to capture as movement, channelled along vulnerable valley floors, would be slow and attacks would have to be made uphill. To make the PLA's task more difficult the Vietnamese had strengthened

Small steps southwards

The Chinese had made some strategic gains. Part of Lao Cai on the Yunnan front was captured and several villages held by units of the Vietnamese 345th and 316A Divisions had fallen into their hands after heavy fighting. Advance elements were moving southwards on Cha Pa and the mines at Gam Dong. Ten villages around Cao Bang, defended by the 346th Division, had been captured and heavy casualties had been inflicted on the Vietnamese 246th Regiment at Soc Giang, the 677th at Cha Ling and the 851st at Da Sha.

The Chinese forces advancing on Lang Son, held by the Vietnamese 3rd and 327th Divisions, had also made some gains. Dong Dang, 3km (2 miles) south of Friendship Pass, fell after successful Chinese assaults against Vietnamese bunkers on surrounding hills. The capture of Hill 379 and the city's railway depot on the 23rd sealed the fate of the town.

By the end of the first week it was clear to Peking

that their punitive action was not going to be the sharp and effective lesson they had hoped for. In restricting their efforts to a limited offensive in the north of Vietnam the Chinese were trying to inflict a severe reversal on regular Vietnamese units without escalating the war. Instead the PLA had been met by local troops who had fought well and contained its advances. The Chinese had to decide, at this stage, between a humiliating withdrawal or redoubling their efforts in spite of mounting casualties, limited territorial gains and growing international condemnation.

In effect there was no choice: Peking decided to continue its offensive in all three battle zones but to concentrate the PLA's main energies on capturing Lang Son. As the site of a major Viet Minh victory in 1950, its capture would be a severe psychological blow to the Vietnamese people and, as the gateway to the Red River delta and Hanoi, a concerted offensive might draw regular units into its defence.

The battle for Lang Son began at 0800 hours on 27 February. For the next week heavy fighting took place on the hills that surround the town, as the Chinese attempted to cut off its defenders from Hanoi. Khou Ma Son, 8km (5 miles) northwest of the town, was captured on the first day, and on the 28th, after the PLA had switched the focus for its attacks to the south, the village of Loc Binh fell. By 5 March the capture of highlands west of Lang Son and Height 413 lying to the southwest had made the Vietnamese position untenable and the town was abandoned. The regional forces pulled out and moved southwards to join up with regular units that had moved up from Hanoi after the government issued orders for the full mobilisation of its armed forces. But the fall of Lang Son effectively signalled the end of the war. The Chinese announced their withdrawal on the night of 5/6 March and two weeks later had recrossed the border largely unhindered by the Vietnamese.

Chinese checked

Although the *People's Daily* of 6 March reported to the Chinese people that the army was withdrawing after 'achieving its goals with complete success', the PLA's performance in the war highlighted major weaknesses in its command structure, tactics and training. Many of its officers had not seen action since the early 1960s and continued to use outdated human-wave tactics, believing that the Vietnamese defenders would be overwhelmed. In fact they did not collapse

Far left: The wreckage of a Chinese Shenyang F-6 fighter (a MiG-19 refit), shot down over Vietnam, is guarded by a Vietnamese militiawoman. Left: Chinese soldiers post warning notices against looting in an occupied Vietnamese town.

Below: A Chinese soldier guarded by his Vietnamese captor. The main brunt of the Chinese invasion was borne by local, second-line Vietnamese troops, and the final withdrawal was in many ways a humiliation for Peking.

main axes of Chinese advance

The Chinese invasion of Vietnam Feb 1979

and inflicted such heavy losses on the initial Chinese attacks that new methods were implemented. The PLA attempted to use coordinated action by artillery, tanks and infantry to destroy strongpoints. However, as the army lacked an efficient communications system the change of tactics enjoyed only a limited success. In contrast the Vietnamese were well-versed in coordinating battle plans between widely-dispersed units operating in difficult terrain.

The PLA advance was also slowed by its reliance on an inflexible and antiquated supply system. Apart from a few lorries, the army's essential logistical support depended on horses and men – it seems that the Chinese had to call off their attack on 18 February in part due to a lack of ammunition at the front. The Vietnamese had much more recent experience in the art of field supply and were able regularly to provide their frontline units with all the necessary war materials.

The quality of the PLA's equipment, neglected during the Cultural Revolution, was also suspect. The T62's armour was poor, making it an easy target for mines or rocket-propelled grenades. The efficiency of many motorised units was put in jeopardy by frequent mechanical failures. Vietnamese equipment, either abandoned by the US or supplied by the Soviet Union, was more reliable and up-to-date. The difficulties over the coordination of troop movements, the poor quality of logistical support, and the unreliability of equipment imposed a degree of stagnation on the Chinese attacks that made them easy targets for small groups of Vietnamese soldiers using hit-and-run tactics.

Both sides appear to have been unwilling to make extensive use of their air forces during the war. The Chinese had 700 planes along the border including MiG-21s, refits of MiG-17/19s and Il-28 bombers. Most were inferior in quality to Vietnam's MiG-23s, F-5A fighters and A-37 ground-attack planes, while the Chinese pilots had neither the experience nor the training to fly precision bombing missions in support of ground attacks over difficult terrain. To make their task more difficult the weather for much of the campaign was cloudy. The Vietnamese had recently strengthened their anti-aircraft defences in the region with supplies of SA-6 and SA-7 missiles from the Soviet Union. Their crews had received the training to make them an effective deterrent. Arguably, the Chinese refrained from use of their air force on the grounds that, if used, it would constitute a major escalation of the conflict.

On balance, both sides scored some points in the 17-day war, but of the two, China emerged with the more tarnished image. Peking's actions alarmed its new-found partners, the United States and Japan, and heightened tensions with the Soviet Union. Its willingness to resort to arms caused concern in neighbouring countries, like Indonesia and Malaysia, whose large Chinese communities could conceivably be used as a pretext for some form of intervention in the future. The dispute also scared off the Indian government when it was seeking to improve a relationship that had been soured by the border war of 1962. In the short term, the Chinese invasion had little effect on Vietnam's capabilities in Kampuchea and Laos. Although two regular divisions were later withdrawn to improve security along its northern border, the Vietnamese offensive against the Khmer Rouge was hardly disrupted.

Exodus from Vietnam

Perhaps the most dramatic consequence of the conflict was a resumption of the exodus of Chinese from Vietnam, this time on an even larger scale and under far worse conditions. Between March and July 1979 some 400,000 Hoa fled Vietnam, 'encouraged' by the authorities. An armada of leaky boats preyed on by pirates and subject to the hazards of the weather, bore the 'boat people' off to China or to an uncertain reception throughout Southeast Asia. In July at the insistence of international humanitarian organisations, the Vietnamese authorities halted what had become effectively a wholesale deportation of an ethnic minority, instituting a more regulated flow of Chinese abroad under better-controlled circumstances. Most Southeast Asian countries were extremely unwilling to accept the refugees, regarding them as an unwelcome and potentially disruptive influx.

Border clashes between Chinese and Vietnamese forces flared up periodically – there were heavy artillery exchanges in May 1981, April 1983 and the early months of 1984 – but there had been no reversion to major warfare by autumn 1984. Any hopes of a settlement of the two countries' differences would appear to depend on a successful rapprochement between China and the Soviet Union.

Ian Westwell

Chemical warfare

From nerve gas to defoliants

The idea of chemical warfare has caused a particular revulsion ever since various gases were extensively used during World War I. For this reason, allegations that one's enemies have employed lethal chemicals have a special propaganda value and, not surprisingly, such accusations are frequently made on the flimsiest of evidence. In the 1980s, for example, the Vietnamese were said to have used 'yellow rain' – a mycotoxin – against Kampuchean rebels and against Meo hill tribesmen in Laos. Yet examination of the evidence proved totally inconclusive – some experts even asserted that the yellow substances retrieved for analysis were the faeces of a particular species of bee.

The stockpiling of chemical weapons by the superpowers and the development of ever more effective varieties is, however, an undoubted reality. The Geneva Protocol of 1925 prohibiting chemical and biological warfare has been adopted by both the United States and the Soviet Union, but the Protocol does not ban the production or development of such weapons, only their use – and both superpowers reserve the right to retaliate in kind if subject to chemical attack.

The gases used in the trench warfare of World War I, such as phosgene, hydrogen cyanide, cynogen chloride and varieties of mustard gas, still form a large part of the world's chemical warfare stocks, particularly in the Eastern bloc. Phosgene was allegedly used by the Soviet-supplied Egyptians during fighting in the Yemen in the 1960s and the Iraqis have carried out at least one experiment with poisonous gas during the Gulf War with Iran. Hydrogen cyanide and cynogen chloride work by binding onto the enzyme in red blood cells which is normally responsible for the removal of carbon dioxide from the system. Phosgene, on the other hand, acts as a lung corrosive and breaks down the tissue into a fatty pulp, thus causing eventual asphyxiation.

The lethality of these chemicals was totally surpassed, however, by others developed during and after World War II. In 1939, Dr Gerhard Schrader discovered Tabun while working in the insecticidal laboratories of I G Farben in Germany. The first so-called G-Agent nerve gas, Tabun (coded GA) was synthesised as a highly toxic organophosphate and proved to be four times more powerful than mustard gas. The military potential of the gas was recognised and under the auspices of the German Army, Schrader went on to synthesise Sarin (coded GB) which in turn proved four times more effective than Tabun. In 1944 Richard Kuhn further developed the G-Agent synthesis and produced Soman, an even more toxic substance. By 1945, the British laboratories at Porton Down had also successfully manufactured all three known G-Agents. It is surprising in the light of these breakthroughs that chemical warfare was not used during World War II – though it is known that Churchill considered it during the height of the invasion scare and that Hitler considered it during the Normandy landings.

The discoveries of the 1940s, however, paled in comparison to the British discovery, made in the ICI laboratories in the mid-1950s, of the nerve gas VX (a methylphosphonothiolate). VX proved to have greater stability than the G-Agents and, ultimately, more killing power. During experimentation in the early stages of its development, an RAF volunteer, Ronald Maddison, had a small drop of VX placed on his forearm during tests at Porton Down. Within a short period he died, surrounded by experts who could not save him.

Both the G-Agents and V-Agents have similar effects on the human body. They combine with a vital blood enzyme, preventing the breakdown of acetylcholine and the transmission of neural commands. Consequently, the build-up of acetylcholine causes initial symptoms of heavy sweating, breathing difficulties and dimming of vision. Uncontrollable vomiting and defecation, convulsions and paralysis are then followed by respiratory failure and death.

By the early 1960s it was believed that the Soviet Union had also developed a V-Agent, known as VR-55, but this was later discovered to be probably a thickened form of the G-Agent Soman (thickening the agent with synthetic polymers reduces evaporation and thus increases its persistence as well as skin absorption). The majority of the Soviet Union's gas stockpile, however, is of the World War I gases (hydrogen cyanide and phosgene), whereas the West has concentrated on developing Sarin and VX.

Research into chemical weapons has not been solely restricted to nerve gases, of course. The major use of chemicals in actual warfare since World War II has been as defoliants, either to expose guerrilla movements by denying them cover or to deny the enemy food supplies by destroying crops. The British employed a herbicide, 245-T, during their counter-insurgency campaign in Malaya in the 1950s, and the Americans made massive use of Agent Orange in Vietnam. The by now well-established long-term effects of exposure to Agent Orange demonstrate how much of the danger of chemical warfare may be incalculable in advance.

The other area of research which has had practical effect is the development of a mild gas for use in controlling civil disturbances. CS gas (orthochlor-obenzalmalononitrile) has emerged as the most usable substance, causing nausea and vomiting in high concentrations but leading to permanent injury only under very rare circumstances. CS gas was also used by the United States in Vietnam, and has reportedly been employed in Afghanistan. A further anti-riot gas, dibenoxazepine has also been developed; it will cause a nettle-sting effect, but has not yet been brought into use.

In the military field, perhaps the most interesting developments are the category of gases known as incapacitants. These are aimed at creating a type of 'bloodless' warfare, severely impairing the enemy's ability to fight but causing only minor casualties; as one American expert put it: 'to cause the enemy to come out singing the star-spangled banner with his hands in the air'. This type of chemical is quite distinct from harassing agents such as CS gas where the effects are brief; a true military incapacitant may be effective for hours or even days. They are intended to kill only in very unusual circumstances and are designed to take effect almost immediately. There are two types of incapacitation which are under

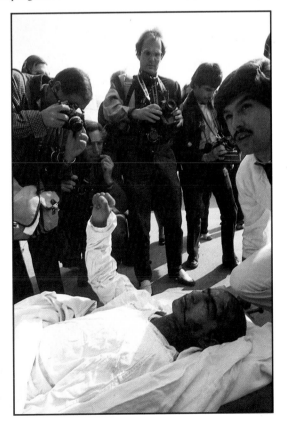

Far left: A US soldier, armed with an M16A1 rifle (with blank firing attachment), on an NBC exercise, wearing respirator, NBC suit and smothered with Fuller's earth (a hydrous aluminium silicate). The charcoal-impregnated clothing offers relatively good protection for 24 hours. Fuller's earth is a standard decontaminant and is noted for its absorption of oily matter and, if added to NBC clothing, may offer enhanced protection in areas of concentrated chemical presence. Centre left: Groundcrew decontaminate a Phantom using a detergent-based mixture dispensed from a portable unit. The probability of NBC warfare taking place has greatly increased the need for such readily portable facilities. Left: An Iranian casualty purported to have been gassed by Iraqi chemical delivery systems.

Binary nerve gas artillery shell

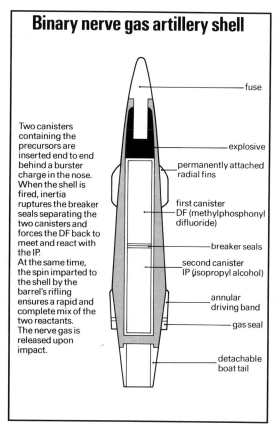

fuse

explosive

permanently attached radial fins

first canister
DF (methylphosphonyl difluoride)

breaker seals

second canister
IP (isopropyl alcohol)

annular driving band

gas seal

detachable boat tail

Two canisters containing the precursors are inserted end to end behind a burster charge in the nose. When the shell is fired, inertia ruptures the breaker seals separating the two canisters and forces the DF back to meet and react with the IP.
At the same time, the spin imparted to the shell by the barrel's rifling ensures a rapid and complete mix of the two reactants. The nerve gas is released upon impact.

consideration: mental and physical.

The physical incapacitation chemicals present the problem of finding substances which will cause a symptom such as muscular paralysis, interference with voluntary control of limbs, unconsciousness or loss of sight. Recent research has attempted to discover selective neuromuscular inhibitors which could, for instance, temporarily deny a soldier the use of his arms or legs, but as yet no effective chemical has been discovered which would be sufficiently selective to avoid the collapse of the breathing muscles.

Greater advances have been made in the field of psychological incapacitants. One of those most commonly investigated was LSD (lysergic acid diethylamide) along with its more potent analogues MLD-41 and ALD-52. LSD was eventually rejected by the United States for military use because of the comparatively high cost of large-scale production and the suspicion that its use might cause long-term genetic damage.

The incapacitant BZ (3-quinuclidinyl benzilate), however, was produced and deployed in chemical weapons. Developed as early as the 1950s, BZ is an extremely potent psychoactive chemical and even small amounts can continue to affect the subject for up to 90 hours. Exposure to the chemical will cause vomiting, mental lethargy and lack of motory coordination within an hour. This will be followed by disorientation and hallucination leaving the victim conscious but incapable of rational thought. Maniacal behaviour may also occur. BZ has now been phased out of Western military arsenals, but research on benzilate derivatives of BZ have continued with the emphasis on physiological effects (such as neutralising nerve ganglions) as opposed to psychological.

The handling and delivery of unstable and lethal chemical substances such as Sarin has always posed problems, but these have been largely resolved by the

Below: Large tracts of the Vietnamese forest destroyed after US spraying operations with Agent Orange. This defoliant was a simple extension of commercial herbicides and was created through the combination of equal parts of the chemicals 2,4-D and 245-T. Its tactical use was illustrated through the extensive defoliation of the Vietnamese forests, thus denying large areas of potential concealment to the communist forces operating from these areas.

development of a binary chemical system. This involves the use of munitions storing two relatively safe chemicals in adjacent compartments, only to mix when delivered to their target. By combining the stable compounds DF (methylphosphonyl) and IP (isopropyl alcohol) Sarin gas is produced. Similarly by combining QL (ethyl 2-diisopropylaminoethyl methyl phosphonite) with NM (a dimethyl polysulphide), the reaction will produce the potent VX gas.

Chemical agents can be accurately delivered into the battle zone by artillery, missiles or aircraft. At present the weapons projected for chemicals delivery by the United States include 155mm and 203mm artillery shells and the 225kg (500lb) Bigeye bomb. It is believed that the Soviet Union deploys chemical warheads, filled with either Soman or hydrogen cyanide, on SS-1 Scud missiles, the SS-N-3 Shaddock and the Frog-7, as well as projecting the use of airborne and artillery delivery systems.

Since the 1960s, when the Soviet Union was very worried by the United States' long lead in the nuclear field, Moscow has taken chemical warfare extremely seriously. In addition to 80,000 specialist chemical troops, the Soviet Union deploys a chemical defence battalion and decontamination companies into each division. All troops are issued with gas masks, protective clothing, chemical detectors and atropine-based antidote deliverance systems. Nato, for its part, has left nothing to chance. In West Germany alone, over 1000 tonnes of nerve gas (much of it in artillery shells) has been stockpiled. Overall US stocks amount to about 42,000 tonnes of chemical warfare agents compared with an estimated Soviet Union stockpile of 30,000 tonnes.

The true effectiveness of chemical weapons on the modern battlefield has yet to be proven. Against troops well prepared for chemical defence such weapons would presumably be less effective than, say, fragmentation shells. The potential effect on large concentrations of civilians without proper protection is, on the other hand, horrific.

Alexander McNair-Wilson

ANTI-AIRCRAFT ARTILLERY

The end of World War II found air-defence artillery at its zenith; every combatant nation had lavished research and manufacturing ability on the provision of large numbers of guns of every calibre from 20mm to 150mm, together with radar and fire-control systems, ammunition and all other relevant equipment. However, the war had also generated the weapon which was eventually to reduce this vast army of guns to a tenth of its wartime strength: the surface-to-air missile (SAM). Under development in Germany, Britain and the United States, SAMs were expected soon to replace the gun as the leading anti-aircraft weapon.

Programmes to update air-defence artillery continued in the postwar period, however, especially as the running down of development budgets slowed missile programmes. In 1944 the US Army had initiated a totally new concept when they specified a 75mm gun with automatic feed and with the radar and fire-control integral to the gun mounting. The idea of an automatic feed had been made possible by the development of the electronic proximity fuze: the major obstacle to rapid fire had lain in the need to set a time fuze before loading every shell, to ensure that the shell would burst within range of its target, but the proximity fuze detected the presence of the target by radio and detonated the shell when it was in the most advantageous position, without requiring any setting before firing.

The US 75mm M51 Skysweeper did not appear until the mid-1950s, since development encountered more obstacles than had been anticipated. The gun was fed by twin rotating magazines and could achieve a rate of fire of 45 rounds per minute (rpm). Alongside the gun, on the mounting, were a tracking radar, a fire-control computer and an optical tracker, so that the entire engagement of the target was in the hands of the gun's crew and they had no need for external sources of data. Skysweeper is still in service with the armies of Greece, Turkey and Japan, but it was replaced in US service in the early 1960s by the Hawk missile.

In general, by the 1960s heavy AA guns of 75mm

calibre or larger had been made obsolete by SAMs. The British experimented with two heavier guns for high-altitude air defence in the 1950s, but they also eventually adopted a SAM, the Bloodhound. Some Soviet heavy AA guns were used in Vietnam around Hanoi and by Arab states in the Middle East during the 1960s and 1970s, but with no great success.

The lighter guns, however, still had a useful service life. Light AA guns, generally of 37mm or 40mm, were common during World War II – everyone had heard of the famous Bofors gun – but the increasing speed of jet aircraft had left them behind by 1950. Hand-operated, they were incapable of swinging fast enough to engage a ground-attack aircraft moving at 800-950 km/h (500-600 mph), so power operation was adopted, first as an 'add-on' to existing guns and then in a purpose-built design when Bofors produced their improved L/70 model in 1951. Such designs were normally used in conjunction with a central fire-control radar and, combined with improvements in shells (giving a greater destructive radius), in the cartridge (giving better velocity and increasing range to 3000m – 9850 feet) and in the rate of fire (now 300 rpm), gave the light anti-aircraft gun a new lease of life. Some examples of other light anti-aircraft guns

Previous page: An M998 Sergeant York during trials in the western United States. Top: An M163 of the US 59th Air Defense Artillery providing protection for the airfield at Baumholder. Above: Inspection of the linked ready-use ammunition of the Vulcan; a variety of ammunition is available for the Vulcan, including armour-piercing.

Left: The M998 Sergeant York prototype. The radar has been developed from that in use on the F-16, the guns are Bofors 40mm L/70 and the chassis is from an M48A5 tank; the prototype was produced by Ford to an army specification demanding mainly 'off-the-shelf' components.

produced since the war are the Oerlikon twin 35mm GDF-002 and the Soviet 57mm S-60, both of which are still in service.

During World War II there were many attempts to achieve a higher mobility for AA guns by putting them onto the chassis of tanks or transport vehicles, thus enabling them to accompany armoured columns. The US Army replaced its wartime M16 and M19 self-propelled AA guns with the M42, which entered service in 1952. This was armed with two 40mm M2A1 cannon (which has proved effective against the armour of PT76 light tanks) and equipped with a lead computing sight. A range-only radar was experimentally installed but no version of this was made. The M42 served with the US Army until 1969 and remains in service with the armies of other nations today.

The advances in electronic and optical techniques

which took place in the 1960s and 1970s made it possible to incorporate micro-computers and similar small electronic devices into practical sights, and also allowed radar sets to be greatly reduced in size until they could be easily accommodated in relatively small gun mountings. One of the first vehicles to take advantage of these developments was the West German Army's Gepard, introduced in 1971. Based on the hull of the Leopard 1 tank, its turret carries surveillance radar, tracking radar, a fire-control computer, and two Oerlikon 35mm belt-fed automatic cannon. The surveillance radar scans all round the vehicle and can detect targets up to 15km (10 miles) away; as soon as it detects a target the crew is alerted and the bearing, range and elevation angle are displayed, together with an indication of whether the aircraft is friend or foe. If it is hostile, then the information is automatically transferred to the track-

Above left: The Bofors 40mm L/70 gun, successor to the famous Bofors m/36; this example has the Bofors Optronic Fire-control Instrument (BOFI) enabling night operation. Above: An M42 of the Lebanese Army in Beirut.

Below: One of the newest types of towed AA guns, the Artemis 30mm system, is made by Hellenic Arms Industries using Mauser guns.

ing radar on the front of the turret, which begins to track the target, releasing the surveillance radar to search for fresh targets.

Information from the tracking radar is now fed to the fire-control computer, which is also informed of wind speed and direction, temperature, barometric pressure and other factors. These are all applied to the target data, and gun elevation and bearing are calculated and passed to the power-operating function which swings the turret and elevates the guns. At this point the commander can, if he wishes, 'take over' the target in his optical sight, or he can leave the tracking radar in control. Whichever is in operation, when the target is within range of the guns the gunner is given a visual signal to open fire. The twin guns combine to produce a rate of fire of 1100 rpm and firing usually begins when the target is about 4km (2.5 miles) away. The level of accuracy is extremely high – so high, indeed, that when the Belgian Army took Gepard into use they complained that it was too accurate and had a compensating factor entered into the computer which distributes the fire around the notional point of aim to introduce a spread of shot and give a greater danger area.

When the US Army came to replace its M42, it incorporated a radar into the M163 Vulcan. Deliveries of this vehicle began in 1968 and it is still produced for export; it has seen action with the Israeli Army and reportedly shot down a Syrian Sukhoi Su-7 during the 1982 invasion of the Lebanon. The M163 is an M113 armoured personnel carrier fitted with a one-man turret, incorporating a lead computing sight and a range-only radar. Capable of firing either 1000 or 3000 rpm, to a range of 1600m (5200 feet), the Vulcan proved unsatisfactory in service and work on a replacement began in 1977.

The US Army introduced the Sergeant York DIVADS (divisional air-defence system) in 1983. This is a modified M48 tank chassis with a turret carrying twin 40mm L/70 Bofors guns, search and tracking radars, optical sight with laser rangefinder, and fire-control computer. The engagement of a target is almost entirely automated; the radar detects and informs the fire-control computer which interrogates the target and computes the firing data, the open-fire range, type of ammunition, burst length and interval, and takes into account target manoeuvres, weather conditions and barrel wear. When all the calculating is done the gunner merely grips his controls and the guns open fire at the computer's command. Two types of ammunition are stored in magazines and can be fed to the guns as necessary; one shell is impact-fuzed, while the other is proximity-fuzed and filled with high explosive and 640 pellets of tungsten alloy so as to give the optimum fragmentation pattern for target damage.

While undoubtedly effective, Gepard and Sergeant York are extremely complex and expensive. They are also large – 47 and 54 tonnes respectively. They are therefore likely to be confined to major armoured formations, and smaller equipments are required for lesser duties. Here the smaller calibre cannons come into play, 20mm and 25mm being the preferred types. The French Panhard M3 VDA is a good example of this class of weapon.

The M3 VDA (véhicule de défense antiaérienne) is a four-wheeled Panhard armoured personnel carrier with a turret devised by the Electronique Serge Dassault company. The turret contains a search radar, an

Top left: A Czech M53/59 self-propelled AA system in action. It is armed with two 30mm M53 cannon. Above: The Panhard M3 VDA was first shown at the 1975 Satory Exhibition; 95 per cent of its mechanical components are identical with those of the AML armoured car. Left: An AMX30 self-propelled AA system advancing through swampy terrain; the twin 30mm guns can fire up to 650 rounds per minute.

Far left, top: ZSU-57s on parade for May Day, 1960. First seen in public in 1957, the ZSU-57 uses a heavily modified T54 chassis. Far left, centre: Considered by some to be one of the finest self-propelled AA systems in the world, the ZSU-23-4 suffers from a tendency to shoot while traversing after firing.

Far left, below: The Soviet 37mm M1939 AA gun was based on the design of the Bofors 40mm m/36. It has seen action in Vietnam and during the Arab-Israeli Wars, and is shown here in the Lebanon.

electro-optical sight, and two 20mm cannon. The search radar is small enough to be carried under a man's arm when removed from the turret, but powerful enough to detect targets at ranges up to 8km (5 miles). It is also capable of tracking a target while still scanning the surrounding area for further targets. Once a target is detected the radar sounds an alarm, interrogates, and if hostile feeds the target range and elevation to the optical sight. At the same time it automatically slews the turret to face the oncoming target, and the gunner then begins to scan vertically with his sight until he acquires the target optically. The fire-control computer, fed with data from the radar, has calculated lead angles and other firing data, and this displaces the visual aiming mark. The gunner now lays his sight on the approaching target, and as soon as it is within engagement range a light flashes in his field of view and electric restraints on firing are switched off. He then opens fire manually while tracking the target, the guns firing at either 200 or 1000 rpm from each barrel.

20mm shells are now thought to be marginal in their effect against modern armoured aircraft, and most designers have begun to move up to 25mm or 30mm weapons which produce a lethal effect but which are still convenient in size and cost. One of the newest systems to be offered is the West German Wildcat, a wheeled gun carrier with a turret mounting two 30mm Mauser cannon. Wildcat has a search radar with a range of 18km (11 miles) and this displays targets on a screen in front of the gunner. It also directs the electro-optical sight unit in the desired direction. A television camera detects the approaching target, locks on to it and begins tracking; a laser rangefinder then measures the range and continues to measure it, so establishing the target's speed. The computer calculates the firing angles and also evaluates the target data and determines the number of shots to be fired in each burst to obtain optimum kill probability. As soon as the target is within range, a signal is given and the gunner can open fire. The reaction time of the system, from detecting an approaching target to being ready to open fire, is about six seconds. The Mauser 30mm gun is also employed in some of the latest towed equipment, such as the Greek-made Artemis and the Italian Breda Twin 30.

It is interesting to compare the Soviet equivalents of these systems. The Soviet Army has used self-propelled air-defence guns since the early 1950s, long before the Western armies began thinking about them, and there are two presently in service, the ZSU-57 and the ZSU-23. The ZSU-57 uses a chassis based on T54 tank components, carrying a large turret armed with two 57mm guns. These guns are the Soviet development of a design which originated in Germany in 1942 but which the Germans never completed. They are fed from four-round clips and have a rate of fire of no more than 70 rpm for each

Above: A Gepard opens fire with its 35mm guns; these can fire either single shots, in bursts or continuously. Left: The Oerlikon 25mm GBM-AO1 naval mount; naval AA guns disappeared from ships with the advent of the SAM but they are now being retrofitted to deal with the anti-ship missile and low-flying aircraft. Centre left: An Oerlikon 35mm GDF-001 of the Swiss Air Force. Below left: Reloading of the automatic replenishers of the Oerlikon 35mm AA gun; rapid fire is of great importance against jet aircraft. Below right: A West German Wildcat which uses the Mauser 30mm AA gun mounted onto the chassis of a Transportpanzer 1. Right: The latest Anglo-French AA gun, the Chieftain-Sabre, uses 30mm AA guns and the AMX30's Oeil Vert surveillance radar.

barrel. The sighting system is simply an optical computing sight, the computing being done by a clockwork mechanism which is wound and primed with estimates of the target's range and speed. Not surprisingly, the ZSU-57 is not considered much of a threat by Western air forces, and it appears to have been phased out of Soviet first line service.

The ZSU-23 is more effective; it is based on a chassis derived from the PT76 amphibious tank, carrying a turret armed with four 23mm automatic cannon firing at a rate of about 900rpm per barrel. There is a dual-purpose radar which can detect targets out to 20km (12 miles); these are displayed on a screen and when one is selected, the radar is switched to tracking mode, though it can only do this once the target is within 8km (5 miles) range. Data is then fed to a computer which calculates firing data and presents it to the gunner, who then points his guns in accordance with this information and opens fire; alternatively he can use an optical sight to acquire the target and open fire. The ZSU-23 is more effective than the ZSU-57, and has replaced it in most Warsaw Pact formations, but it still falls short of current Western techniques.

In spite of the missile, the air-defence gun is still a useful weapon. One reason, as already explained, is that the gun mounting and sighting systems have been vastly improved due to modern electronic technology; another reason is simply that a 30mm explosive shell will bring down an aircraft or helicopter just as surely as a shoulder-fired missile and at about one thousandth of the cost. An air-defence gun system may be expensive to buy, but its running costs are infinitely cheaper than those of a missile system, and where the targets can be expected to come thick and fast, this makes a great deal of difference.

No area of the world has escaped the influence of the superpower conflict between the United States and the Soviet Union. Even in Africa, where neither of the superpowers has traditionally had any substantial interests, the 1970s and 1980s saw a mounting tide of superpower involvement, both military and diplomatic. The situation was complicated by the involvement of the former colonial powers – all part of the Western bloc but not necessarily identical in interests and policies with the United States – and of South Africa, officially a pariah on the international stage, but often an important element in plans to promote Western interests.

In the 1960s, the first decade of independence for most African states, the superpowers played little part in the continent's affairs. The new African states chose an ideological option, normally either clearly socialist or capitalist, and depending on their ideology received military aid from the West or the East. Apart from Egypt – marginal to African affairs – the Soviet Union found itself backing Algeria, Somalia, Guinea, Mali, the Congo (ex-French Congo, not to be confused with the ex-Belgian Congo), and Benin by the end of the decade. With the exception of Algeria, this aid was very small-scale in military terms. Other independent countries remained largely tied to their former colonial power, receiving training and equipment in continuity with colonial days. Soviet and ex-colonial aid could be combined – as Nigeria showed during the Biafra war – because Soviet policies did not involve any serious effort to dictate the behaviour of its clients.

Only in the crisis in the ex-Belgian Congo (now Zaire) from 1960-65 did the two superpowers confront one another, as the US backed General Mobutu (now Mobutu Sese Seko) through the CIA, while the Soviet Union first supported Prime Minister Patrice Lumumba and then aided his successors in rebellion in the country's eastern provinces. Mobutu won, and maintaining his rule over the vast area of Zaire has remained a fixed objective of US policy since.

It is significant that this early case of superpower involvement followed on the failure of the colonial power, Belgium, to control the independence process. It was the collapse of the Portuguese colonial empire in 1974-75 that raised the level of involvement to a new height. It not only brought three new states to the pro-Soviet camp in Africa – Angola, Mozambique and Guinea-Bissau – but it also saw the arrival of some 20,000 Cuban troops on African soil. The motives of the Soviet Union in despatching the Cubans to Angola have been much discussed, with far-ranging plans of domination in the region often alleged. In fact, the move showed the usual opportunism of either of the superpowers presented with a chance to extend its influence. The Soviet decision was undoubtedly affected by the extreme willingness of Fidel Castro's government to become involved, and by the wide support the intervention could expect through much of black Africa because of the presence of South African troops on the other side.

The US response to the Angolan crisis showed considerable incoherence. Having backed the Portuguese against the guerrillas before independence, and then chosen to give CIA support to Holden Roberto's Zaire-based contenders for power in Angola, the United States withdrew from the challenge when the Soviet Union upped the stakes. Secretary of State Henry Kissinger, who had previously guided US

Africa in the Cold War
Superpower involvement from Cairo to the Cape

policy into a guarded encouragement for white supremacy in southern Africa, now embarked on a vigorous reshaping of the US approach. In collaboration with the South African government, Kissinger set out to achieve settlements of the guerrilla wars in Rhodesia and Namibia, fearing obviously that a guerrilla victory might introduce still further pro-Soviet regimes to the region. In September 1976 this direct US diplomatic intervention produced the attempt at an 'internal settlement' in Rhodesia, but both there and in Namibia guerrilla war continued .

Africa was now clearly established as a US foreign policy priority, but the new administration of Jimmy

Top: USAF F-111s fly over Egypt during a Rapid Deployment Force exercise. Above: A Soviet-supplied T34/85 on the streets of Luanda, capital of Angola. Both superpowers stepped up their involvement in Africa from the mid-1970s, bringing a new Cold War dimension to a continent already scarred by colonial wars and by racial and ethnic conflicts.

Above: US Secretary of State Henry Kissinger (left) with South African Prime Minister B. J. Vorster. After the collapse of the Portuguese colonial empire in 1974-75 had allowed Soviet influence to penetrate Angola and Mozambique, Kissinger embarked on an active diplomatic campaign to prevent a repetition of these events elsewhere in southern Africa, working closely with the South African government.

Carter in 1977 at first sought to align itself more with black opinion in its pursuit of a liberal policy based on 'human rights'. Leading administration figures proposed taking Africa out of the context of superpower confrontation. Andrew Young, the black US ambassador to the UN, went so far as to describe the Cubans as 'an element of stability and order' in Angola.

Although this statement provoked much hostile comment in the United States, it addressed itself to a real aspect of the African situation which policymakers could not ignore, namely the overwhelming desire of Western economic interests for stability above all else. Almost all black African countries were extremely weak economically, and more or less fully dependent on the West for finance and the exploita-

tion of their resources. Thus Angola, for example, proved perfectly willing to cooperate with the foreign companies mining its diamonds and petroleum, and the companies in their turn found the regime, despite Marxist ideology and the Cuban presence, a quite satisfactory partner. Algeria was a major recipient of Soviet arms, but this did not stop the Americans pursuing deals for important supplies of natural gas with its socialist government. In these and other cases, the West had a clear economic interest in maintaining the status quo, whatever the implications for the superpower strategic balance.

The Russians rush in

The unclear nature of the interests involved influenced the reaction to the next major demonstration of Soviet activity on the continent – the rush of Cuban troops, equipment and Soviet advisers to Ethiopia in 1977. As an independent state of long standing, with no ex-colonial power to look after it, Ethiopia had become a recipient of American military aid. But President Carter was hostile to aiding the Marxist post-1974 regime, with its appalling human rights record. It was the US decision to cut off military supplies in February 1977 which opened the door to the Soviet Union. The Russian decision to transfer support from Somalia to Ethiopia was once more largely a demonstration of opportunism, and it once more showed a sensitivity to African opinion – Somalia was guilty of trying to change Africa's sacred post-colonial boundaries.

The United States immediately took up the opportunity to gain a position of influence in Somalia, but refused to back the Somalis in their invasion of Ethiopia. Effectively, a chance for a Cold-War style confrontation, with the ultimate aim of forcing a withdrawal from Ethiopia by the Soviets and their allies, was ducked. Despite expressions of indignation over Soviet and Cuban activities, the dominant impression given was that the US administration was not altogether sorry to see the communist forces taking on the costly and difficult business of holding Ethiopia together.

But the temper of the Carter administration was changing, as the story of the two Shaba crises in 1977 and 1978 reveals. The first of these incursions into southern Zaire elicited only a token gesture of US support for the Mobutu regime, leaving France and Morocco to defend Mobutu. In 1978, by contrast, the

The Soviet/Cuban presence in the 1980s

MOROCCO
TUNISIA
WESTERN SAHARA
ALGERIA
LIBYA
EGYPT
MAURITANIA
MALI
NIGER
CHAD
SUDAN
DJIBOUTI
SENEGAL
GAMBIA
GUINEA BISSAU
GUINEA
SIERRA LEONE
LIBERIA
IVORY COAST
UPPER VOLTA
GHANA
TOGO
BENIN
NIGERIA
CAMEROON
CENTRAL AFRICAN REPUBLIC
ETHIOPIA
SOMALIA
UGANDA
KENYA
RWANDA
BURUNDI
EQUATORIAL GUINEA
GABON
CONGO
ZAIRE
TANZANIA
ATLANTIC OCEAN
ANGOLA
ZAMBIA
MALAWI
MADAGASCAR
NAMIBIA
MOZAMBIQUE
BOTSWANA
ZIMBABWE
SOUTH AFRICA
SWAZILAND
LESOTHO

| | Soviet/Cuban advisory force |
| | Soviet/Cuban combat force |

Left: Mozambican leader Samora Machel shares a joke with a Chinese military adviser. Despite the hostility between China and the Soviet Union, Machel was able to combine aid from both communist sources.

Below: Cuban soldiers man a Soviet M-46 130mm field gun during the Ogaden War in 1977. The presence of Cuban troops in Angola and Ethiopia was the most visible sign of Soviet influence in Africa. The use of Cubans enabled the Russians to keep their own forces free of combat involvement.

second incursion provoked accusations of Cuban and Soviet involvement, and brought US diplomatic and logistical backing for French intervention.

The need to block 'Soviet expansionism' in Africa developed into a fixed plank of US foreign policy – and certainly the evidence of Soviet penetration of a traditionally Western sphere of influence during the 1970s had been impressive. As well as countries already mentioned, Libya had become a major recipient of Soviet arms, helping make Russia the biggest single supplier of weaponry to the continent. It was easy to interpret Libyan and Algerian support for Polisario guerrillas in the Western Sahara, or Libyan backing for rebel forces in Chad, as extensions of Soviet expansionist policy.

As what has been termed 'the second Cold War' gathered pace, with the Soviet intervention in Afghanistan in December 1979 and the election of President Ronald Reagan's hardline administration in 1980, the United States moved more positively into Africa. This was not only a counter to Soviet advances, but also a back-up to American policy in the Persian Gulf – Africa's eastern seaboard provided the best launchpad for rapid intervention in the region. By 1984, Egypt, Sudan, Somalia and Kenya had all granted the Americans base facilities in return for economic and military aid (although this specifically excluded any support for Somali territorial ambitions against Ethiopia). In North Africa, the United States took over from France as

Morocco's main backer in its war against Polisario and was granted the use of military facilities in exchange. Libya became the object of heavy American pressure, even resulting in an air battle in the Gulf of Sirte in 1981, and the advance of Libyan forces in Chad in 1983 met a stern US response, although it was the French who actually provided the troops to defend the West's perceived interests.

In southern Africa, the Reagan administration committed itself to cooperation with the South Africans in an effort to retrieve some of the ground lost in the 1970s. The two countries worked out a common policy on Namibia, linking South African withdrawal from that territory with Cuban withdrawal from Angola. The fragility of both Angola and Mozambique in the face of South African destabilising techniques forced them into humiliating negotiations, since their Soviet backers were incapable or unwilling to guarantee their regimes against their enemies. The success of this aspect of US policy was tempered, however, by the adverse effect on black African opinion of the close association between America and the white supremacist Pretoria regime.

In terms of the superpower balance, the US could be well satisfied by the developments of the 1980s, although it seemed unlikely that Soviet influence could be rolled back in the foreseeable future. The relevance of the Cold War perspective to African affairs remains questionable, however. The conflicts that exist in Africa grow out of local ambitions, ideological commitments and ethnic divisions, which the superpowers can opportunistically exploit in pursuit of their global interests, but which remain essentially apart from their concerns. **R. G. Grant**

Prophet of revolution
Colonel Gaddafi's Libya

In January 1984, Libya attempted to block the re-admission of Egypt to the Islamic Conference organisation. By February, however, Libyan policy had shifted to an acceptance of Egyptian readmission, and by early March Colonel Muammar Gaddafi was even proposing the union of the two countries. Colonel Gaddafi announced that the Libyan-Egyptian border would be opened on 28 March and warned that this decision would be enforced, if necessary by a march on Cairo – in other words, if the new friendliness were not accepted, it would be imposed by force.

Libyan foreign policy since Colonel Gaddafi came to power in September 1969 has been littered with similar examples of apparently illogical, contradictory and frankly opportunistic behaviour, which has often invited the charge of adventurism. However, although Libyan behaviour since 1969 has not been untouched by imperial dreams and an element of megalomania, it nevertheless displays a fundamental consistency which has its roots in Libya's traditional position in the Arab world, in Gaddafi's Bedouin origins and in the nature of the society he has tried to create.

Libya has traditionally been regarded with a degree of contempt by the rest of the Arab world. Its tiny population is seen as unsophisticated and its desert territory as remote and isolated. The tribal and colonial history of Libya makes it difficult for Libyans to regard themselves as a coherent nation, and they suffer from a sense of inferiority in regard to their neighbour, Egypt, which remains the intellectual and cultural powerhouse of the Arab world.

The Arabs have been colonised and villified by Europe, which has totally underestimated their cultu-

ral heritage. In this respect, Libya suffers doubly by being regarded by its Middle Eastern neighbours in much the same way as the Arab world generally is regarded by the former colonial powers. This does not, however, produce a coherently unified Libyan response, but rather two contradictory impulses, pulling in opposite directions. On the one hand, Gaddafi seeks recognition and acceptance by the Arab nations he regards as natural allies to support an important Libyan role in regional and global affairs. On the other hand, he regards conservative and powerful Arab states, such as Egypt and Saudi Arabia, as having betrayed the Arab cause through alliances of expediency with Western Europe and the United States.

Gaddafi sees himself as the heir of Egyptian President Gamal Abdel Nasser's pan-Arabism, and

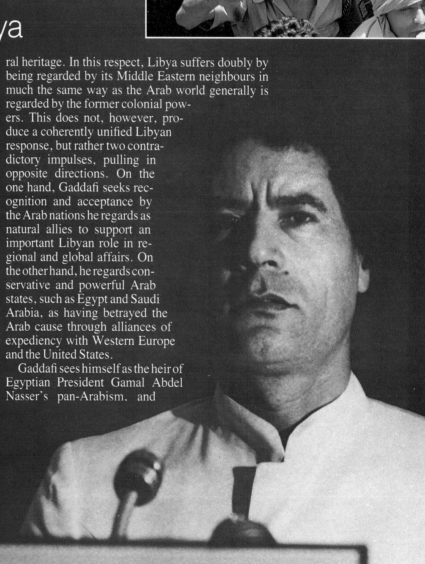

CHAIRMAN الرئيس

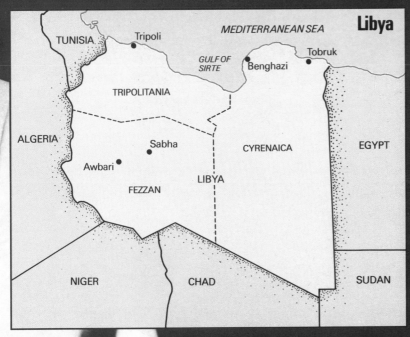

has therefore repeatedly sought to unite Libya with its Arab neighbours – so often that the whole idea has become debased and devalued, and few now take such treaties seriously, or expect them to last. The September 1984 unity agreement with Morocco – a long-standing enemy – was a diplomatic coup for both sides, and sent a political shock throughout the whole region, but was not regarded as likely to fare better than previous agreements with Egypt, Syria, Sudan and Tunisia.

Though the motives for Gaddafi's pursuit of such alliances during his early years in power were more purely based in Nasserite pan-Arab principles, he later showed just as much concern with sheer survival, and his primary aim was to prevent Libya's total regional isolation. The alliance with Morocco, for example, came after a year of growing rapprochement, but was given added impetus by the refusal of Tunisia and Algeria to allow Libyan accession to the treaty of fraternity and concord which they had signed in March 1983.

Similarly, Gaddafi's sudden pursuit of friendship with Saudi Arabia was largely due to the weakening of his position within the Organization of African Unity, and his desire for Saudi diplomatic support. The value of that rapprochement was indicated in early 1984, when the Saudi embassy in London assumed responsibility for the representation of Libyan interests in Great Britain after London severed diplomatic relations with Tripoli, following the murder of WPC Yvonne Fletcher in front of the Libyan People's Bureau in St James's Square.

Gaddafi denounces countries such as Saudi Arabia and Egypt for failing to achieve Arab unity, for failing to prosecute the struggle against Israel, and for their close ties with the West, but at the same time he realises that he has to live with them. Egypt is still by far the most important Arab nation, and Saudi Arabia ultimately controls the price of oil, which provides Libya's sole source of vital foreign exchange. Gaddafi's rage and frustration at being snubbed by his neighbours – for example, being excluded by President Anwar Sadat from the preparations for the 1973 Yom Kippur War – are tempered by realism and expediency.

A further influence upon Libyan foreign policy has been the society which Colonel Gaddafi has attempted to create since the 1969 revolution, modelled upon the ideas contained in his own Green Book. By the standards of that work, Libyan society has reached the state of perfection, and therefore all its acts are above blame and themselves perfect; thus Libya can act outside the norms of international behaviour. The liquidation of Libyan dissidents living abroad is not regarded as criminal, whatever the laws of the country in which the killings take place. Tripoli's indignation at the arrest, conviction and imprisonment of its deadly agents is therefore not entirely devoid of sincerity.

Nor is the claim that the Libyan government should not be held responsible for the actions of such killers totally insincere. Libya insists that these assassins are acting as individuals and not on orders from Tripoli, and indeed there is an element of truth in this. Gaddafi's Libya ostensibly operates on the Green Book principle of 'direct democracy' by which policies are determined by the people acting directly, and there is a convention that Colonel Gaddafi does not decide policy himself. Libya is ostensibly ruled by popular congresses which exist at both the local and national levels. Gaddafi is portrayed as simply the charismatic figurehead of the revolution. In practice, however, Gaddafi overrules any decisions which go against his own wishes, such as when he countermanded the rejection of universal military service by the General Popular Congress in February 1984.

Because, in theory at least, Gaddafi is not the sole arbiter of Libyan policy, there exists a certain room for manoeuvre for various factions, which vie for influence by operating abroad against political opponents. Individual bombings and killings may therefore be the work of such factions, although they would nevertheless be in line with Gaddafi's own policy of killing dissident exiles - 'stray dogs' – announced in February 1980. Growing internal and external Libyan opposition has, since Gaddafi's 'stray dogs' speech, focussed Libyan covert foreign policy on the elimination of dissidents. During the 1970s, however, Libya also provided assistance to terrorist organisations such as the IRA, the Italian Red Brigades and the Japanese Red Army. This support was motivated not only by sympathy for the revolutionary aims of these movements, but also by a desire to discomfort the great powers, whom Gaddafi saw as enemies of the Arab people.

Libyan relations with the United States have deteriorated seriously since early 1980, for example. American public opinion was enraged by Libyan public support for the Iranian seizure of American hostages in Tehran in November 1979 and the Reagan administration quickly denounced Gaddafi as a terrorist; Libya was openly identified as a target for 'destabilisation'. The dogfight over the Gulf of Sirte on 19 August 1981, during which two Libyan fighters were shot down by two US carrier-based F-14 Tomcats, was probably a deliberate act of provocation by the United States, motivated by a desire to 'tweak Gaddafi's nose'.

The incident prompted Libya to move even closer to the Soviet Union, which had been courting Colonel Gaddafi for many years. This seemed to provide the United States with evidence that Gaddafi was merely a stooge of Moscow, but this was, in fact, completely false. Gaddafi had first approached Moscow for arms

Above: Youthful supporters of Colonel Gaddafi's revolutionary government demonstrate their enthusiasm for the regime. Officially Libya is run on the principle of 'direct democracy', but opponents of Gaddafi receive short shrift.

Main picture: Colonel Muammar Gaddafi, charismatic leader of the Libyan 'Jamaharyia' ('state of the masses'), photographed as Chairman of the Organization of African Unity (OAU) in 1982. Unfortunately for Gaddafi, a split in the OAU prevented the holding of the summit meeting he was to have chaired.

Left: The baggage area of Heathrow airport, wrecked by an explosion at the time of the 1984 siege of the Libyan People's Bureau in London. Libyan-inspired terrorists have been active throughout Western Europe, but London in particular has been the scene of a number of assassinations by Libyan hit-squads. Gaddafi has also backed terrorist groups such as the IRA.

Above: A Libyan pilot, shot down over Chad, answers questions at a press conference in N'Djamena. Above centre: Libyan troops, captured by Chad government forces in October 1979. As well as supporting rival factions in Chad's endemic civil war, Gaddafi has committed his own troops several times to the fighting there. Libya has also occupied a strip of northern Chad since 1973.

supplies in 1973, but Libya was far from a Marxist-Leninist state or a Soviet satellite. Colonel Gaddafi remains fundamentally opposed to Marxism, because of its atheism and because it presents a universalist threat to Islam, with which it is in direct competition. Gaddafi was delighted when President Sadat expelled the Soviet advisers from Egypt in 1972. Nevertheless, Libya's links with the Soviet Union are much closer now than when the United States began to display such open hostility.

The Soviet Union is now Libya's major source of arms, but Gaddafi is willing to buy from anyone who has for sale the equipment he needs. The Libyan appetite for military equipment is huge, and by 1984 estimates, Tripoli spends some $3 billion a year on weapons. Libya has become one of the most militarised societies in the world, and it seems clear that Gaddafi intends to replace the army, which he sees as a possible threat to his position, by a militia including all Libyans, both male and female, between the ages

of 16 and 54. Gaddafi believes that a revolutionary people must be a 'people in arms' capable of guaranteeing its own security. This is one reason why Libya is such a great consumer of arms; another, equally important, is that lack of adequate servicing produces a high rate of equipment failure and wastage.

Libya procures weapons, however, not simply for its own defence, but also in order to be able to pursue an aggressive foreign policy. From 1977, for example, Libya provided arms and Libyan bodyguards to the Ugandan leader Idi Amin, and Libyan troops took part in the fighting against the Tanzanian invasion of Uganda in 1979. To the West, Amin was no more than a bloody dictator, but to Gaddafi he was both an anti-Israeli Muslim and the authentic voice of black Africa, staunchly opposed to colonialism.

The Saharan region of North Africa was the area of most active Libyan involvement, as Gaddafi sought to realise his dream of unity with the Arab states of the North African Maghreb as well as the broader and more ambitious aim of unity with the predominantly Muslim but non-Arab states of the Sahel to the south. Gaddafi has sought by means of diplomacy, economic aid, military assistance, subversion and even open military intervention to establish the basis for a Muslim Saharan republic to include Chad, Senegal, Niger, Mali and Gambia. Gaddafi's fundamental impatience and adventurism have been most clearly shown by his rapid and erratic alternation between efforts to woo the established governments of these countries and when these failed, or progress was too slow for his taste, support for attempts to overthrow them.

In January 1984, for example, Libyan attempts to improve relations with neighbouring Tunisia were undermined by simultaneous support for anti-government riots. Earlier Libyan interference within the region includes the public approval given by Gaddafi to the 1971 and 1972 attempted coups against King Hassan of Morocco; involvement in the overthrow of the Diori government in Niger in 1974; suspected support for the 1980 riots in northern Nigeria, as well as involvement in the military coup in Upper Volta in the same year. During 1981, the government of Gambia accused Libya of supporting an attempted coup against it.

Libya has been accused of involvement in coup attempts in Senegal, Mali and the Sudan, and has been one of the chief backers of the Polisario guerrilla movement in its war against Morocco in the Western Sahara. The main area of Libyan activity has been in Chad, however, and has included the outright annexation of the Aouzou strip in northern Chad, occupied by Libyan troops since 1973, backing for pro-Libyan factions in Chad's endemic civil war, and outright military intervention during 1980-81 and again in 1983-84. The reasons for Libyan intervention in Chad have been more complex, and have included a long-standing claim to the Aouzou strip, assigned to Libya under the Laval-Mussolini treaty of 1935 which was, however, never implemented. Libya is also interested in securing control of Chad's rich deposits of uranium as a guarantee of continued independence when its own oil stocks run out.

The present oil glut has created new economic problems for Libya, and her oil revenues have been cut from approximately $22 billion in 1981 to around $9-10 billion in 1984. Foreign exchange reserves dropped during the same period from some $9 billion to about $2 billion. Not only may the build-up of arms stocks have to slow down, but mounting internal opposition to Colonel Gaddafi, indicated by an attempted coup on 8 May 1984, may well make the Libyan leader's position increasingly vulnerable.

Hugo Gurdon

Below: Soviet-built SA-3 Goa surface-to-air missiles, mounted on ZIL-157 transporters, take part in a military parade through the streets of Libya's capital, Tripoli. Colonel Gaddafi built up an imposing arsenal of advanced military equipment, financed by Libya's large oil revenues.

Dogfight

The Gulf of Sirte incident, 1981

In 1981, the forces of the United States dealt a sharp reminder to Colonel Gaddafi's Libya that the most intense revolutionary rhetoric was no substitute for technological superiority during a brief but decisive air battle over the Mediterranean Sea.

In 1973, Gaddafi had claimed the Gulf of Sirte as Libyan territorial waters. Previously considered international waters, the Gulf was regularly used by the US Sixth Fleet as a training area. The Gulf is a large expanse of sea – some 240km (150 miles) north to south and 450km (280 miles) east to west – and US naval units continued to use it during the late 1970s; but during the crisis over the detention of the US hostages in Tehran from November 1979 President Carter forbade the US Fleet to sail south of the 32° 30' north parallel – the line of latitude Gaddafi had claimed as his maritime border. The Libyan leader had publicly proclaimed his support for the actions of the Iranians; it was considered that he might have close links with Iran's new regime and it was felt that nothing should be allowed to exacerbate the situation.

By the time that Ronald Reagan assumed office as US president in January 1981, however, the hostages were home and the US, having been held to ransom and then humiliated during the fiasco of a failed rescue attempt, was in no mood to endure further blows to its pride from radical Middle Eastern regimes. In the spring of 1981 Vice-Admiral William Bowden, commander of the Sixth Fleet, requested permission to ignore the Carter precedent and to penetrate south into the Gulf of Sirte. The request, classified as sensitive, was passed first to the US Navy's commander-in-chief Europe at Vaihingen in West Germany, then to the US chief of naval operations in Washington and finally on to the chairman of the joint chiefs of staff Air Force General David Jones. The idea was then formally placed before the National Security Council (NSC). The proposal was well received by the NSC during a meeting in June and a majority agreement was reached that the Carter abstention should not be allowed to be seen by the Libyans as an accepted precedent. Following a further meeting of the NSC on 14 July, the US decision to stage a major naval exercise in the disputed waters was taken with the unanimous approval of President Reagan and his senior advisers.

Three days later, Rear-Admiral James Service was summoned to the Pentagon. He was briefed on the various confrontation risks that might arise from a US naval presence in the Gulf of Sirte and was formally warned that his pilots were only to engage in self-defence manoeuvres and on no account were they to open fire unprovoked. Service then returned to Naples where he joined the fleet commander, Admiral Bowden, to begin planning the forthcoming operation.

On 17 August 1981, a naval force comprising 14 cruisers and destroyers and two aircraft carriers, USS *Forrestal* and USS *Nimitz* (carrying about 150 aircraft between them), sailed into the Gulf of Sirte. During the first two days of the exercise the *Nimitz,* using a five-radar computer-linked defence system with a range of 800km (500 miles), spotted Libyan 'intruders' 72 times. Despite a US warning that live ammunition would be used during the exercise, the Libyan aircraft were intent on flying into airspace over the Gulf. Given that the Gulf of Sirte was, at the very least, international waters, Libya's action was not an unusual procedure for a country with a large foreign naval presence involved in manoeuvres off its coast. It seems, however, that the Libyans were intent on disrupting the exercise, forcing the Americans to desist from the use of live ammunition through the risk of hitting a Libyan aircraft.

The US response to the presence of Libyan aircraft was always the same. Fighters already patrolling or launched from the deck of the *Nimitz* – an F-14 Tomcat can reach a height of 6000m (20,000 feet) from a deck launch in under two minutes – would intercept the Libyan aircraft and force them away from the area after identifying themselves to the Libyans and noting down the Libyan aircraft fighter

Above: An Su-22 Fitter in flight. This basic and somewhat primitive aircraft was widely supplied to air forces thoughout the world by the Soviet Union. Adapted from the Soviet Su-7, the Fitter has a lower-rated engine and less advanced avionics.

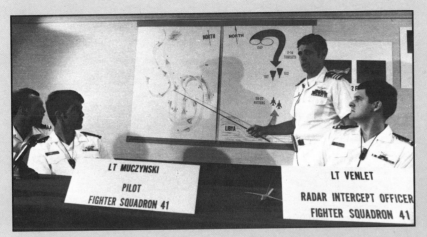

Above: The US personnel, both pilots and radar operators, directly involved in the Gulf of Sirte incident, explain the sequence of events at a press conference held aboard the USS *Nimitz.*

Below: Grumman F-14 Tomcats of the crack Black Ace squadron on the flight deck of the *Nimitz.* The F-14, which first flew operationally in March 1974, is undoubtedly one of the world's most formidable multirole fighters. It can detect and attack targets some 160km (100 miles) distant and has a maximum speed of 2517 km/h (1564 mph).

designations. Usually the Libyans responded by returning to mainland airspace.

On 19 August, however, the Libyan response was completely different. Shortly after 0700 hours, the *Nimitz's* radars locked onto and identified two Soviet-built Libyan Su-22s heading into the Gulf. The two fighters were also spotted by a US Hawkeye early-warning reconnaissance aircraft patrolling above the Gulf at 21,000m (70,000 feet). At the same time, two F-14 Tomcats from the Black Ace squadron (considered the best fighter group in the US Navy) which was based on the *Nimitz,* were on a routine patrol. As the Su-22s closed, the Tomcats were ordered to intercept. With the two Tomcats heading straight towards them, the Libyans fired off one missile, passed underneath the Tomcats, banked steeply and fired another. The Libyan pilots should certainly have known that their missiles would not hit. In the first place, the Atoll missiles with which the Su-22s were armed are heat-seeking missiles which could not possibly lock-on to an oncoming aircraft. Secondly, even if the US pilots allowed the Libyans to manoeuvre into an attacking position behind them, the F-14's extraordinary performance would make it an

unlikely casualty. With a maximum speed of Mach 2·3 (2517km/h – 1564mph) the F-14 could easily outrun an Atoll missile within 8km (5 miles). It also mounts an extremely sophisticated electronic defence system which not only warns the pilot when an enemy arms his missiles prior to firing, but will also predict enemy aircraft movements and issue attack information which is projected onto a head-up display in front of the pilot. Given these capabilities, the skill of the American pilots and their aircrafts' manoeuvrability and speed, the point has been raised by military experts that the Americans may well have been luring the Libyans into a trap from which they could not hope to escape. It could not have eluded the notice of the Reagan administration that such an event could substantially decrease Gaddafi's international prestige.

Following the strict regulations relating to offensive and defensive actions, the US pilots, once fired upon, were free to take action. With a 480km/h (300 mph) speed advantage over the Su-22s, the Tomcats had little difficulty in manoeuvring behind the Libyans who were already fleeing towards the coastline. Allowing just a little time for the Libyans to move away from the sun (which could affect the accuracy of heat-seeking missiles), the US pilots opened fire with Sidewinder missiles. One Su-22 erupted in flames. The second was also hit but the missile failed to detonate and the pilot ejected safely.

In the wake of the incident, diplomatic protests were launched by both sides. The attempted use of the Sixth Fleet to overawe Gaddafi served only to strengthen his wayward anti-Americanism and he lost no time in using the incident to enhance his self-proclaimed image as champion of the Third World. Conversely, for pro-Western countries the incident provided a comforting demonstration of American military presence. Whether they had in fact planned to provoke such an encounter or not, the US administration was clearly not displeased with the military success against one of their least favourite regimes.

Alexander McNair-Wilson

Polisa

The struggle for the Western Sahara

Spain formally withdrew from the Spanish Sahara, a territory lying between Morocco and Mauritania on the northwest coast of Africa, on 26 February 1976, an action which was followed by a complex and long-running conflict with wide international ramifications. Both Morocco and Mauritania had claims on the Spanish Sahara, while the territory offered Algeria a useful route to the Atlantic for the iron ore mined at Gara Djebilet. Although it was sparsely populated, the area was of considerable economic importance because of the phosphates it contained. Morocco already controlled 40 per cent of the world's phosphate market, and possession of the Spanish Sahara would give her perhaps 20-25 per cent more. If, however, the area became an independent state, as the Spanish planned, Morocco's share of the world market could be substantially reduced. It is also likely that the Moroccan government recognised that concentration on an external dispute might help reduce internal unrest.

In 1974 Morocco and Mauritania had secretly agreed to partition the Spanish Sahara. The Spanish government, negotiating in the uneasy atmosphere accompanying Franco's last illness, concluded a secret agreement with the Algerian-backed guerrilla group Polisario – the Popular Front for the Liberation of Saguiet el Hamra and Rio de Oro – under the terms of which Polisario would take over following Spain's withdrawal. A United Nations commission took a similar line, reporting that the population of the area favoured independence rather than union with Morocco.

Spanish resolve did not survive intense Moroccan pressure. In the 'Green March' of November 1975, some 350,000 unarmed Moroccans marched across the border into the Spanish Sahara, and the following month the Spanish government agreed that the territory should be divided between Morocco and Mauritania when Spain withdrew. As the Moroccans and Mauritanians took over, much of the population departed to refugee camps in Algeria. Polisario claimed that this exodus was voluntary, and had involved most of the population, which it estimated at 150,000 people; the Moroccans maintained that it was provoked by Polisario, and that in any case the majority of the population – some 75,000 according to their figures – had remained. The partition of the area, now known as the Western Sahara, was completed in April 1976. The Moroccans took the lion's share, the richer and more populous northern sector, which became the Moroccan provinces of El Aaiun, Smara and Boujdour, while the Mauritanians obtained the smaller southern sector, the south of Tiris el Gharbia.

The partition was fiercely resisted. Polisario

rio

Left: Well-protected against the harsh weather of the Sahara, a Polisario fighter cradles his FN FAL rifle. Polisario guerrillas have proved tough and self-reliant in their war against Morocco. Below left: Supporters of Polisario in exile in Algeria show the movement's flag.

fighters immediately began operations against the occupying forces, and Algerian support for Polisario produced at least one serious clash between Algerian and Moroccan regular troops at Amgala, leading to fears of war between Algeria and Morocco. Diplomatic pressure accompanied these military efforts. The government-in-exile of the Sahraoui Arab Democratic Republic (SADR) was set up in Algeria in March 1976, and by November 1980 the SADR had been recognised by 27 states.

The Mauritanian Army, small and inexperienced, found the war increasingly costly, despite the fact that the Moroccans agreed, in May 1977, to send 9000 men to assist it. The Mauritanian economy was severely damaged by droughts, as well as by Polisario attacks on the extremely vulnerable Zouerate-Nouadhibou railway line, upon which Mauritania depended for the export of her iron ore. Many Mauritanians were closely related to the Sahraouis and had no enthusiasm for the war. They were, by contrast, extremely suspicious of the Moroccans, who had until quite recently claimed sovereignty over Mauritania, as well as over the Western Sahara. In July 1978 there was a military coup in Mauritania, and Polisario immediately announced a unilateral cease-fire with the Mauritanians. A flurry of negotiations followed, but fighting between Moroccan forces and Polisario continued unabated. France intervened with air support for the Moroccans, deploying Jaguars and Bréguet Atlantic reconnaissance aircraft in December 1978, operating from Dakar, Senegal.

In August 1979 the Mauritanians agreed to withdraw from the Tiris el Gharbia, their sector of the Western Sahara, and thereby to end their war against Polisario. There were pro-Moroccan demonstrations in the area's only town, Dakhla (formerly Villa Cisneros). The Moroccans maintained that these were genuine indications of popular feeling, while Polisario claimed that they were manipulated by Moroccan agents. Both sides moved forces into the Tiris el Gharbia: on 11 August there was a sharp battle at Bir Enzaran, between advancing Polisario elements and a Moroccan column moving up from

Mauritania to Dakhla. The Moroccans lost about 175 men – half as many as Polisario – and their forces occupied the area.

The Moroccan armed forces, rising steadily in size from 50,000 in 1975 to 89,000 in 1978 and 116,000 in 1981, embarked upon the dual strategy of attacking Polisario bases and constructing a lengthy fortified line to seal off much of the disputed territory against Polisario incursions. In October 1979, for example, the Moroccans mounted Operation Uhud, in which some 6000 men, with air and artillery support, moved

Above: Carrying portraits of King Hassan II, unarmed Moroccans march into the Spanish Sahara in the carefully stage-managed 'Green March' of November 1975. Morocco's takeover of the Western Sahara after the departure of the Spanish colonial power in 1976 was immensely popular with the Moroccan people.

A royal survivor

Morocco's King Hassan II has been a major beneficiary of the war in the Western Sahara, using it to bolster his sometimes perilous hold on power.

In the early 1970s he faced not only the challenge of popular agitation but also opposition from right-wing officers who twice attempted to assassinate him. On 10 July 1971 about 1400 army cadets led by rebel officers attacked the royal palace during the king's birthday celebrations, killing 90 guests, including the Belgian ambassador, but Hassan escaped unscathed. In a second attempt, on 16 August 1972, four Royal Moroccan Air Force F-5s attacked the king's B-727 jet but failed to shoot it down. Despite damage to two engines and a wing, the aircraft landed safely and the king was spirited away before the F-5s carried out a follow-up strike.

The Spanish Sahara question offered an excellent opportunity for Hassan to rally both right-wing officers and the mass of the population. The 'Green March' of unarmed civilians into the Sahara in November 1975 was a brilliant publicity coup, even though the marchers turned back only a few kilometres across the border, before confronting the Spanish forces mobilised to meet them. Ever since, Hassan has enjoyed almost total domestic support for his Western Sahara policy, despite the heavy casualties and financial costs of the continuing war.

against Polisario strongholds in the Djebel Ouarkziz. In the first half of 1981 the Moroccans concentrated on the building of the 500km (300-mile) barrier, running from Zag at the northeast end of the Djebel Ouarkziz to Boujdour on the coast, with particular attention being paid to the defence of the 'useful triangle', the phosphate-mining area around El Aaiun, Smara and Bou Craa. Polisario strove to disrupt the construction of this line, and there were a number of serious clashes which gave rise to the usual conflicting claims. Nevertheless, the fortifications were completed in May 1982, and the phosphate mines at Bou Craa were reopened.

Encouraging guerrilla action

Morocco consistently blamed Algeria for encouraging Polisario, and, after Mauritanian withdrawal from the Tiris el Gharbia, Mauritania too was soon accused of supporting the guerrillas. In the summer of 1980 Moroccan aircraft attacked targets inside both Algeria and Mauritania, and in March 1981 the latter complained that Morocco had supported an unsuccessful coup against the Mauritanian government. This was reorganised shortly afterwards, to include more members who favoured a policy of neutrality in the war in the Western Sahara, and no action was taken on a suggestion by Libya's Colonel Gaddafi that Mauritania and the SADR should be merged. In late 1981 and early 1982 Polisario launched a number of large-scale attacks on Moroccan positions in the Western Sahara, some of them very close to the Mauritanian border. The Moroccan government accused Mauritania of permitting the attacks to be mounted from its territory, but Mauritania steadfastly denied these allegations. The Moroccans also discerned Libyan involvement, and mounted a diplomatic campaign against Libya.

By this stage the conflict had assumed far-reaching international importance. The Americans tended to see the regime of King Hassan II of Morocco as a powerful force for stability in northwest Africa, and the political complexion of Polisario and its major

backers reinforced American prejudices in this respect. Nevertheless, there was considerable congressional opposition to an arms sale agreement in 1980 which promised the Moroccans $235 million of military hardware, including helicopters and aircraft. Opponents of the deal argued that the Moroccan Army was not capable of making the best use of modern weapons and warned that Moroccan attacks on Algeria or Mauritania would escalate the war. The election of President Reagan was followed by prom-

Above left: Polisario guerrillas are accustomed to coping comfortably with desert conditions. Above: Moroccan armoured vehicles have frequently proved vulnerable to guerrilla attacks.

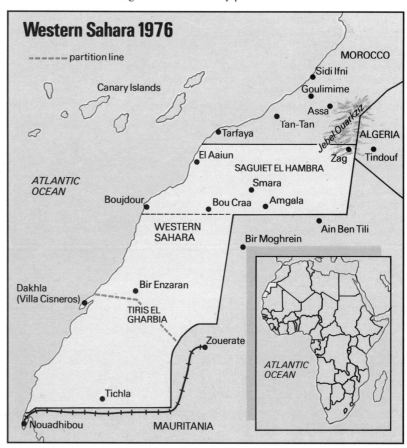

Western Sahara 1976

- - - - - - partition line

MOROCCO

Canary Islands

Sidi Ifni
Goulimime
Assa
Tan-Tan
Tarfaya
ALGERIA
El Aaiun
Zag
Tindouf

ATLANTIC OCEAN

SAGUIET EL HAMBRA

Smara

Boujdour
Bou Craa
Amgala

WESTERN SAHARA

Ain Ben Tili

Bir Moghrein

Dakhla (Villa Cisneros)
Bir Enzaran

TIRIS EL GHARBIA

Zouerate

ATLANTIC OCEAN

Tichla

Nouadhibou
MAURITANIA

Above: A motorised column of the Moroccan Army prepares to set out on patrol from El Aaiun in August 1979. The presence of a Soviet-built ZU-23 anti-aircraft gun mounted on the back of this Land Rover is a reminder that, although backed by the West, the Moroccans still employ some Soviet equipment.

Below: The ability of Polisario to shoot down Moroccan aircraft showed the sophistication of their weaponry. Below right: Polisario leader Mohammed Abdel Aziz (centre) with the OAU president Edem Kodjo.

ises of further arms supplies, including 180 M60 tanks. King Hassan visited the United States in May 1982, by which stage American military aid to Morocco was running at some $30 million a year. United States policy was defined as being 'aimed at limiting the risks of escalation and supporting a military balance in the region'. Numerous American officials visited Morocco in 1982, and took pains to point out that a full-scale Moroccan campaign against Mauritania might easily result in Mauritania having to accept Soviet aid. Thus, while the United States is prepared to support Morocco, she is anxious to prevent a widening of the conflict.

France, the former colonial power in North Africa, has continuing interests in the region. As well as carrying out air attacks on Polisario units which had raided French-manned mines in Mauritania, French military engineers helped the Moroccans to restore essential services in Dakhla after the Moroccan takeover of the Tiris el Gharbia, French instructors

helped train the Mauritanians, and French equipment, particularly AMX13 light tanks, and EBR-75, AMX-10 and AML-90 armoured cars, makes up an important segment of the Moroccan Army's inventory. However, France was understandably reluctant to alienate the African states which backed Polisario, in particular Algeria, and in 1982 she allowed Polisario to open a bureau in Paris. In March 1981, when the UN Human Rights Commission censured Morocco's 'persistent occupation' of the Western Sahara, France abstained from voting. France strove to maintain this policy of even-handedness by temporarily suspending the supply of arms in March 1982, though in January 1983 President François Mitterand visited Morocco and spoke in favour of a referendum amongst the people of the Western Sahara, a solution generally favoured by Morocco.

The Organization of African Unity (OAU) has provided the backcloth against which many of the diplomatic moves in the dispute have been played out.

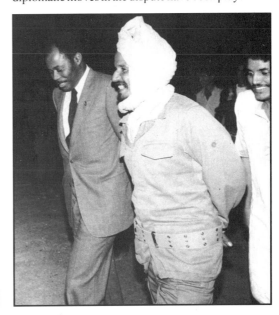

In March 1979 a five-man commission of the OAU reported in favour of a ceasefire followed by a referendum and at the Nairobi OAU summit in June 1981 King Hassan promised a referendum. The major obstacle confronting this, however, was his government's refusal to negotiate with Polisario. Another committee repeated the demand for a referendum, again without success. The SADR seemed, meanwhile, to be gaining strength. It was formally admitted to the OAU in February 1982, though the arrival of its delegation resulted in a walk-out by Morocco and many of her supporters. However, the relative inactivity of Polisario forces during the period from February to July of that year probably reflects the fact that there was considerable hope for a negotiated settlement. But the question of negotiation between Morocco and the Polisario continued to be a stumbling-block, and the dispute had a damaging effect upon the cohesion of the OAU. A serious crisis was averted when, in June 1983, the SADR 'voluntarily and temporarily' decided not to participate in the OAU's 19th summit meeting. This body adopted a nine-point resolution advocating, amongst other things, a referendum under the auspices of the OAU and a request for a UN force to monitor a ceasefire. Both Morocco and Polisario hailed this as a victory. Morocco pointed out that the resolution did not mention the SADR by name, and reiterated its wish to have a referendum as soon as possible, while Polisario maintained that the resolution acknowledged its demands for direct negotiations with Morocco.

This apparent diplomatic stalemate mirrors a military stand-off in the Western Sahara. Polisario forces, despite the fact that they now have some heavy equipment and have shown themselves capable of mounting large-scale operations, are unlikely to make much impression on Moroccan fortifications. Conversely, Polisario columns seem to enjoy a wide measure of freedom of movement to the southeast of the defensive line, and Western journalists who have accompanied them have reported that these tough, self-reliant fighters seem perfectly prepared to fight on in a war which offers no quick or easy victories.

Richard Holmes

Above: Polisario troops guard Moroccans captured during the battle of Guelta Zammour. A 3000-strong Polisario mechanised unit, supported by surface-to-air missiles engaged and defeated the Moroccan 4th Regiment. The action showed the scale of the challenge to Morocco.

The battle of Guelta Zammour

Although we tend to think of Polisario troops as guerrillas, they are capable of mounting major operations and of operating sophisticated equipment. On 13 October 1981, 3000 Polisario fighters attacked the town of Guelta Zammour, 40km (25 miles) from the Mauritanian frontier, with 50 armoured personnel carriers and 12 T54 tanks. Polisario sources claimed that the garrison, the 2000-strong Moroccan 4th Regiment, suffered very heavy casualties. The Moroccans, for their part, admitted only the loss of 100 men, and maintained that their crack 6th Regiment defeated the Polisario force on the following day. The fighting certainly went on for some days, and the truth probably lies between the two conflicting claims.

Of particular importance was the acknowledged Moroccan loss of one C-130 transport plane and two Mirage F-1 fighters, allegedly shot down by Soviet missiles manned by non-African personnel. The Moroccans were disturbed by the appearance of the tanks and anti-aircraft missiles – though whether these were SAM-6s, SAM-8s or SAM-9s was never made clear – and by the fact that the attack seemed to have been launched from inside Mauritania. General Ahmed Dlimi, then commanding Moroccan troops in the Western Sahara, announced that his forces had responded by bombing targets inside Mauritania.

Key Weapons

ARMOURED CARS

The armoured car is not only the oldest type of fully automotive armoured fighting vehicle (AFV), but also the one which has changed least since it was conceived. At the end of World War I, such design features as good ground clearance and dual capacity front-and-rear steering were all established and since then the only important changes have stemmed from expanding technology which has provided improved performance and better armament. However, the purpose-built armoured car is a comparatively recent innovation, the first generation being tailored to fit existing commercial vehicle chassis; the first significant breakthrough was made in 1929 by Daimler-Benz with an experimental vehicle known as the ARW-MTW (Achtradwagen-Mannschafts-transportwagen, or eight-wheeled personnel carrier) in which each wheel was independently driven and suspended.

The Daimler scout car and the Daimler armoured car, which equipped the British armoured car regiments for several years after World War II, both owed a great deal to the ARW-MTW. Work on the former, a turretless 3048kg (6720lb) four-wheel drive vehicle with pre-selected transmission, began in 1937; nearly 7000 were built, being used for reconnaissance and liaison duties. The Daimler armoured car was a scaled-up version of the scout car weighing 7610kg (16,800lb) and mounted a turret armed with a 2-pounder gun and a co-axial machine gun; the 2-pounder armour-piercing performance could be improved by fitting a Littlejohn adaptor, which applied squeeze to the shot, so causing it to accelerate beyond its normal muzzle velocity.

During the period in which Great Britain granted independence to her former colonies, her armoured car troops were regularly employed on counter-insurgency tasks in various parts of the world, notably during the long but successful war against communist guerrillas in Malaya. In 1947 the War Office, as it then was, issued a requirement for the Daimler scout car's replacement; named the Ferret, it entered service in 1952 and was again manufactured by the Daimler

Previous page: A Ferret Mk 2/3 in Northern Ireland. Above: A Ferret Mk 2/6 fires a Vigilant ATGW. Right: The flotation screen raised on a Ferret Mk 4. Below left: A Saladin exercising on Salisbury Plain. Below right: A Saladin of 17/21st Lancers on patrol in Cyprus.

Company. In many respects the Ferret was very similar to its predecessor, but it was better protected, was larger, had a longer wheelbase and possessed a much superior cross-country performance. The Ferret Mark I, like the original Daimler scout car, was turretless, but the Mark II and subsequent Marks were fitted with a turret mounting a single machine gun, and in the early 1960s some Mark IIs were armed with four Vickers Vigilant ATGWs (anti-tank guided weapons), two in launching racks on either side of the turret and two stowed in the hull. The later Mark IV, weighing 5400kg (11,905lb) possesses a flotation screen and the more recent Mark V has a redesigned turret armed with four Swingfire ATGWs ready to fire, and two reloads. The Ferret is still operational with the British Army, and with many Commonwealth armies and some other countries. It has proved highly suitable, not only for its intended roles, but for peacekeeping missions as well.

The War Office also ordered the Daimler armoured car's replacement, the Saladin, in 1947 but Alvis, the manufacturers, did not go into quantity production until 1958. The reason for this was that the Malayan Emergency diverted those resources which had been earmarked for the Saladin into building the Saracen armoured personnel carrier, which employed the same six-wheel torsion bar suspension, and for which there was an urgent demand. The Saladin/Saracen suspension possessed steering on the leading four wheels and could simultaneously lose one wheel on each side to mine damage and still remain mobile. Armed with a powerful 76mm gun – from which the Scorpion light tank's main armament was developed – and a co-axial machine gun, the Saladin served with distinction throughout the fighting in the Radfan and the Aden Emergency, the Indonesian confrontation with Malaysia, and the Nigerian civil war. It remains one of the most successful armoured car designs ever built and has been purchased by several Commonwealth and foreign armies as well as by the West German Border Police. It weighs 11,590kg (25,550lb), is powered by a Rolls-Royce B80 engine producing 160 bhp, has a maximum speed of 72km/h (45mph), and is manned by a crew of three.

The most recent addition to the British armoured car fleet is the Fox scout car, which was intended to replace the Ferret in the 1970s, although in fact the latter remains in service. While the layout of the two vehicles is very similar, the Fox has a two-man turret armed with a 30mm cannon; alternative versions, with a one-man turret, are armed with either a 25mm Hughes Chain Gun or the Milan ATGW system. Secondary armament consists of one 7·62mm GPMG (general-purpose machine gun). Like the Scorpion series, the Fox is constructed with aluminium armour and employs the same Jaguar 4·2 litre engine. It weighs 6386kg (14,080lb), has a maximum speed of 105km/h(65mph), and is capable of operating within a temperature variation of -25°C to +50°C (-13°F to +122°F). The vehicle was designed with air-portability in mind and three can be carried aboard a C-130 Hercules transport.

After World War II the US Army continued to use the six-wheeled M8, armed with a 37mm gun and co-axial machine gun, until the early 1950s; used by the French, it saw much action in Vietnam. The US then lost interest in armoured cars, their duties being carried out by light tanks or small armed but unarmoured wheeled vehicles with a good cross-country performance. However, in the early 1960s the Cadillac Gage Company developed its Commando Multi-Mission Vehicle, which could serve equally well as an armoured car or as a wheeled armoured personnel carrier. The Commando can be fitted with a variety of turrets and weapon systems to suit its user's requirements – reconnaissance, convoy escort, internal security, and so on. It is powered by a Chrysler 361 engine producing 200 bhp and has a top

Top: The Fox armoured car suffers from a high centre of gravity and drivers require special steering training. Centre: A Fox adapted to carry the Milan ATGW. Above: The US M8 armoured car, made by the Ford Motor Company.

speed of 88km/h (55mph); it can also swim without preparation, being propelled by the tread of its own tyres when afloat. In addition to serving with the US Army, the Commando has proved popular with the armies of a number of Third World countries.

By the end of 1941 the Soviet Union's fleet of BA armoured cars had virtually ceased to exist and it was not until almost 20 years later that the next Russian design appeared. This was the amphibious BTR-40P, later redesignated the BRDM-1; it contains a number of interesting features, including two pairs of retractable wheels in the centre of the chassis which can be engaged on difficult going, a central tyre-pressure control system, and a single hydrojet propulsion unit for use when afloat. Several types have been developed, the standard model mounting a 7·62mm machine gun, others with mountings for Snapper, Swatter and Sagger ATGWs. The BRDM-1 has a maximum speed of 80km/h (50mph) and a crew of between two and five, depending on type. In the early 1960s a replacement for the BRDM-1 entered service, the BRDM-2 (also known as the BTR-40 P2). It has a more powerful engine and a turret. Otherwise, it is almost identical to the BRDM-1.

When the West German Bundeswehr was formed it was forced to rely exclusively on imported equipment for several years before its own designs were ready to take the field. When they did, several of them were comparable in appearance and concept to AFVs with which the German Army had ended World War II although, of course, there was a marked improvement in performance. This was especially true in the case of the amphibious Spähpanzer Luchs (Lynx), which appeared in 1975 and has a similar suspension to the old SdKfz 234 armoured car series, which was in turn descended from the original ARW-MTW. The Luchs weighs 19,500kg (42,990lb), is manned by a crew of four, and is driven by two large propellers when afloat. It is armed with one 20mm cannon and a 7·62mm machine gun in a ground/air mounting, the turret being designed by Rheinmetall. Despite its size and weight, the vehicle is remarkably quiet on the move, a most important consideration during reconnaissance.

The postwar French Army found itself in a similar situation and for a while relied on British and Amer-

Top left: The Commando V-150. Centre left: The Commando Scout. Left: The Commando V-300. The Commando series of vehicles has proved to be very popular with countries that want an inexpensive and flexible AFV on a limited budget. It is in service with, among others, the armies of Bolivia, Malaysia, Turkey and Saudi Arabia.

ican wheeled AFVs and such pre-war designs of its own as had survived in France's colonial territories, the latter including the rear-engined four-wheel drive Panhard Model 178, which dated from 1935 but which was justly regarded as being advanced in its day. Another remarkable design of the period was the eight-wheel drive Panhard Model 201, on which work commenced in 1937. By 1940 a prototype existed: this was shipped to French North Africa to prevent its capture, and the plans were destroyed. The car itself was lost in the Sahara but in 1945 the ideas contained in its design were revived in the Panhard Model 212, which is better known as the EBR (Engin Blindé de Reconnaissance). Production of this symmetrical design began in 1950. The vehicle can be driven from identical positions at either end, and is powered by a 12-cylinder horizontally opposed Panhard 12 H 6000 engine which is only 220mm (8·5in) high and is housed under the floor of the fighting compartment. The front and rear wheels are fitted with conventional pneumatic rubber tyres, but the centre four are large metal discs, heavily flanged and with deep grousers, and can be raised when running on surfaced roads. Early marks were armed with a 75mm gun, most commonly mounted in the same oscillating FL-10 turret as the AMX13 light tank, but the vehicle was up-gunned in the late 1960s with a 90mm gun firing fin-stabilised ammunition. The car is manned by a crew of four and has a

maximum speed of 105km/h (65mph). It saw much active service during the war in Algeria, as did an APC version, the EBT-ETT. The French are now producing a replacement for the Panhard EBR known as the AMX-10RC which uses many of the same components as the AMX-10P mechanised infantry combat vehicle. It weighs 15,000kg (33,075lb), has a top speed of 85km/h (53mph) and is armed with a 105mm MECA gun.

The French experience in Algeria led to the de-

Above: The Spähpanzer Luchs demonstrates its wintertime cross-country performance. The crew comprises two drivers (one at the front, the other at the rear), a commander and a gunner.

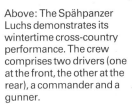

Above left: The Panhard AML with the H-90 turret. It also comes in three variants with a 60mm mortar, one with a 30mm cannon, plus AA and anti-tank versions. Above right: This Panhard EBR is in service with the Moroccan Army; the EBR has steering on the front and rear wheels.

Left: A BRDM-2 on an exercise. Right: A BRDM-1 with a PT76 in the background. The Soviet Army does not expect its reconnaissance units to fight and therefore provides them with small, lightly-armed and fast vehicles that try to avoid combat.

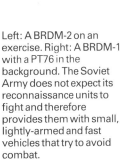

Below: Eland Mk 5s of the South African Army in Namibia. Bottom: A Brazilian Engesa Cascavel; it can be fitted with the French H-90 turret shown here or other armaments.

velopment of the Auto-Mitrailleuse Légère, or AML Panhard Model 245. This light armoured car is similar to the British Ferret, with which it has competed very successfully in the arms markets of the world since 1961. With such sales potential in mind, Panhard have developed a variety of turrets and armaments to suit their customers' needs, including versions mounting a 90mm gun, a 60mm mortar, 30mm automatic cannon and several ATGWs; a licence to produce the AML has been granted to the South African company Sandock-Austal Ltd which uses the name Eland for the vehicle. The basic AML weighs 5500kg (12,125lb), has a crew of three and a maximum speed of 100km/h (62mph); it is air-portable and can be lifted by the larger helicopters. The Argentine Army shipped a squadron of 90mm AML Model Cs to the Falkland Islands during the 1982 conflict but these did not operate outside Port Stanley and took little or no part in the fighting.

Other nations, including Belgium and Brazil, have also produced their own armoured cars, but these tend to be variations on existing themes or designed solely for internal security duties. In general, since 1945 it has been the former colonial powers which have made the greatest use of the armoured car, in the counter-insurgency role where the use of tanks would have been uneconomic, if not undesirable. In this area, the armoured car has a marked advantage over tracked AFVs of every kind since it denies the insurgents the propaganda coup of claiming that the security forces are using 'tanks' and therefore excessive force against the population – an important consideration, of which the Soviet Union has failed to take adequate account in its handling of disturbances among its allies. In this light, it is easy to understand why the armoured car has proved to be such a valued tool in the hands of successive UN peacekeeping missions. Again, being cheaper to buy and maintain than tanks, armoured cars are the ideal AFVs for Third World nations with strictly limited defence budgets. As to their use in any major conflict, they now possess greater mobility and firepower than ever before, but the extent of their involvement will depend upon the nature of the fighting.

The fall of the Shah

The Iranian revolution 1978-79

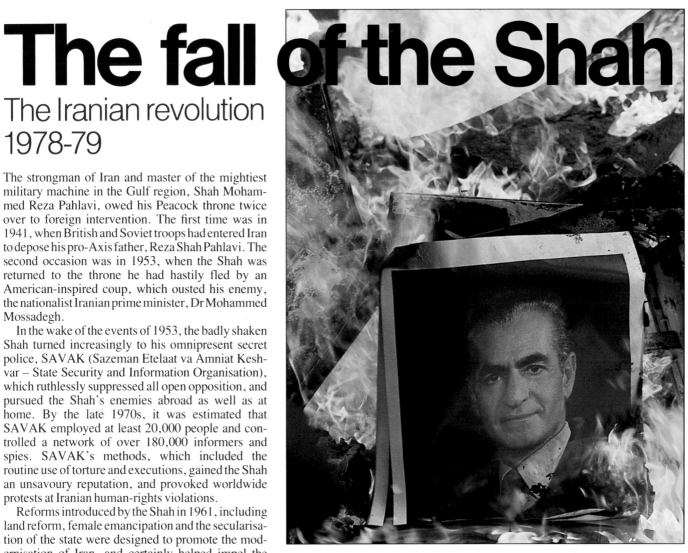

The strongman of Iran and master of the mightiest military machine in the Gulf region, Shah Mohammed Reza Pahlavi, owed his Peacock throne twice over to foreign intervention. The first time was in 1941, when British and Soviet troops had entered Iran to depose his pro-Axis father, Reza Shah Pahlavi. The second occasion was in 1953, when the Shah was returned to the throne he had hastily fled by an American-inspired coup, which ousted his enemy, the nationalist Iranian prime minister, Dr Mohammed Mossadegh.

In the wake of the events of 1953, the badly shaken Shah turned increasingly to his omnipresent secret police, SAVAK (Sazeman Etelaat va Amniat Keshvar – State Security and Information Organisation), which ruthlessly suppressed all open opposition, and pursued the Shah's enemies abroad as well as at home. By the late 1970s, it was estimated that SAVAK employed at least 20,000 people and controlled a network of over 180,000 informers and spies. SAVAK's methods, which included the routine use of torture and executions, gained the Shah an unsavoury reputation, and provoked worldwide protests at Iranian human-rights violations.

Reforms introduced by the Shah in 1961, including land reform, female emancipation and the secularisation of the state were designed to promote the modernisation of Iran, and certainly helped impel the country into the 20th century. But at the same time, this 'White Revolution' alienated the powerful Muslim clergy, who not only lost their own extensive landholdings, but also denounced the reforms as anti-Islamic. The most prominent of these Muslim traditionalists was the Ayatollah Ruhallah Khomeini, who used his position as a respected teacher of Islamic theology as a propaganda platform against the Shah. The clash between the clergy and the Shah reached a peak in 1963, when the storming of Khomeini's theological school in Qom by Imperial Guards triggered off widespread riots and demonstrations. Khomeini was arrested and many demonstrators killed; the Shah denounced what he called an alliance of 'black reactionaries' (the Muslim clergy) and 'dark red forces' (the communist Tudeh Party). Khomeini continued actively to oppose the Shah after his release in March 1964, but failed to mobilise mass support and became increasingly isolated. By November 1964, the Shah felt strong enough to order Khomeini's expulsion from Iran. After a brief period in Turkey, Khomeini settled in Iraq, where he spent the following 14 years as a political exile, denouncing the Shah and all his works.

A second source of opposition to the Shah emerged in 1965, with the foundation of the Sazeman-e-Mujahidin-e-Khalq-e-Iran (People's Mujahidin Organisation of Iran) by a small group of left-wing Muslim graduates of Tehran University. Several had

Iran

taken part in the 1963 pro-Khomeini demonstrations, but later moved beyond Khomeini's conservative traditionalism to a radicalism derived from a combination of Islam, Marxism and the example of Third World national liberation movements. The Mujahidin soon developed close links with the Palestine Liberation Organisation, in whose camps they received their first military training, and by 1971 they were beginning to lay the foundations for an urban guerrilla movement. Their first operations included the assassination of a senior American military adviser and of the Tehran chief of police.

The organisation quickly became the number one target for SAVAK, and by late 1971 the entire leadership had been captured – by May 1972 they had all been either executed or tortured to death. The blow was severe, but the Mujahidin simply went deeper underground, rebuilding their shattered organisation and gradually learning the dangerous lessons of urban guerrilla warfare. As the Mujahidin organisation grew it began to cooperate with the Marxist Fedayeen-e-Khalq in a series of terrorist operations aimed at showing that resistance to the Shah was possible, and that SAVAK was not invincible.

Both the Mujahidin and Fedayeen were able to tap the growing reservoir of discontent with the Shah's new Iran which was widespread not only among the urban poor and the growing working class, but also among the affluent and socially privileged middle class which was itself largely a product of the Shah's programme of modernisation. The corruption and ostentation of the Shah's court contrasted dramatically with the condition of the large numbers of unemployed urban poor, who had been drawn to the shanty towns, such as those which surrounded Tehran, by the lure of work and a share in the prosperity of an increasingly remote and Westernised society. Their disillusionment combined with the desire of the expanding educated administrative and industrial middle class for a share in the power which remained concentrated exclusively in the hands of the Shah, who did little to win support outside of the elite, but increasingly alienated opinion by the brutality of his suppression of all dissent.

Pressure for a liberalisation of the Iranian regime

came increasingly from her main ally and arms supplier, the United States, after the election of Jimmy Carter to the White House in 1976. President Carter saw Iran as a test case for the human-rights orientated foreign policy which he hoped to initiate for the United States. American pressure did persuade the Shah to introduce a number of liberalising measures, including the announcement of free elections to be held in the summer of 1979.

The American-inspired liberalisation, however, unleashed a wave of protests against the regime, which became caught in the classic dilemma of modernising autocracies, which find that each step towards liberalisation is seen as a sign of weakness, and each reassertion of authority as a provocation to new protests and opposition. The trigger for the protests was a government-inspired press attack on the Ayatollah Khomeini which appeared on 7 January 1978. The attack followed shortly after the mysterious death of the Ayatollah's eldest son, which many attributed to SAVAK, and led to demonstrations in the religious centre of Qom which were fired on by troops, causing many deaths.

The 40-day mourning period laid down by the Shi'ite religion was widely observed, and its end was marked by a renewed round of demonstrations and clashes between protestors and security forces. In Tabriz, over 100 demonstrators were either killed or wounded by the police, and the enraged crowd attacked cinemas and banks as the symbols of the Westernised Iran the Shah hoped to construct. This anti-Western nationalist Islamic aspect of the opposition to the Shah was encouraged by cassette recordings of messages from Khomeini which were being illicitly distributed throughout the country, calling on the

Previous page: As the fires of Islamic revolution swept Iran during the winter of 1978-79, the power of the Shah turned to ashes. Left-wing and fundamentalist opponents of the Shah united in huge mass demonstrations which led to bloody confrontations with the Iranian Army. Above: A victim of the first such clash in Tehran on 4 September 1978. Top: The Jaleh Square massacre on the following day led to the deaths of 500 demonstrators and convinced many of the need to overthrow the Shah.

Top right: The austere figure of the Ayatollah Khomeini became the universal symbol of the opposition to the Shah. Right: The Shah responded by employing troops against unarmed demonstrators, but the willingness of many to accept martyrdom only demoralised the army and hastened the final collapse of the regime.

faithful to rise up against the Shah as their religious duty.

The depths of the latent distrust and hatred which existed towards the Shah were most clearly illustrated after an arson attack upon the crowded Rex cinema in Abadan on 19 August 1978, during which some 600 people were burned to death. Although subsequent evidence pointed strongly to the responsibility of fanatical Islamic fundamentalists, many Iranians accepted without question the allegation that the attack had been carried out by the Shah's agents in order to discredit the opposition. The Rex killings initiated a new wave of attacks on banks and cinemas, and protest demonstrations took on the character of fanatical confrontations with the security forces, each yielding its own crop of martyrs, and the continually repeated 40-day mourning periods were transformed into a process of organisation and propaganda, resulting in ever larger protests which the security forces were increasingly powerless to prevent.

Demonstrations and death

The first mass demonstrations to be held in Tehran took place on 4 September 1978, when over 100,000 people took to the streets in an unprecedented challenge to the Shah. The government reacted by banning all demonstrations, but was unable to prevent a second march on 7 September. The regime responded by placing the capital under martial law, and soldiers were ordered to shoot to kill.

The following day, however, demonstrators again assembled in the Jaleh Square in south Tehran. The Tehran correspondent of the French newspaper *Le Figaro* described what followed, as the soldiers opened fire: 'This is not a fight; this is a massacre. A firing squad at work. The street one minute beforehand darkened with people, is strewn with bodies, shoes, trampelled banners, the wounded crawling toward each other, struggling to reach each other.' An estimated 500 demonstrators had been slaughtered. It was a turning point that marked the transition from protest to revolution.

Tehran University, which reopened towards the end of September, became the organisational centre for revolutionary activity, and the virtually open base

of the Mujahidin and Fedayeen guerrillas who not only helped organise demonstrations and meetings, but also trained many people in the use of weapons. Meetings, exhibitions and the production of a torrent of propaganda material transformed the university into a blatant challenge to the Shah's authority. On 4 November a rally of over 100,000 high school and university students was attacked by units of the Shah's Imperial Guards – 65 demonstrators were killed and up to 400 wounded. Tehran witnessed the most violent protests yet, and by the following day a nationwide state of martial law had been imposed.

The prime minister, Sharif Emami, who had been appointed as a half-hearted gesture to liberalisation, was removed from office, and the Iranian chief of staff, General Azhari, took his place. Tehran University was occupied by troops and control of the campus became a key issue in what was rapidly becoming an all-out struggle for power between the Shah and the loose opposition coalition that ranged from Islamic fundamentalists loyal to Ayatollah Khomeini, through moderate liberals of the National Front, to the more radical Mujahidin and the pro-Moscow communists of the Tudeh Party. While a group of lecturers occupied classrooms at the university, students staged a sit-in at the Ministry of Education from 23 December, which escalated to massive demonstrations involving over 400,000 when troops shot and killed one of the student protesters on 26 December.

The flight of the Shah

The martial law regime appeared increasingly desperate as the various strands of the opposition united behind the austere and intransigent figure of Ayatollah Khomeini, now based in Paris. Isolated incidents of fraternisation between troops and demonstrators began to be reported, and anti-Shah slogans were chanted nightly from the rooftops in a constant provocation to the army patrols in the streets below. General Azhari, who had suffered a heart attack late in December, was replaced as prime minister by former opposition National Front politician Shapur Bakhtiar on 29 December, but the situation had already deteriorated far beyond cosmetic cabinet changes. On 13 January 1979, demonstrators marched on the occupied university and took it over as the 'Central Fort of the Revolution'. Three days later the Shah and his wife left Iran by air for the final exile.

Within hours the news of the Shah's departure had reached the streets of the capital, where hundreds of thousands demonstrated their joy and relief. The Bakhtiar government continued to oppose change by armed force, however, and the runway of Tehran airport was blocked by army tanks in order to prevent the much heralded return of Khomeini. By 1 February the runway barriers had been removed, however, and the Ayatollah landed to the rapturous reception of the people of Tehran, who lined the route of his triumphant entry into the capital in their millions.

Two centres of authority now existed in Iran: that of the Shah, represented by the totally isolated person of Prime Minister Bakhtiar; and that of Ayatollah Khomeini, to whom the majority of the Iranian people now looked for leadership, and who appointed Mehdi Bazargan as prime minister of a provisional government on 5 February. The armed forces remained for the most part loyal to the Shah, however, and formed a last barrier to a peaceful transition. A final bloody

resolution appeared inevitable.

The uprising which sealed the fate of the Shah's regime was set in motion by events which occurred at an Iranian Air Force base at Farahabad, in south Tehran. A filmed report of the arrival of Khomeini in Tehran being shown on television was greeted by a group of air force technicians and cadets with chanted slogans in support of the Ayatollah. Imperial Guards loyal to the Shah who were present attacked the airmen and laid siege to them in their barracks.

News of the fighting at Farahabad spread rapidly throughout the capital, and the airmen appealed for help against the Imperial Guards. Armed Mujahidin and Fedayeen rushed to the scene of the fighting, and took up positions to the rear of the Imperial Guards who suddenly found themselves under attack from all sides. The airmen distributed weapons from their armoury to the large numbers of civilians who had come to their aid, and fighting became general throughout Tehran as the revolutionaries moved to cut off units of the Imperial Guards which were moving to the support of their comrades.

The insurgents, armed with light automatic weapons and molotov cocktails, faced the tanks of the Iranian Army, but the morale of the government troops had already been weakened by the months of confrontation with fanatical unarmed demonstrators who had welcomed martyrdom in the fight against the Shah. Resistance began to crumble, and by 11 February the insurgents were moving over to the offensive

Above: Left-wing guerrillas and armed supporters of the Ayatollah round up agents of SAVAK, the Shah's hated secret police. Above centre: The arrival of Khomeini at Tehran airport on 1 February 1979 to a rapturous welcome.

Top right: The bodies of Iranian generals, supporters of the Shah, killed by the firing squads of the new Islamic Republic. Right: The Shah flees Iran on 16 January 1979. After taking refuge in a number of countries, including the United States, he finally died of cancer in Egypt in July 1980.

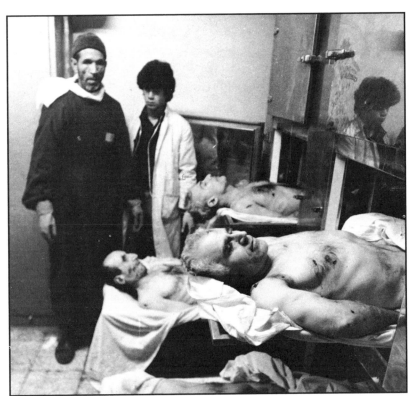

and had begun to attack SAVAK buildings, police stations and the capital's five main military bases. News of the insurrection had already spread to the rest of Iran and fighting broke out in all the country's major cities. Late on 11 February the fall of Tehran to the insurgents was announced on radio and television. The rule of the Shah was at an end.

The triumphant Islamic revolution now turned to the grim business of visiting retribution upon the senior army officers who had been responsible for propping up the Imperial regime and for the bloody suppression of opposition. General after general faced firing squads of the new Revolutionary Guards who had taken over responsibility for security. Loyal to Ayatollah Khomeini, they were distinct from the guerrilla groups which had played such an active part in the fighting, and provided the Islamic fundamentalists with the means to impose their stamp on Iran.

Divisions within the anti-Shah coalition soon began to re-emerge when the Shah himself had been removed from power. Though the Tudeh Party continued to support the socially conservative but violently nationalistic and anti-Western Islamic Republic established in the wake of the revolution (until the Muslim fundamentalists themselves turned on the communists and destroyed them), conflict with the Mujahidin and with Iran's various national minorities soon exploded into open warfare. The Mujahidin, driven once more underground, resorted to terrorist tactics in a violent struggle over the course of the Iranian revolution, while national minorities, such as the Kurds, who had played an active part in the struggle against the Shah, found that their hopes of equality and self-determination were to be shattered against the even more aggressive Persian chauvinism of Iran's new Islamic rulers. The 1979 revolution had substituted a dictatorship of the Mullahs for the autocracy of the Shah – a dictatorship which in many respects was even more brutal than that which it had replaced. **Walter Hoffmann**

Chronology 1976-80

EUROPE AND NORTH AMERICA
1976
January
5   Northern Ireland Ten Protestant textile workers killed by terrorist group at Whitecross, Armagh.
May
9   West Germany Red Army Fraction leader Ulrike Meinhof found dead in her prison cell.
28   United States concludes treaty with Soviet Union on the control of underground nuclear explosions for non-military purposes.
July
21   Eire British ambassador Christopher Ewart-Briggs assassinated.
November
1   United States Jimmy Carter elected president.

1977
January
12   Northern Ireland Secretary of State Roy Mason announces the 'Way Ahead' policy – 'Ulsterisation'.
May
11   Soviet Union and United States begin SALT II talks in Geneva.
16   Soviet Union Leonid Brezhnev becomes president as well as general secretary of Communist Party.
17   Nato agrees to a 3 per cent annual rise in defence spending.
23   Netherlands South Moluccan terrorists seize hostages in train and school.
June
11   Netherlands Dutch Marines and police release hostages from South Moluccans.
30   United States President Carter announces cancellation of B-1 bomber programme.
July
7   United States President Carter reveals neutron bomb in production.
September
5   West Germany Industrialist Dr Hanns-Martin Schleyer kidnapped by Baader-Meinhof group.
October
13   West Germany Lufthansa flight hijacked to Mogadishu, Somalia, by West German and Palestinian terrorists, demanding release of Baader-Meinhof prisoners.
18   West Germany GSG9 anti-terrorist squad successfully assaults hijacked aircraft at Mogadishu. Three Baader-Meinhof leaders, including Andreas Baader, found dead in their cells.
19   West Germany Kidnapped industrialist Dr Schleyer found dead.
November
2   Soviet Union President Brezhnev offers to halt nuclear testing.

1978
January
4   Britain Representative of PLO in London Said Hammami assassinated.
February
17   Northern Ireland Fire bomb at La Mon restaurant kills 12.
March
16   Italy Aldo Moro, five times prime minister, kidnapped by Red Brigades.
May
9   Italy Body of Aldo Moro found.
September
15   Britain Baader-Meinhof terrorist Astrid Proll arrested in London.

December
13   United States announces resumption of diplomatic relations with China.
23   United States and Soviet Union SALT talks end without agreement.

1979
March
22   Netherlands British ambassador assassinated by IRA.
30   Britain Airey Neave MP assassinated by INLA.
May
4   Britain Margaret Thatcher becomes first woman prime minister.
18   United States and Soviet Union Presidents Carter and Brezhnev sign SALT II treaty in Vienna.
August
27   Ireland Earl Mountbatten killed by terrorist bomb at Mullaghmore in the Irish Republic; 18 British paras killed by terrorist bombs at Warrenpoint in Northern Ireland.
December
6   Netherlands Dutch parliament rejects Nato plan for stationing of cruise missiles in the Netherlands.
12   Nato approves stationing of 572 missiles in Europe.

1980
January
1   United States President Carter recalls US ambassador from Moscow following Soviet invasion of Afghanistan.
April
28   Europe European Campaign for Nuclear Disarmament (END) founded.
30   Britain Iranian embassy seized by terrorists.
May
4   Yugoslavia President Tito dies after long illness.
5   Britain SAS commandos storm Iranian embassy and release hostages.
June
19   Britain Government announces intention to deploy cruise missiles at Greenham Common and Molesworth.
September
12   Turkey Demirel government overthrown in military coup led by General Kenan Evren.
October
24   Poland Independent trade union organisation 'Solidarity' recognised by government.
November
4   United States Ronald Reagan elected president.

SOUTHEAST ASIA
1976
June
24   Vietnam officially reunified.
30   Thailand South East Asian Treaty Organisation (Seato) closes Bangkok headquarters and ceases to exist.
October
20   Thailand Military coup.

1978
November
3   Vietnam and Soviet Union sign a Treaty of Friendship.

December
27   Vietnam sends troops into Kampuchea.

1979
January
7   Kampuchea Vietnamese troops occupy Phnom Penh, and set up government under Heng Samrin.
February
17   Vietnam Chinese troops invade the northern provinces of Vietnam.
23   Vietnam Soviet military supplies airlifted to the Vietnamese.
March
5   Vietnam Long San abandoned to Chinese forces after fierce fighting.
6   Vietnam Chinese begin withdrawal from Vietnam.
20   Vietnam Chinese withdrawal completed.

SOUTH ASIA
1976
June
29   Seychelles gains independence, remaining in Commonwealth.

1977
April
21   Pakistan Martial law imposed in major cities.
June
5   Seychelles President Mancham overthrown in bloodless coup.
July
4   Pakistan Army takeover under General Zia ul-Haq.

1978
April
27   Afghanistan Daoud government overthrown in coup; Noor Mohammed Taraki comes to power at head of Marxist regime.

1979
July
Sri Lanka State of emergency in response to Tamil revolt.
September
17   Afghanistan Taraki ousted by Hafizullah Amin.
November
21   Pakistan US embassy in Islamabad burnt down.
December
24   Afghanistan Soviet aircraft deliver combat troops to Kabul airport as five divisions mass on frontier.
27   Afghanistan Amin killed in Soviet assault on presidential palace. Babrak Karmal flown in by Soviets to take his place.

1980
January
1   Afghanistan Soviet force of some 60,000 men in the country; fighting continues throughout the year.

EAST ASIA
1976
September
9   China Death of Mao Tse-tung.

1978
May
11   China and Soviet Union Troops clash on the Ussuri River.
June
5   China halts aid to Vietnam.
August
12   China and Japan sign treaty of peace and friendship.

1979
January
28   China Deputy prime minister Deng Hsiao-ping begins official visit to the United States.
October
26   South Korea President Park assassinated.

MIDDLE EAST
1976
April
9   Lebanon Syrian regular troops intervene in Lebanese civil war to prevent a Muslim/Palestinian victory.
July
3-4   Israel mounts a successful rescue mission to Entebbe, Uganda, where Israeli passengers on a hijacked Air France flight are being held hostage by West German and Palestinian terrorists.
November
15   Lebanon Syrian troops enter Beirut as guarantors of an Arab peace agreement to end the civil war; fighting subsides.

1977
July
21   Libya and Egypt engage in border clashes.
November
22   Israel President Sadat of Egypt addresses the Israeli Knesset in Jerusalem.

1978
February
19   Cyprus Egyptian commandos unsuccessfully storm a hijacked aircraft at Larnaca.
March
14   Lebanon Large-scale thrust by Israeli forces into the south of the country (Operation Litani).
22   Lebanon UN peacekeeping force (UNIFIL) despatched to the south Lebanon.
June
13   Lebanon Israeli forces withdraw from south Lebanon.
24   North Yemen President Ghashmi assassinated.
26   South Yemen President Rubayi Ali deposed and executed by pro-Soviet opponents.
September
5-17   Egypt and Israel Camp David summit during which Prime Minister Begin, President Sadat and President Carter devise a 'framework for peace'.
8   Iran Martial law declared in Tehran and 11 other cities after widespread demonstrations against the Shah.
28   Israel The Knesset approves the Camp David agreement.
October
27   Egypt and Israel Begin and Sadat awarded Nobel Peace Prize.
November
3   Egypt suspended from the Arab League.
December
20   Lebanon Israel attacks Palestinian bases.

1979
January
16   Iran The Shah leaves the country in the face of relentless mass demonstrations.
February
1   Iran The Ayatollah Khomeini returns from exile.
16   Iran Pro-Shah generals executed.

March
26   Egypt and Israel sign peace treaty in Washington.
31   Malta Final withdrawal of British Navy.
April
1   Iran declared an Islamic Republic.
October
23   United States Ex-Shah of Iran flown to New York for cancer treatment.
November
4   Iran Students occupy the US embassy and take the staff hostage.
14   Iran United States freezes all Iranian assets.

1980
January
27   Israel and Egypt reopen their border.
April
9   Lebanon Israeli troops move in.
24-25   Iran US Delta Force carries out abortive attempt to free the embassy hostages in Tehran (Operation Eagle Claw).
July
27   Egypt Death of ex-Shah of Iran.
September
4   Iran attacks Iraqi border villages in escalation of border clashes.
22   Iran Start of Gulf War as Iraq invades Iran.
23-25   Iran and Iraq launch crippling air strikes against each others' oil refining installations.
October
13   Iran Khorramshar falls to Iraqi forces; Abadan besieged by land.

SOUTH AMERICA
1976
August
1   Trinidad and Tobago gain independence within the Commonwealth.

1977
August
11   Panama United States agrees to hand over the Canal to Panama by the year 2000.

1978
August
7   Honduras Military coup.
September
11   Nicaragua Martial law imposed through much of the country as Sandinista guerrillas increase pressure on government of General Somoza.
November
24   Bolivia Military coup.

1979
May
4   El Salvador Guerrillas seize French and Costa Rican embassies.
17   Nicaragua President Somoza flees to the United States leaving Sandinistas in control of the country.
October
17   El Salvador Colonels seize power, impose martial law.
November
1   Bolivia Military coup.

1980
March
24   El Salvador Archbishop Romero assassinated at altar in San Salvador.

AFRICA
1976
February
9   Angola MPLA/Cuban forces capture UNITA 'capital'. Nova Lisboa.

15   Angola FNLA/mercenary force finally driven from northern Angola by MPLA/Cuban advance; MPLA in effective control of the country.
13   Nigeria General Murtala Mohammed, head of state, assassinated.
March
3   Mozambique closes border with Rhodesia, imposes sanctions.
June
16   South Africa Rioting in black township of Soweto, Johannesburg.
July
3-4   Uganda Israeli airborne troops rescue hostages from Entebbe airport.

1977
February
3   Ethiopia Lieutenant-Colonel Mengistu Haile Mariam seizes power in palace coup.
24   Ethiopia United States halts arms supplies.
March
10   Zaire Shaba Province invaded by Katangese gendarmes from Angola.
July
24   Somalia launches full-scale invasion of the Ogaden area of Ethiopia.
September
12   Ethiopia Somali forces capture Jijiga.
October
18   Somalia Rescue of Lufthansa flight hostages at Mogadishu by West German GSG9.
November
4   South Africa UN security council imposes mandatory arms embargo.
26   Ethiopia Soviet airlift of Cuban troops and weapons to aid Ethiopia in the Ogaden War.

1978
February
7   Ethiopia launches major offensive in the Ogaden.
March
9   Somalia announces total withdrawal from Ethiopian territory.
May
1   Angola Major incursion by South African troops.
12   Zaire Second invasion of Shaba from Angola.
18-25   Zaire French legionnaires paradrop into Kolwezi to rescue white hostages and defeat Shaba invasion.
July
10   Mauritania Coup brings Lieutenant-Colonel Salek to power.
30   Mozambique South African troops attack guerrilla bases.
August
30   Namibia UN plan for Namibia accepted by SWAPO, rejected by South Africa.

1979
April
11   Uganda Kampala occupied by force of Tanzanian troops and Ugandan exiles; Amin overthrown.
June
4   Ghana Flight-Lieutenant Rawlings takes power in military coup.
September
5   Rhodesia launches ground and air attacks into Mozambique.
20   Central African Republic France overthrows 'Emperor' Bokassa and installs David Dacko as president.
December
21   Rhodesia Treaty on preparations for independence signed at Lancaster House in London.

1980
March
4   Rhodesia/Zimbabwe Robert Mugabe's ZANU party wins overall majority in elections.
April
18   Zimbabwe becomes independent state.
June
16-19   South Africa Serious rioting in Soweto.

Left: Militant Islamic students burn the American flag on the roof of the US embassy in Tehran, November 1980. The students seized the embassy and took 66 US citizens hostage, demanding the return of the Shah to face a revolutionary tribunal.

The Iranian hostage crisis

On Sunday, 4 November 1979 some 400 militant Islamic students occupied the United States embassy in Tehran, capital of Iran, and took 66 American citizens hostage. Three more US officials on a visit to the Iranian Foreign Ministry were also taken prisoner. The occupation appears to have surprised not only the Americans – who had not long before abandoned on grounds of cost a plan to 'harden' the embassy compound – but also the revolutionary leaders themselves. Nevertheless, Ayatollah Khomeini and his allies in the Islamic Republican Party (IRP) were quick to back the action of the students, seizing the opportunity that it presented to undermine the liberal government headed by Prime Minister Bazargan and push forward their project of institutionalising the power of the Islamic clergy.

Anti-American fervour, fomented by the revolutionary clergy, had run high in Iran since the flight of the Shah and the collapse of the hated Pahlavi regime in the preceding February. Indeed, on 14 February, only three days after the fall of the Pahlavi government, the American embassy had been briefly occupied by Fedayeen-e-Khalq guerrillas. Since the end of the first occupation the American diplomats had been 'protected' by a contingent of Revolutionary Guards who were, however, disavowed by the government.

On 22 October the ailing fugitive Shah was admitted to the United States to receive medical treatment, and this provided the militant students with their immediate pretext for the seizure of the hostages. In return for freeing them, the students demanded that the US return the 'treacherous Shah' to Iran to stand trial, rejecting any possibility of negotiation. The US government had maintained relations with Bazargan's government throughout this period in the hope that it would be able to survive the pressures of Islamic fundamentalism, but in the aftermath of the occupation Bazargan resigned and the Revolutionary Coun-

cil, an alliance of Islamic factions, took over the government. The new government confirmed that they were not prepared to negotiate the release of the hostages; in theory at least the students occupying the embassy were acting independently. The Americans were therefore obliged to try to negotiate with the students through intermediaries.

US President Jimmy Carter had publicly rejected any notion of military intervention to free the hostages (reduced in number to 53 in the embassy compound by the release of 13 people by 20 November) but with the American public clamouring for a solution to the crisis, and the 1980 presidential election on the horizon, it is hardly surprising that he did in fact consider the military option from the very beginning of the crisis. The US naval presence in the Gulf of Oman was stepped up and a special unit, Delta Force, under Colonel Charlie Beckwith, was charged with developing a plan to retake the embassy by force.

In 1962 Charlie Beckwith, as a young captain in the Green Berets, had been posted to Britain for a year to train with the SAS. He had been impressed with their counter-insurgency methods and on his return he had begun a campaign for a similar American unit to be set up. After seeing active service in Vietnam, Beckwith continued to press for an SAS-type unit to be set up with a counter-insurgency and counter-terrorist role, until finally in 1977 he was given command of a new detachment of Special Forces: the 1st Special Forces Operational Detachment – Delta. When the crisis broke in November 1979 Beckwith was given a chance to test his new force.

Although Beckwith's men had been trained to assault buildings occupied by terrorists and free civilian hostages, none of this training had anticipated the immense problems presented by the situation in Iran. Instead of operating on friendly territory, Delta Force would have to move deep into the Iranian interior.

Above: The American hostages were subject to intense psychological pressure, and were often blindfolded and displayed before television cameras and anti-American crowds.

Below: The occupied embassy became the focus for violent anti-American demonstrations which swept Iran in the wake of the Islamic revolution.

Tehran. A refuelling stop in the desert would have to be arranged.

At each stage of the planning of the operation – code-named Operation Eagle Claw – new difficulties emerged, and each solution made the operation more complex. To make matters worse, there was a shortage of good intelligence. When the crisis broke, there had been no American agents in Iran except those who were attached to the embassy and were now among the hostages. An ex-CIA agent, code-named 'Bob', was quickly briefed and inserted into Iran, followed by four more Department of Defense agents. But there was no time to train them properly and none of them was able to speak the main local language, Farsi. Nevertheless the quality of intelligence began to improve and Delta Force were able to build up a detailed picture of the buildings in the embassy compound. Not until late in the planning, however, was it discovered that all the hostages were being held in the Chancellery building. The American agents were also able to supply details of the dispositions of the Revolutionary Guards.

When Delta Force deployed to Egypt on 21 April 1980, after months of training, the 72-man team that had been agreed on in December had expanded to over 130, plus a detachment of Rangers to secure an airfield for the withdrawal. In addition to the Sea Stallion helicopters, eight in number, the operation involved C-130 transports, tankers and gunships, and two C-141 Starlifters with fighter cover for the final evacuation.

And any solution to the logistical difficulties would have to preserve the element of surprise – once American forces were detected in Iran there could be no mistaking their objective.

Early suggestions that Delta Force should parachute into Tehran or drive there in trucks from Turkey were dismissed as unrealistic. Helicopters would certainly be needed to evacuate the hostages once the embassy had been taken, and so it was decided to use them on the way in. Naval carrier-based RH-53D Sea Stallion helicopters with a long-range heavy-lift capability, piloted by Marines, could be launched from the Gulf of Oman, but despite their long range they would be unable to cover the whole distance to

Delta Force and 'Desert One'

The plan for Eagle Claw called for the Delta Force assault team to be landed at 'Desert One', a desert road 320 km (200 miles) southeast of Tehran, by three troop-carrying MC-130s accompanied by three EC-130 fuel tankers. Thirty minutes later they would be met by eight Sea Stallions launched from the carrier *Nimitz*. The assault force of 118 men and their equipment would be loaded onto the helicopters, and after the refuelling was complete Delta Force would be flown on to a hide-site near Tehran, arriving before sunrise. The helicopters were then to be moved to a second site and concealed to await the call to evacuate the Force and the rescued hostages. It was agreed that unless at least six of the Sea Stallions were available the operation would not be viable and would have to be aborted.

Meanwhile, Beckwith and his men would be led by two of the Department of Defense agents to a wadi some 8km (5 miles) from the landing zone and spend the day in hiding. After sunset two of the agents would return with two vehicles. Six drivers from Delta Force would drive to Tehran, pick up six Mercedes trucks and return to the wadi while Beckwith carried out a reconnaissance. Finally, Delta Force would divide into separate elements and drive to Tehran by separate routes.

Sometime after 2300 hours the leading contingent would drive up to the embassy and take out two guard-posts with silenced handguns. Two elements of Delta, Red and Blue, following close behind, were tasked to climb over the embassy walls, secure different sections of the compound and free the hostages, killing any armed Iranians they encountered. Meanwhile, White Element was to secure the outside of the embassy and cover the withdrawal. The assault on the buildings in the compound would be signalled by a

gigantic explosion as the wall of the compound was blown up. At approximately the same time a special 13-man assault team would attack the Foreign Ministry building and free the hostages there.

By now, the Sea Stallion helicopters would be circling to the north of Tehran and at a signal from Delta's air officer they were to begin landing either in the compound or in a nearby soccer stadium. The whole operation would be covered from above by two C-130 gunships whose massive firepower could be called down to halt any response by the Iranian armed forces. The Sea Stallions were to ferry hostages and assault teams to Manzariyeh airfield, 55km (35 miles) to the south, where a contingent of US Rangers would be defending a flight of C-141 Starlifters waiting to airlift everyone out of Iran.

The plan was almost unbelievably complex, and yet everyone involved thought that it could work. The go-ahead was given and Delta Force was air-lifted to the island of Masirah in the Gulf of Oman on Thursday, 24 April. At 1630 hours, dressed in Levi's and black field jackets, Delta Force boarded the C-130 transports. An hour and a half later the first aircraft took off and set its course for Desert One.

The first stage of the operation went smoothly. The aircraft successfully eluded the Iranian ground radar system and the leading transport landed at Desert One; the Ranger Road Watch Team deployed and secured the flanks of the site and Delta Force moved into position. Then, unexpectedly, a large civilian Mercedes bus arrived along the road with its headlights blazing. Blue Element surrounded it as Beckwith fired a shot at one of its tyres. The passengers were ordered off, searched and placed under guard. As a second Ranger force was deploying to the west of Desert One, another civilian vehicle, a petrol tanker, drove up. One of the Rangers fired an M72 Light Anti-tank Weapon, and the tanker burst into flames.

The US rescue plan
24-25 April 1980

CASPIAN SEA

Tabriz

Tehran
Garmsar
Hide Site
Manzariyeh
Qom
Desert One
Esfahan

IRAN

USSR

AFGHANISTAN

TURKEY
KUWAIT
Shiraz

Zargos Mountains

THE GULF

PAKISTAN

SAUDI ARABIA

OMAN

helicopter launch from USS Nimitz

MASIRAH ISLAND

→ Sea Stallion helicopter flight path
→ C-130 flight path
→ C-141 flight path

Left: Sikorsky RH-53 Sea Stallion helicopters on the deck of USS *Nimitz* prepare to take part in the hazardous mission to free the US hostages. Below left: Colonel Charlie Beckwith, Delta Force commander, who led the rescue operation. Main picture: The burnt-out wreckage of a C-130 destroyed in a collision with a Sea Stallion at 'Desert One' inside Iran. By the time this collision took place – killing eight men – Delta Force had already abandoned the hostage rescue bid. Below right: The hostages, released as the result of a negotiated settlement in January 1981, returned to a hero's welcome in the United States.

A truck drove up behind the tanker and the tanker driver jumped out of his blazing vehicle, got into the truck, and was driven off at speed. The Road Watch Team failed to stop it.

The remaining troop-transports and 'fuel-birds' arrived one by one and Delta Force deployed and settled down to wait for the helicopters. They were due to arrive in 30 minutes. After an hour there was still no sign of them and it was clear that Delta would be unable to reach the hide-site before first light, which was due at 0530 hours. After an hour and a half the first helicopter arrived; five more appeared during the next 30 minutes. The last two never arrived at all. The helicopters had encountered appalling dust storms, which had caused the delay. The two that failed to arrive suffered mechanical and electrical failures.

There was now no margin for error: with only six helicopters, the operation depended on every one of them. Although the risk of discovery was mounting every minute, Beckwith decided to continue. The Sea Stallions were refuelled and loaded. Delta was ready to move out of Desert One, and then, with the operation already ninety minutes behind schedule, Beckwith was told that only five of the helicopters were flyable. Eagle Claw was doomed and Beckwith ordered a withdrawal.

The withdrawal plan was for everyone to off-load and rejoin the C-130 transports. The five Sea Stallions would then fly back to the *Nimitz*. At 0230 hours preparations were complete. The C-130 pilots had started to gun their engines when the first helicopter lifted off. As the wind gusted around, the helicopter banked to the left, slid backwards and hit the C-130 with Blue Element on board, before bursting into flames. A huge conflagration ensued with flames reaching far into the sky and Redeye missiles exploding in all directions. Miraculously, all of Blue Element managed to disembark as the C-130 caught fire. Eight men crewing the C-130 and the Sea Stallion were killed. Boarding the remaining aircraft, Delta Force swiftly abandoned Desert One, leaving five helicopters intact on the ground.

The failure of the mission was a humiliation for the United States and especially for President Carter. When the Shah died in July 1980 the immediate issue behind the hostage-taking was resolved, but the revolutionary students announced further conditions. They sought the return of the Shah's assets in the US to Iran and a series of humiliating apologies and undertakings on the part of the US government – conditions that President Carter was unable to meet.

Nevertheless, the crisis was finally resolved by negotiation in January 1981, after an agreement was reached between the US and Iran in Algiers. The hostages returned to the United States, to a hero's welcome. So not only had the 'military solution' proved a disastrous failure – it had in the final analysis proved unnecessary. It is, of course, impossible to say with certainty if the operation could possibly have succeeded, but a plan of such complexity inevitably risks failure. In the event, it was the use of helicopters – notoriously unreliable aircraft at any time – in desert terrain where they were all the more likely to fail, that resulted in a disaster that probably cost Jimmy Carter the presidency.

Barry Smith

Rapid deployment
The US prepares for intervention in the Gulf

The idea of a quick-reaction military force, capable of worldwide deployment, had first been suggested by Secretary of Defense Robert McNamara during the Kennedy administration. McNamara had drawn the essential lesson of the 1962 Cuban missile crisis that advantage in sub-nuclear superpower confrontations went to the side which could deploy a decisive local conventional military superiority. Such a capability would also help prevent an escalation of such confrontations to the nuclear level.

It was not until 1977, however, when President Jimmy Carter issued a directive (Presidential Directive No. 18 – PD18) to the Joint Chiefs of Staff, that the first practical steps were taken to create such a force. In the general mood of post-Vietnam depression there was much opposition to this initiative, and progress was at first slow. The rapid deterioration of relations with the Soviet Union during the late 1970s and the Iranian revolution of January 1979, which overthrew the United States' closest and most important ally in the Gulf region, provided the context for a more active application of PD18, however. In August 1979 the Joint Chiefs produced proposals for the establishment of a unified operational command aimed at the development of a force ready to respond to threats to US interests in the Gulf.

Events in the region proceeded apace. The seizure of the US embassy hostages in Tehran on 4 November 1979 created a mood of extreme hostility to Iran which swept the United States during the winter of 1979-80. The Soviet intervention in Afghanistan in December 1979, added to the anti-American hysteria of Khomeini's Iran, seemed to pose a direct threat to Western oil supplies from the Gulf and to the stability and security of pro-Western countries there. President Carter's State of the Union message on 21 January 1980 contained a clear commitment to the security of the Gulf, and indicated a US readiness to defend its interests there by military force if absolutely necessary.

On 1 March 1980, the headquarters of the Rapid Deployment Joint Task Force (RDJTF) was set up at McDill air force base, Tampa, Florida, in bunkers previously occupied by the Strategic Air Command. McDill was also the headquarters of the US Readiness Command (REDCOM) to which the RDJTF was subordinated. The first commander of the RDJTF was Lieutenant-General Paul X. Kelley of the US Marine Corps, later to command the United States contingent in Beirut.

A unified command

At first the RDJTF was little more than a skeleton HQ, but by 10 October 1981 it had been transformed into a separate task force with joint command and control of forces designated to it, and on 1 January 1983 the RDJTF became a separate unified command. Known as the US Central Command (CENTCOM), theoretically equal in status to the European and Pacific commands, it had a 977-strong HQ organisation and was responsible for all military operations in the Southwest Asian theatre.

From the beginning, the RDJTF faced special difficulties inherent in the task it had to fulfil. The essential problem was how to transport a sufficient number of highly trained, well equipped men from the continental United States where they were based to Southwest Asia rapidly enough to counter any local or external threat to stability. The sheer distances involved in such an enterprise and the magnitude of the resources required would have defeated any other nation than the United States. Logistics were the main

Above: A US Marine M60 tank practising an assault landing during exercises in the Middle East.

limitation to operations, and therefore occupied a central position in RDJTF planning.

In US Fiscal Year 1983, the US Military Airlift Command (MAC) and Tactical Air Command (TAC) had some 512 C-130 Hercules, 234 C-141 Starlifters, 70 C-5 Galaxies and 12 KC-10 Extenders, to which could be added some 109 cargo and 215 passenger aircraft of the Civil Reserve Air Fleet (CRAF). Nevertheless, it was still only possible to airlift 30 per cent of the RDJTF's sole quick-reaction paratroop unit, the 82nd Airborne Division, at any one time to the Gulf region, and that only if stopover facilities were available at some friendly base along the way. The total payload of the MAC would not be capable of transporting the RDJTF-assigned 24th Infantry Division in less than five weeks, and once in action that division would need 1000 tonnes of supplies every day to remain combat-effective.

The US sought to reduce these difficulties by adopting a policy of prepositioning supplies in the region, ready for local transportation and use. Prepositioning applied to equipment of all kinds, includ-

ing fuel, ammunition and vehicles. Supplies were held at secret locations in the Middle East, on the territory of friendly countries as well as on a number of ships permanently based at Diego Garcia in the Indian Ocean. Until 1984 these ships constituted a Near-Term Prepositioning Force (NTPF) of 18 vessels, but from 1984 RDJTF planning provided for the establishment of a larger operation, comprising three Maritime Prepositioning Ship (MPS) task forces by 1986. Each MPS task force was to carry sufficient supplies for a highly mechanised Marine Amphibious Brigade.

Plans for the airlift of troops and equipment into the region, as well as the permanent presence of prepositioned material, demanded the availability of local military and naval facilities. By 1983, such facilities existed in Oman at Sib on the Gulf of Oman and on Mazirah island; at a number of points on the Saudi Arabian Gulf coast, including Dharan; at the Egyptian Red Sea

Right: US airborne troops jump from a C-130 Hercules during Bright Star exercises in Egypt. Above: Paratroops of the 82nd Airborne Division prepare to board a C-130. Equipped with desert-camouflage uniforms and the new Kevlar helmet, they form the quick-reaction spearhead of the RDJTF. Left: An M113 APC being dropped by parachute during desert exercises.

port of Ras Banas and in the Western Desert; at Mombasa in Kenya; and Berbera and Mogadishu in Somalia. The key base for the RDJTF remained the British-owned island of Diego Garcia in the Indian Ocean, from which not only supply vessels but also carrier task forces and Strategic Air Command B-52s could operate.

While strategic and tactical airlift would supply RDJTF combat troops with logistic support in the short-term, and the MPS task forces in the medium-term, the long-term logistical back-up to operations in Southwest Asia would have to come from a greatly enhanced sealift capability routed around the Cape of Good Hope, and delivering men and material from the US East Coast in some 30 days. A Sealift Readiness Program was initiated in 1979, which provided for the gradual replacement of commercially-hired vessels with purpose-built ships, to include roll-on/roll-off container ships and fuel and water tankers. Sealift would also provide an alternative method of transporting troops to the Gulf, in vessels such as the SL-7 high-speed container ship.

High-profile exercises

Each stage in the development of the RDJTF was accompanied by extensive and exhaustive exercises to test the logistical system under operational conditions, and to train the designated troops in the special techniques of warfare demanded by Southwest Asian conditions. These exercises were seen by the United

Above: US Army Sikorsky UH-60A Black Hawk helicopters transporting jeeps during Bright Star in the Egyptian desert. The RDJTF depends heavily upon the cooperation of allies in the Middle East to overcome its enormous logistical problems.

States not only as a routine military training programme, but as a demonstration to both allies and potential enemies that the RDJTF was an effective military force. RDJTF exercises were therefore high-profile political occasions, as well as a military necessity.

The first exercise combined both political and military aspects to an exemplary degree. Within a month of President Carter's 1980 State of the Union message, a Marine Amphibious Task Force, including four vessels, led by the amphibious assault ship USS *Okinawa* and carrying some 1800 men, left the Pacific for the Indian Ocean for manoeuvres with Carrier Task Force 70 on station in the Arabian Sea. Since then similar Marine Task Forces have been rotated to the Arabian Sea to maintain a permanent presence there. The operation was a clear signal of America's determination to defend its interests in the Gulf region by military force if necessary.

Subsequent exercises have taken place in the United States – in the California desert (Gallant Eagle, March 1982) and in Nevada (Reforger series) – and in the Middle East (Bright Star series and Jade Tiger). The first Bright Star exercise in November 1980 involved the deployment of 1400 troops of the 101st Air Assault Division and of the 502nd Infantry (24th Division) in Egypt for joint training with the Egyptian armed forces. Bright Star 82 saw the deployment of 6500 US troops in Egypt, and units of Rangers and Special Forces to Somalia and Sudan, while 1000 Marines were landed in Oman.

Joint exercises in the Middle East with friendly local forces immeasurably increased the combat readiness of RDJTF troops, and ironed out many problems arising from the adaptation of US equipment to the harsh conditions associated with desert warfare, but the high visibility of such operations, while demonstrating the seriousness of the American commitment to the region, also increased political pressures on Arab governments cooperating with the Americans. US backing for Israel left pro-Western Arab governments involved in RDJTF exercises or providing the RDJTF with base facilities open to internal criticism as being tools of Israel's most powerful ally. This problem has led to attacks on the RDJTF concept from some of the European Nato countries, who regard it as a further destabilising influence upon an already troubled region.

Robin Corbett

Major forces available to the RDJTF

Units	Station
US Army	
(XVIII Airborne Corps)	
82nd Airborne Division	Fort Bragg
101st Air Assault Division	Fort Campbell
24th Infantry Division (Mechanised)	Fort Stewart
6th Air Cavalry Brigade	Fort Hood
9th Infantry Division	Fort Lewis
US Air Force	
(HQ 9th Air Force)	
Seven tactical fighter wings (TFW), including	
1st TFW (F-15 Eagles)	Langley AFB
27th TFW (F-111Ds)	Cannon AFB
49th TFW (F-15 Eagles)	Holloman AFB
347th TFW (F-4E Phantoms)	Moody AFB
354th TFW (A-10As)	Myrtle Beach AFB
366th TFW (F-111As)	Mountain Home AFB
Strategic Projection Force	
57th Air Division, SAC	Minot AFB
US Navy	
3 Carrier Battle Groups	including one on-station in Indian Ocean
1 Surface Action Group	
1 Amphibious Ready Group	
5 Squadrons (P-3 Orions)	
Near Team Prepositioning Force	Diego Garcia
US Marine Corps	
Marine Amphibious Forces, including	
1st Marine Division	Camp Pendleton
7th Marine Amphibious Brigade (NTPF)	Camp Pendleton
3rd Marine Aircraft Wing	MCAS El Toro
1st Force Service Support Group	Camp Pendleton
Joint Warfare Task Force	
Rangers and Special Forces	JFK Center (Fort Bragg)

Key Weapons

AIR-TO-AIR
MISSILES

From its origins in the last years of World War II, the air-launched missile has become a fundamental element in aerial combat. Originally seen as primarily an interceptor's weapon, the class has diversified so that today missiles are found in the air-to-air, air-to-surface, anti-shipping and anti-tank roles.

Current air-to-air missiles (AAMs) can be subdivided by their means of guidance: the two most commonly employed systems are infra-red (IR) and semi-active radar (SAR) homing. Infra-red missiles (also known as heat-seeking missiles) are equipped with a seeker unit sensitive to the IR radiation generated by a target's engine exhaust and airframe. The first generation of IR missiles was affected by poor seeker discrimination and might home onto the sun or any other intense heat source instead of the true target. The missiles were restricted to firing into the rear arc of an aeroplane where the IR radiation generated by the target's engine exhausts was strongest. Current IR weapons have been designed to overcome these limitations; their seeker units respond only to the pattern of IR wavelengths associated with aircraft, and their increased sensitivity enables them to be launched even from directly head-on to a target and still lock on to the radiations – this is known as all-aspect capability.

Missiles with SAR homing require a radar on the launching aircraft to illuminate the target with radio waves; they then locate the target using an internal radio receiver that generates steering commands. The SAR weapon has the advantage of an all-weather capability and can engage targets beyond visual range, but the need for the launching aircraft to have its radar locked-on to the target throughout the missile's flight limits the number of targets that can be engaged by one aeroplane. To surmount this problem, the newest generation of radar-guided missiles is provided with its own integral radar seeker: the launching aircraft directs the missile towards its target, but in the final stage the missile's own radar takes over.

One of the most widely used IR air-to-air missiles is the American AIM-9 Sidewinder. Developed by the US Naval Weapons Center at China Lake, California, the Sidewinder first entered service in May 1956 and by 1983 a staggering total of 158,000 AIM-9s had been produced in 13 separate versions. The initial models, the AIM-9A and AIM-9B, were primitive by today's standards because of the poor sensitivity of their seeker units. Such missiles were the first AAMs to be used in combat, during clashes between Nationalist Chinese F-86s and communist Chinese MiG-17s over the Formosa Strait during 1958.

The development of the Sidewinder may be seen in terms of generations, each of which has improved the missile's performance. Following on from the initial models, the second generation comprised the AIM-9D to the AIM-9J and introduced a number of technical improvements on the original design; this generation achieved its highest degree of sophistication in the AIM-9H which brought solid-state electronics to the seeker unit, double delta control surfaces that give improved manoeuvrability, and a limited all-weather capability. In 1977, the AIM-9L launched the third generation of the Sidewinder and probably represents the ultimate development of the type. The AIM-9L can be recognised by its pointed delta control surfaces and is the first all-aspect and all-weather member of the family. The type achieved considerable attention during the Falklands War

where it formed the primary armament of the Royal Navy's Sea Harriers and was responsible for the majority of the 25 kills credited to the aeroplane.

The AIM-7 Sparrow is the dominant SAR missile in the air forces of the United States and its allies. Starting life as Project Hot Shot in 1946, the missile entered service during 1956. The first model, known as the AAM-N-2 Sparrow I, used a 'beam riding' guidance system, following the radar beam locked-on to the target by the launch aeroplane's radar. Sparrow I only saw limited service and it was with the Sparrow III that the AIM-7 came into wide-scale use.

Sparrow III switched to SAR guidance and entered service as the AIM-7C during 1958; the main production variant has been the AIM-7E, some 25,000 of which have been built. The AIM-7E has seen considerable combat service, notably in Vietnam, but has proved to be far from the ideal missile. The Sparrow has been found to be unreliable and of less value in a

Previous page: An AIM-9J Sidewinder on the pylon of an F-5E belonging to a USAF 'Aggressor' squadron. Top: An AIM-9E is loaded onto an F-8C Crusader on an aircraft carrier off Vietnam in 1967. Above: This F-15 is carrying AIM-9Ls on its wingtips and AIM-7Fs under the fuselage.

Below: An F-15A of the 48th Fighter Interceptor Squadron fires its last AIM-7F. The AIM-7 Sparrow has not proved as successful as hoped in actual combat.

dogfight than the Sidewinder but despite its shortcomings it has been the subject of major development in both the UK and Europe.

In the UK, British Aerospace combined the AIM-7E airframe with a new monopulse seeker unit to produce a more effective weapon. Development of the 'UK Sparrow' began in 1969 and, as the Sky Flash, it entered service with the RAF during 1978. In American service the AIM-7E was superseded by the AIM-7F during 1977, but it was not until 1982 and the introduction of the AIM-7M that the US Air Force had a Sparrow which could match a Sky Flash.

The other important AAM to enter service during the 1950s, along with the Sparrow and Sidewinder, was the Hughes AIM-4 Falcon. It entered service in 1956 and was developed into eight versions, four of which employ SAR guidance and four IR. The basic design was further developed as the AIM-26 Super Falcon, two models of which were produced, the AIM-26A with nuclear warhead and the AIM-26B with a high explosive one. Both types were designed for the defence of the continental United States but the AIM-26B was also supplied to Sweden as the Rb27.

The Hughes AIM-54 Phoenix, which entered service in 1974 on the F-14As of the US Navy, began life in 1960 as a development of the Falcon. It is representative of the trend towards AAMs with greater range and less dependence on the launch aeroplane. In order to achieve the required range and independence, the Phoenix uses SAR guidance until it is within 20km (12.5 miles) of its target, when it switches to an on-board active radar for the remainder of the flight. When the AIM-54 is combined with the F-14A and its AN/AWG-9 fire-control system, it probably represents the most complex AAM system in service.

Some of America's Nato allies have produced their own AAMs. The first British AAM was the Firestreak, developed by de Havilland Propellers in conjunction with various official agencies. Entering service with the Royal Navy and the RAF in 1958, Firestreak carried a 23kg (50lb) warhead and used a relatively complicated IR system both for guidance and as a proximity fuze. During 1964, an improved Firestreak – Redtop – entered service combining an

Right top: A Swedish Draken interceptor with two Falcons under the wing and two Super Falcons under the fuselage (Swedish designations are Rb28 and Rb27, respectively). Right centre: An AIM-54C Phoenix fired by an F-14; together, the Phoenix and the Tomcat are a formidable combination.

Left: A Tornado ADV (Air Defence Variant) prototype carrying four Sky Flash missiles. Above: The Red Top missile will be phased out of service with the Lightning.

improved seeker with an even larger warhead and it will remain in RAF service until the complete withdrawal of the Lightning interceptor.

In 1975 the Matra R550 Magic IR missile entered service with the French Air Force. Magic began development in 1968 and two versions of the basic weapon have appeared, with the Mk2 incorporating an improved seeker and new rocket motor. The R550 saw action during the Falklands War with the Argentinian Air Force and is also in service with the Iraqi Air Force against the Iranians.

One of the newest missiles in service is the Matra Super R530, developed from the earlier R530 which proved unsatisfactory in service. The R530 could use either IR or SAR guidance, depending on the seeker unit installed, but the Super R530 is restricted to SAR guidance. The Super R530 is produced in two versions, the F and the D: the former entered service on the Mirage F1 in 1980 and the latter is scheduled for introduction on the Mirage 2000 in 1986. The R530 and the Super R530 have done well in the export market and the R530 has been used operationally by

Argentina, Iraq, Israel and Pakistan.

In a programme similar to the British Sky Flash, the Italian firm of Selenia Industrie Elettroniche Associate has developed a multi-role missile using SAR homing, the Aspide. Although the configuration is the same as that of the AIM-7, the Aspide features a new motor, a new seeker unit and reconfigured nose, and control surface geometry. The Aspide entered

Above: An Su-15 armed with AA-3 missiles; it was this combination of aircraft and missile that shot down flight KAL 007 of Korean Air Lines in 1983. Right: Two AA-6s mounted on the wing pylons of a Libyan MiG-25. Below: A MiG-21MF carrying AA-2 missiles on the outer wing pylons and AA-8 missiles on the inner wing pylons.

Right: A Mirage F1 carrying the R550 Magic on its wingtip and the Super R530F on its wing pylons.

Below: An R550 flies away from the Mirage 2000 that has launched it. Inset: An R530 mounted on a French Navy F-8E Crusader

service in 1978 and will replace the AIM-7 on the F-104S and possibly on the Tornado.

The Soviet Union introduced its first AAM in 1958; it was dubbed the AA-1 Alkali by Nato analysts. Development work on the missile probably began during 1950 and the mature weapon was used to arm both the MiG-17PFU and the MiG-19FM interceptors. There has been some disagreement over the type of guidance system used by the AA-1 but it is now generally believed to have used SAR or to have been a 'beam rider'; indeed, both systems may have been used as the weapon was developed in six separate models during its service life and it is common Soviet practice to employ different guidance systems in the same basic airframe. As far as is known, Alkali was withdrawn from frontline service in 1978 but it is believed to be still in use as a training round by the Soviet Air Force.

The second generation of Soviet AAMs entered service about 1961 and consisted of three types: the AA-2 Atoll, the AA-3 Anab and the AA-5 Ash. In its initial form the AA-2 was a straightforward copy of the American AIM-9B Sidewinder but it has followed its own path of development. Used primarily in the MiG-21, the Atoll has been built in very large numbers and produced in both IR and SAR forms. During

the early 1970s, Hindustan Aeronautics began producing IR models of the weapon under licence in India and there are also reports of a Chinese version. In 1967 a new variant was identified, known in the West as the AA-2-2 Advanced Atoll, part of a new generation of missiles using differently shaped and enlarged control surfaces; it also appears to have been developed in both IR and SAR forms. The Advanced Atoll is used on both late-model MiG-21s and a number of MiG-23 variants. As a whole, the AA-2 family is the most widely used Soviet AAM and examples of both generations are in service with the air forces of at least 29 countries.

The AA-3 Anab was the Soviet Union's first long-range, all-weather AAM and has been used on the Yak-28P, the Su-11 and the Su-15. Both IR and SAR versions have been developed, the SAR models using continuous wave target illumination generated by the Skip Spin fire-control system. A second generation Anab, the AA-3-2 Advanced Anab, was identified during 1972 and is still the primary armament of the 700 or so Su-15s which remain in service with the Soviet Air Defence Force.

The AA-5 Ash is a Soviet Air Defence Force-only weapon and is believed to have been developed specifically for use with the Tu-28P interceptor.

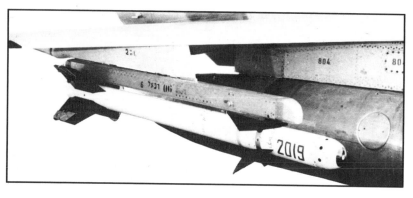

Above: The Shafrir's appearance demonstrates well its descent from the Sidewinder. Proven in combat, the Shafrir is fairly inexpensive in comparison with other missiles, costing only about $20,000. The Shafrir is carried on Israeli Mirages, Neshers (like this one) and Kfirs.

Initial Ash models used SAR guidance, employing the Tu-28's Big Nose radar for target illumination, but by 1965 an IR model was introduced to complement the radar weapons and both models remain in service. This very large AAM was used to arm the earliest models of the MiG-25 Foxbat as well as the Tu-28.

The Soviet AA-6 Acrid entered service during 1970 and like the AA-5 appears to have been designed exclusively for a single aircraft type, in this case the MiG-25. The Acrid has been produced in both IR and SAR forms and has been supplied to Libya and possibly Algeria as well. The Acrid is now being withdrawn in favour of the AA-7 on the newest MiG-25, the Foxbat-E. The AA-7 was developed between 1971 and 1974 and represents the third generation of Soviet AAM; it has been developed in both IR and SAR versions. The radar version has an unusual fixed external reception antenna array in place of the more usual internal scanner. The AA-7 is most frequently seen on the MiG-23 in Soviet and allied air forces.

The AA-8 Aphid entered service in 1976 as a replacement for the Atoll family. A very compact weapon, the Aphid appears to have been developed in both IR and SAR forms and has been carried by the MiG-21, the MiG-23 and the Yak-36MP.

Outside Nato and the Warsaw Pact, the major producer of indigenous designs is Israel whose Rafael Armament Development Authority produces the Shafrir and its successor, the Python. These IR AAMs have seen considerable operational service. The Shafrir, based on the design of the early Sidewinder, entered service in 1969 and the Israeli Air Force has claimed 200 kills with the missile. In 1982 a development of the Shafrir, the Python, was used operationally for the first time during the invasion of the Lebanon; this new weapon features a more sophisticated seeker and is an all-aspect weapon. Armscor of South Africa have developed the V3 Kukri which has a helmet-mounted sight to designate the target, while CTA Instituto de Atividades Espaciais of Brazil are developing the Piranha; both of the missiles are IR seekers.

Developments in AAMs in the 1980s are tending towards ever more sophisticated and complex missiles. Missile engineers are now aiming to produce missiles with either a 'fire and forget' capability or 'look-down shoot-down' capability and preferably both. Fire and forget missiles have pre-programmed inertial guidance for the initial stages of flight and an active radar for homing onto the target. Look-down shoot-down capability is provided by installing missiles with radars which discern the Doppler effect of an aeroplane at a lower altitude and also suppress static echoes from the ground. The AIM-54 Phoenix is a look-down missile as is the Sparrow replacement in development (the Hughes AIM-120A); the Soviets now have an operational look-down missile – the AA-9 – and are developing the AA-X-10; both of these could be used against cruise missiles. Also under development in the United States is the Vought ASAT (Anti-SATellite) which could be launched by an F-15 against enemy satellites. All these high-technology missiles seem very impressive, but during the Vietnam War the AIM-7 Sparrow had a kill rate of about 10 per cent, and the Falcon could only achieve seven per cent.

Nato air-to-air missiles

Type	Length	Speed	Range
AIM-9L Sidewinder	2.85m (112in)	Mach 2.5	17.7km (11 miles)
AIM-7E Sparrow	3.7m (144in)	Mach 4	44km (28 miles)
Sky Flash	3.7m (144in)	Mach 4	50km (31 miles)
AIM-4A Falcon	2m (78in)	Mach 2.8	8km (5 miles)
Firestreak	3.2m (125in)	Mach 3	8km (5 miles)
Red Top	3.3m (131in)	Mach 3.2	12km (7.5 miles)
AIM-54A Phoenix	4m (158in)	Mach 5	200km (124 miles)
R550 Magic	2.8m (109in)	Mach 3	10km (6 miles)
Aspide	3.7m (144in)	Mach 4	100km (62 miles)
Super R530	3.5m (139in)	Mach 4.6	35km (22 miles)

Soviet air-to-air missiles

Type	Length	Speed	Range
AA-1 Alkali	1.9m (74in)	Mach 1	8km (5 miles)
AA-2 Atoll (IR)	2.8m (110in)	Mach 2.5	6.5km (4 miles)
AA-2 Atoll (SAR)	2.9m (114in)	Mach 2.5	6.5km (4 miles)
AA-3 Anab (IR)	4.1m (161in)	Mach 2.5	19km (12 miles)
AA-3 Anab (SAR)	4m (158in)	Mach 2.5	24km (15 miles)
AA-5 Ash (IR)	5.5m (216in)	Mach 3	21km (13 miles)
AA-5 Ash (SAR)	5.2m (204in)	Mach 3	55km (35 miles)
AA-6 Acrid (IR)	6.3m (248in)	Mach 4	25km (16 miles)
AA-6 Acrid (SAR)	5.9m (232in)	Mach 4	80km (50 miles)
AA-7 Apex (SAR)	4.6m (181in)	Mach 3	40km (25 miles)
AA-8 Aphid (IR)	2.2m (85in)	Mach 3	5.5km (3.5 miles)

In the Bear's hug

Soviet influence in Afghanistan up to 1979

Backward and weak, Afghanistan was the cockpit of Anglo-Russian rivalries in Central Asia throughout the 19th century. Twice invaded by British troops, Afghanistan suffered the humiliation of having her foreign relations, such as they were, controlled by the British Viceroy of India from 1880 until 1920, when she was able to take advantage of the Bolshevik revolution and the consequent disruption of the balance of power in Asia to win back her independence.

Throughout the inter-war period, from the 1921 Russo-Afghan Treaty of Friendship onward, Kabul sought to preserve her independence by balancing the Soviet Union and Britain against each other. The post-World War II Cold War provided a particularly rewarding context for the continuation of this Afghan balancing act, with Kabul coaxing large amounts of economic aid from the American and Russian rivals. Exploiting the emergence of an unaligned group of newly independent Third World states during the 1950s to reinforce her own position, Afghanistan resisted American pressure to join the Baghdad Pact (Cento), even though Washington had made continued arms deliveries dependent upon a more pro-Western policy in Kabul.

In consequence, Afghanistan turned to the Soviet Union and Czechoslovakia for arms supplies. The government of General Mohammed Daoud Khan, a cousin of Afghanistan's King Zahir Shah, who had become prime minister and minister of defence after a military coup in 1953, signed a $25 million arms contract with the Kremlin in 1956. Daoud, who favoured a programme of economic development and less reliance upon the West, also negotiated a $100 million Soviet loan to finance Afghanistan's first Five-Year Plan, and in 1961 established military training programmes with the Soviet Union and Czechoslovakia. A border crisis with Pakistan led to the fall of Daoud in 1963, however, and in 1964 a new liberal constitution was introduced which provided for an elected parliament and a free press, both conditions which stimulated the formation of a number of new political parties.

Among these was the Marxist People's Democratic Party of Afghanistan (PDPA), founded on 1 January 1965 under the leadership of Noor Mohammed Taraki, a self-educated intellectual from a nomad family who had become a communist during the 1930s while working as a clerk in Bombay. The PDPA temporarily united a number of left-wing groups, but split in July 1967 as bitter rivalry developed between Taraki and the younger Babrak Karmal, a student leader.

While Taraki bragged of his humble origins, Karmal was the son of a general, and had connections with the Afghan royal family. There was also an element of ethnic conflict behind the split – the Taraki faction, named after the PDPA newspaper *Khalq (The People)*, was essentially Pushtun, while Karmal's supporters, named after another newspaper, *Parcham (Banner)*, tended to come from the Tajik and other

Above: A Soviet soldier stands guard over traffic on a mountain road in Afghanistan. The weakness of the pro-Moscow regime in Kabul, and its inability to contain the Mujahidin insurgency which had already seized control of large areas of the Afghan countryside, convinced the Soviet Union that direct intervention was vital to prevent the emergence of a hostile, pro-Western government on its southern border.

non-Pushtun ethnic groups. More fundamentally, Karmal rejected Taraki's uncompromising radicalism, and favoured a gradualist approach to the problem of revolution in backward Afghanistan.

The late 1960s and early 1970s saw the rapid destabilisation of parliamentary government in Afghanistan. On 17 July 1973 Daoud seized power in a coup carried out largely by young Soviet-trained officers and supported by the Parcham group. He declared Afghanistan a republic and became the country's first president; the fact that he was himself a member of the royal family tended to blunt royalist opposition. At first, the Daoud regime appeared innovative and reforming; a number of Parchami ministers were appointed and land-reform was instituted. Soon, however, Daoud packed off his left-wing supporters to the provinces and began to move towards a more conservative and dictatorial regime. In July 1975 freedom of the press was suppressed, and with it all opportunity for open political dissent. Disenchanted with their former ally, the Parchamis reunited with the Khalq faction in July 1977.

A fragile alliance

The reconstituted PDPA remained a fragile alliance of two distinct factions, however. As preparations for a left-wing coup advanced during the winter of 1977-78, Hafizullah Amin, a former school-teacher who had become a Marxist while studying in the United States in 1958, was entrusted with the establishment of an underground organisation within the armed forces, but he ensured that the officers he recruited would be loyal to his own Khalq faction.

There were political assassinations and rumours of plots throughout the latter half of 1977, and on 17 April 1978 Mir Akbar Khyber, a leading Parchami theoretician and writer, was assassinated in Kabul. Though the killers were never identified, the PDPA was quick to blame the CIA, and Akbar's funeral two days later was transformed into an angry demonstration outside the US embassy.

Daoud was alarmed by these protests, and sought to decapitate the Parcham and Khalq groups by arresting their leaders during the night of 26 April. But Amin, who had already laid plans for a coup, had

Mohammed Daoud Khan (above left) was killed along with most of his family when the Marxist People's Democratic Party, led by Noor Mohammed Taraki (above right), overthrew his government during the Saur revolution of April 1978. Taraki's Khalq faction soon dominated the government and armed forces, but real power gradually fell into the hands of Hafizullah Amin (above), who had Taraki arrested and murdered in the autumn of 1979. The overthrow of Taraki probably decided the Kremlin to put into operation its plan for military intervention in Afghanistan.

Right: Soviet military advisers sight-seeing in Kabul. Even under Daoud, the Afghan armed forces had been trained and equipped by Moscow, but after the 1978 revolution, the Soviet presence increased dramatically. Opposite: Supporters of the Marxist government carrying portraits of Taraki demonstrate in Kabul.

time before his own arrest to give the order for the secret members of the PDPA within the armed forces to move into action. The coup itself, which began at 0600 hours on 27 April 1978, was led by Colonel Abdul Qader, deputy commander-in-chief of the Afghan Air Force, and met only brief, if fierce, resistance from units loyal to Daoud. The president was killed, along with at least 17 members of his family and a number of senior officers and ministers, when the presidential palace was stormed by armoured units led by Khalqi officers.

The PDPA leaders, released from prison, were soon in control of the Saur revolution, as it was called, and dominated the Revolutionary Council which constituted the government of the Democratic Republic of Afghanistan proclaimed on 30 April. While the PDPA moved swiftly to purge the administration of suspected opponents, and began to place its own members in the most important positions within the ministries and armed forces, rivalry between the Parcham and Khalq factions soon resurfaced.

Though Karmal and Amin were both deputy prime ministers in a government headed by Taraki, the Khalqis were far stronger within the armed forces. As disagreements over the pace of political and social change became more open, the first arrests of Parchamis took place during June 1978, signalling the end of the Parcham/Khalq coalition. On 5 July, Karmal and a number of his supporters were demoted, and sent into virtual exile as ambassadors in Eastern Europe. There they remained under the protection of the Soviet Union, which was evidently critical of the Khalq radicalism that was rapidly alienating all support within Afghanistan.

After the fall of the Parchamis, the Khalq-dominated government pushed ahead with a number of radical and widely unpopular reforms, which were imposed on the reluctant countryside by Khalqi militants backed by squads of soldiers. Usury was banned in order to lift the crippling burden of debt borne by large numbers of poor peasants, but no alternative source of credit was provided. The peasants were unable to buy seed and tools, business confidence was undermined, and a fall in investment created an economic slump and unemployment. An attempt to regulate marriage, reducing the traditional bridal price to a token sum and setting minimum ages for marriage, proved totally unenforceable in the backward and suspicious countryside. A decree published in November sought to break up all large landholdings in an attempt to mobilise the rural poor behind the Saur revolution, but in a country where approximately 60 per cent of land was cultivated by its owners the reform merely provoked resistance.

Out of control

By mid-1978 there were already several opposition groups based among the growing number of Afghan refugees in Pakistan. In Afghanistan itself, locally based armed opposition sprang up throughout the country, and by the spring of 1979 large areas were beyond government control. Insurgency spread to the cities in March 1979, when a demonstration of armed peasants escalated into a general uprising in the town of Herat. The rising was joined by elements of the Herat garrison and was only crushed after the deployment of large numbers of tanks, helicopter gunships and Ilyushin-28 bombers, which pounded the city into submission, at the cost of over 5000 casualties. The insurgents had themselves massacred several hundred Khalqi officers and officials, and tortured to death some 50 Soviet advisers and their families.

Resistance spread to Kabul when a popular rising broke out in the city's Shi'ia quarter on 23 June. Crushed by the Khalq-dominated garrison, the rising led to mass arrests of Shi'ites and other suspects. A more serious event occurred on 5 August, when commando and tank units mutinied at the Bala Hissar fort in Kabul in a suicidal attempt to arrest the government. Loyal troops from the Pal-e-Charkli

barracks smashed the rebels with helicopter gunships and tanks, killing over 400.

As the situation deteriorated Taraki rapidly lost influence to the more ruthless Amin, who took over as prime minister and minister of defence in a cabinet reshuffle in July 1979. The conflict between Taraki and Amin climaxed in a bloody shootout in the presidential palace on 16 September, after which Taraki disappeared. It was first announced that he had retired from the presidency for health reasons, and later, on 6 October, that he had died. It was widely rumoured in Kabul, however, that Taraki had been arrested and strangled on Amin's orders.

Though Amin sought to lay the blame for earlier excesses at the door of Taraki, and some conciliatory gestures were made to opposition opinion, the Kabul regime was by now totally isolated, and depended for its existence upon the massive Soviet military and economic aid that was pouring into the country. However, although Moscow continued to provide Amin with military equipment, advisers down to company level in the Afghan Army, and a contingent of combat troops who may have taken part in operations against rebel forces, it is probable that preparations for intervention began as early as March 1979.

Western experts suggest that the high-level Soviet military mission which toured Afghanistan in the wake of the Herat rising drew up an operational plan for a possible intervention under cover of a detailed survey of the military assistance required by the Afghan armed forces to counter the mounting rebellion. The threat of growing instability in the Gulf region in the wake of the Iranian revolution, coupled with the possible spread of militant Islamic fundamentalism through Afghanistan into the Muslim Central Asian republics of the Soviet Union itself, sharpened the Kremlin's perceptions of a security threat on its southern flank. The evident inability of the Kabul regime to stabilise the situation led to the preparation of contingency plans, but it was almost certainly the overthrow of Taraki which finally decided the Soviet Union to intervene. By early December the wheels had already been set in motion.

Robin Corbett

Above: Mujahidin rebels at prayer. The radical Marxism of the post-1978 government offended many of Afghanistan's traditionalist tribesmen. Poorly armed and unorganised, the Mujahidin nevertheless forced the Afghan Army onto the defensive and dominated much of the countryside.

Below: Afghan Army soldiers advancing into a Mujahidin-held area. Although well-equipped, the government troops lacked initiative and morale was low. Many deserted to the rebels, and the government was unable to enforce conscription in the hostile countryside.

Takeover

The Soviet invasion of Afghanistan

In October 1979, the head of Soviet Ground Forces, General Ivan Pavlovsky, and a team of 60 senior Soviet commanders visited Afghanistan to conduct a thorough tour of inspection of the war against the anti-government guerrillas in which the Afghan Army was being extensively supported by Soviet advisers. It now appears, however, that this mission was at least partly used as cover for a detailed reconnaissance in preparation for a possible Soviet military intervention.

Military intervention was not the Soviet Union's favourite option as a response to the Afghan crisis. The Soviet leaders were determined to ensure the continued existence of a pro-Soviet regime in Kabul and restore government control over the country, but they thought these goals could be achieved by the Afghan Army if the unpopular Prime Minister Hafizullah Amin could be replaced. Their hopes of establishing a more moderate government capable of winning back popular support collapsed, however, in September 1979 when President Noor Mohammed Taraki, on whom they were counting, was killed by Amin.

The Soviet Union had provided the Afghan Army with massive military aid to counter anti-government guerrillas; now they were forced to become more deeply involved. Two goals existed for intervention: to replace Amin by a ruler more acceptable both to the Russians themselves and hopefully to the Afghans, and to repress the anti-government rebellion by an effective use of military force. By November a forward headquarters had been established at the 40th Army HQ at Termez on the Afghan-Soviet border, under Marshal Sergei L. Sokolov, Soviet first deputy minister of defence. It was complete with a satellite communications station which maintained a direct link with the ministry of defence in Moscow.

The final decision to intervene was almost certainly taken at the 26 November meeting of the Soviet Politburo. Three days later, units of the elite 105th Guards Airborne Division began to arrive at Ferghana in the Soviet Central Asian republic of Uzbekistan, and by 6 December there were already three battalions concentrated there.

Meanwhile, Moscow still attempted to persuade Amin to cooperate in his own downfall. On 29 November Lieutenant-General Viktor Paputin flew to Kabul for talks with Amin, presumably in an effort to induce him to stand down in favour of the Soviet candidate for head of the Afghan government, Babrak Karmal (at that time living in exile under Soviet protection), or possibly to secure his agreement to

invite Soviet troops into Afghanistan, under the terms of the Soviet-Afghan Treaty of Friendship signed in December 1978. Evidently, Amin refused to cooperate, and his refusal sealed his fate. By 10 December the Soviet Union had moved a 600-strong armoured unit to their forward position at Ferghana, and between 11 and 15 December a large force of transport aircraft was concentrated around Moscow and in Central Asia. Combat aircraft were moved to positions along the Afghan border and the 103rd Airborne Division based at Vitebsk, Byelorussia, and the 104th at Kirovabad, Azerbaijan, were placed on alert. Western diplomats reported sighting elements of a Soviet combat battalion in Kabul for the first time on 12 December, and the US State Department issued a warning to Moscow against any interference in Afghan affairs.

By mid-December, the call-up of reservists in the Military Districts bordering Afghanistan was in full swing. The forces earmarked for the operation were drawn mainly from units stationed in the Central Asian and Turkestan Military Districts, and though these units were initially far below combat strength, their mobilisation was rapid. In less than two weeks,

Top: Soviet leader Leonid Brezhnev with his Afghan protégé Babrak Karmal. Moscow hoped to defuse the crisis in Afghanistan by installing the moderate Karmal in place of the dangerously independent radical Amin. Above centre: Soviet troops patrol Kabul in a BMP APC. Above: The overall commander of the operation to take over Afghanistan, Marshal Sergei L. Sokolov.

an estimated 100,000 troops from several motor rifle divisions, along with their full complements of armour and artillery were concentrated at two key crossing points along the border.

On 20 December, the armoured unit based at Ferghana moved south to secure the strategic Salang Tunnel, north of Kabul, through which the bulk of Soviet supplies to the Afghan regime passed, and through which the main Soviet forces assigned to the invasion would have to advance. But full-scale intervention came only after the completion of the Soviet logistical build-up at base areas along the Afghan border on 23 December.

At 2300 hours on 24 December, units of the Soviet 105th Airborne Division began to land at Kabul airport where they established a bridgehead. At the same time, Soviet troops began to fly into the airbase on the outskirts of Kabul at Bagram which was already virtually under the control of Soviet troops and advisers stationed there. They also flew into bases at Shindand, 100km (65 miles) south of Herat, and at Kandahar, in southern Afghanistan. Over the next two days, an almost continuous airlift, carried out by

some 400 military transports and Aeroflot planes, brought the number of Soviet combat troops in Kabul to approximately 5000.

In addition, there were already some 1500 Soviet military advisers in the Afghan capital, who persuaded many Afghan units to which they were attached that the Soviet build-up was part of a large-scale exercise, for which they issued blank ammunition, effectively disarming much potential opposition. Afghan armoured units were immobilised by being recalled for servicing, or by having their batteries removed. These measures clearly show that the Soviets were aware of the probable strength of anti-Russian feeling in the Afghan armed forces, but at the same time the Soviet Union was supporting the Afghan Army in its war against the Islamic guerrillas and therefore the arrival of Soviet troops at various locations occasioned little surprise.

At 1900 hours on 27 December Soviet troops in Kabul went into action to take control of the political situation. Key points were seized, including the Afghan ministry of the interior, which housed the headquarters of Amin's much-feared secret police, the central telephone exchange and the Makroyan housing district, which was allotted to Soviet advisers. A column of BMD armoured personnel carriers (APCs) from Bagram, supported by ASU-85 assault guns, surrounded the Darulaman Palace on the southern edge of Kabul, where Amin was defended by an Afghan tank regiment.

Below: A Soviet Antonov An-22 transport aircraft being unloaded at Kabul airport. Following the December 1979 invasion Soviet garrisons were established in all the major Afghan cities, and large amounts of equipment were flown in as the Soviet Army attempted to prop up the unpopular Kabul regime.

The events that followed at the palace remain disputed. It would appear that Lieutenant-General Paputin made a further attempt to persuade Amin to resign or to justify the Soviet invasion by issuing a request for military intervention, and that during heated discussions one of Amin's bodyguards shot Paputin dead. What is certain is that the palace was stormed by Soviet paratroopers and in the ensuing gunfight Amin was killed. This was a profound embarrassment to Moscow, since it made a mockery of their claim to be acting in support of the Afghan government.

By 2300 hours on 28 December the centre of Kabul was firmly under Soviet control. It was announced that Babrak Karmal had been 'elected' secretary-general of the People's Democratic Party of Afghanistan (PDPA) and would head an 11-man Revolutionary Council in place of the 'traitor' Amin, who was now accused of having been an agent of the CIA, and of having prepared a massacre of Soviet personnel in Kabul to be linked to an appeal for Western intervention. In the light of continuing guerrilla activity, Karmal requested Moscow to render urgent political, moral, military and economic assistance. The new regime pledged to honour the Muslim faith and to bring the 'executioners' of Amin's secret police, who were alleged to have murdered some 25,000 Afghans, to trial.

As units of the 105th Division tightened their grip on Kabul by closing its international airport and severing telephone links with the outside world, a further four Soviet divisions crossed the country's northern border. The 66th and 357th Motor Rifle Divisions based at Kushka moved on the provincial capitals of Herat and Kandahar in the northwest and south of Afghanistan. Two others, the 201st and 360th, advanced over the kilometre-wide Amu Darya (Oxus River) south of Termez by pontoon bridge. Their role was to link up with elements of the 105th Division pushing north from Bagram towards the Salang Tunnel. Both columns were accompanied by BTR-60 APCs, T54 and T62 tanks and artillery. Air cover was provided by MiG-23 fighter-bombers.

Opposition to the invasion forces was, for the most part, insignificant. Although there were reports of Afghan units at Beshkar and Qargah military bases near Kabul refusing to obey Soviet advisers and of the 8th Division putting up a stiff resistance, estimates of 2000 casualties were probably exaggerated. However, in the following months up to 50 per cent of the army, some 40,000 men, are believed to have deserted. Although the majority fled to the security of their native villages, many joined the guerrillas.

The occupation of several provincial capitals was followed by a period of consolidation involving the arrival of more troops and the building of armed camps. The presence of the 16th and 54th Motorised Rifle Divisions brought the number of troops in the country up to 80,000. Tajbek Palace on the outskirts of Kabul became the headquarters of the 40th Army. Having insufficient troops to assure complete control of Afghanistan, the Soviets attempted to dominate urban areas and protect their lines of communication. Divisional headquarters were established along the circuit of main roads that linked Kabul, Herat and Kandahar. The 357th Division was based in Kabul.

Inset: A column of Afghan Army T62 tanks mounted on transporters. Soviet strategy was to maintain control of the main Afghan towns and roads, while employing Afghan forces for the bulk of counter-insurgency operations. Re-equipped and reorganised, the Afghan Army nevertheless remained of doubtful military value.

with elements in Herat; the 360th in both Kandahar and Herat; and the 16th in the northeast town of Kunduz. The 66th and 105th Divisions were also stationed in Herat, but detached units held Jalalabad and Shindand.

Large bases, usually built around military airfields, were set up outside provincial capitals, while outposts of battalion or company strength protected strategic towns, such as Doshi in the northeast, or key bridges and tunnels. The Soviets concentrated their efforts at the Salang Pass, where a 3km (5 mile) long tunnel – the main supply route to the USSR – was recognised as being particularly vulnerable to guerrilla attack.

In the first few weeks after the invasion the Soviet command tried to minimise its casualties and maintain a low profile by using the Afghan Army against the Mujahidin. Most Soviet units stayed in their barracks and only emerged at night to patrol urban areas. However, by February 1980 wholesale desertions and ill-discipline in the Afghan Army forced an escalation in the Soviet role. On the 25th, as a precursor to the relegation of the Afghan Army to garrison duties, both armies were placed under a unified command. The arrival of BM-21 rocket launchers and armoured Hind Mi-24 helicopter gunships, as the weather improved for both ground and air activity, heralded the start of a major spring offensive. In preparation for their use a large logistical base was under construction at Pol-e-Khomri, 160km (100 miles) north of Kabul. Helicopter facilities at Ghazni, Jalalabad and in the capital were also expanded, and a draft of all eligible male Afghans over 21 was designed to free Soviet troops from garrison duties.

Hounding the guerrillas

By March, elements of both armies were actively engaged against the guerrillas in three key areas: around Herat, near the border with Iran in the west; in the eastern provinces of Nangarhar, Paktia and Nuristan adjacent to Pakistan; and in the central Hazarajat region. All were well-established centres of resistance and, being mountainous with easy access to towns and roads, particularly suited to guerrilla operations. The offensive had two aims: first, the Mujahidin were to be pushed out of strategic valleys, such as the Panjsher and Kunar, from which many of their attacks were made, thus denying them the food and shelter afforded by local villages. Secondly, Afghanistan's borders with its Muslim neighbours were to be patrolled to prevent the influx of supplies.

From 29 February until the beginning of June, the Soviets concentrated their efforts in the southern province of Nangarhar. A series of offensives were launched from Jalalabad and the garrison towns of Chaga-Sarei, Baricot and Asmar lying along the Kabul-Pakistan highway, against guerrilla strongholds in the Peck and Kunar valleys. Tanks and APCs, supported by artillery, moved along the valley floors as helicopters strafed and MiG-23s napalmed suspected rebel positions. Although the valleys were temporarily cleared and several villages destroyed, the slow-moving army units were never able to deliver a knock-out blow. The guerrillas melted away into the mountains to prepare for further attacks.

The arrival of a large number of tribesmen in the mountains around Kabul during the first week of June forced the Soviets to switch their attention to the countryside immediately surrounding the capital. To provide supplies the Soviet transport command flew

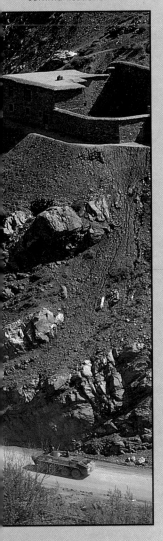

Left: A Soviet APC, destroyed in a mountain ambush. Below: Afghan and Soviet army convoys such as this one in the Salang Pass were extremely vulnerable to Mujahidin attacks. Soviet losses were often heavy, and large-scale operations were mounted to destroy rebel units which threatened Soviet communications.

Left: Mujahidin fire on government troops during a battle in the Afghan mountains. The Soviet intervention greatly increased support for the guerrillas, both within Afghanistan and internationally. The Mujahidin received arms and finance from Egypt, China and the USA, and were able to strengthen their control of the rural areas.

12 sorties a day into Bagram, and on 3 June a column of 200 armoured vehicles manned by Soviet and Afghan soldiers launched a three-day attack in the Kah Danan area. A week later the battle switched to the mountains running from the town of Pagman, 20km (12 miles) west of Kabul, to Carikar, 50km (30 miles) to the north. About 1000 rebels were killed and 200 wounded as troops recaptured Pagman, Chari-e-Kari and Kalantar.

The direct use of Soviet troops highlighted major weaknesses in the training of the Soviet Army. Mountain warfare against an elusive foe required close air support, good reconnaissance and a stamina that many units were unable to provide. Some 40 per cent of the invasion force, drawn from the Turkestan and Central Asian Military Districts, were of Muslim origin. Their reliability was questionable and reports of fraternisation with Afghans caused concern amongst senior commanders. The much-publicised withdrawal of 5000 men in June 1980 appears to have been an attempt to give the occupation force a more reliable ethnic mix. There were also shortcomings in the Soviet command structure. The need for independent action by small groups placed a burden on junior officers and senior NCOs that their training made them ill-prepared to meet.

Ill-equipped for counter-insurgency

Much of the equipment used in conventional warfare by motorised divisions proved unsuitable for counter-insurgency operations. Soviet tanks and APCs were prone to mechanical failure in harsh winter conditions; anti-aircraft batteries were established at air-bases and convoys provided with ZSU-23 automatic AA cannon though there was virtually no danger of air attack. It seems that Soviet operational planners failed initially to make sufficient allowance for the particular needs of troops fighting a guerrilla war, and that until the disintegration of the Afghan Army they may have hoped that it, rather than the Soviet Army, would bear the brunt of the fighting.

Afghan resistance to the occupying forces relied on traditional hit-and-run operations, with the guerrillas periodically moving out of their mountain positions to attack isolated outposts or convoys. The Hazarajat region, virtually inaccessible to ground forces and occupying a central position within the country's road network, contained many prime ambush sites. On 31 May, for example, a convoy on the road between Herat and Kandahar was hit. One fuel tanker was destroyed and 70 personnel captured. Other areas also provided fruitful hunting grounds. One part of the road from Kabul to the Salang Tunnel was so dangerous that it was dubbed 'death mile'.

Wherever attacks on convoys took place they followed a similar pattern: in mountainous areas avalanches were started to block the road whilst elsewhere bridges were blown or mines laid, and as Soviet troops left the protection of their APCs they were subjected to fire from the surrounding hillsides. Before any response could be organised the guerrillas melted away. At night rebels wore down the morale of troops stationed in isolated outposts by constant sniping attacks. In towns, PDPA officials were killed and their offices ransacked, and isolated soldiers on patrol were frequently stoned or knifed to death. Other incidents were more spectacular: at the end of May three Russian soldiers were killed in a grenade attack on the Makroyan housing complex in Kabul.

Although security was particularly tight in urban areas and an 11pm curfew cleared the streets, opposition was not stifled. Nightly, cries of *Allah-u-Akbar* (God is Great) echoed defiance, and crudely written *shabnama* or night letters, posted up at street corners, urged unrest. A call for a general strike to begin on 21 February was answered solidly by the shopkeepers of Kabul's Old Bazaar. The next day saw mass demonstrations and attacks on police stations. Martial law was imposed and Soviet troops sealed off the Russian embassy before attempting to restore order. Mass arrests followed and up to 300 civilians were killed in street battles. During the second anniversary of the 1978 April Revolution, anti-government demonstrations led by schoolgirls were bloodily suppressed by the Afghan Army. In-fighting between the Khalq and the ruling Parcham factions of the PDPA was claiming 10 lives a day by June.

The effectiveness of Afghan resistance was also seriously undermined by the lack of coordination between rival factions. The need for a well-organised military structure and commanders with the ability or prestige to provide leadership was at a premium. Yet long-standing tribal animosities and the tribesmen's fiercely guarded individuality worked against them, and their lack of discipline was often their undoing. In their desire for loot and weapons they often stayed too long at the scene of a successful ambush and fell prey to marauding helicopter gunships. Perhaps the Mujahidin's most serious weakness was the shortage of modern weapons. Many relied on 100-year-old muskets and the accurate, but outdated, British Lee Enfield rifle. Soviet assault rifles taken from deserters or captured from convoys augmented their firepower, but ammunition remained in short supply. The Soviet use of helicopters from the spring of 1980 highlighted the rebels' lack of heavy weapons.

In retrospect, it appears that the Soviet military had three operational priorities during the period immediately after the Afghanistan invasion: the protection of PDPA officials, the control of key urban areas and the destruction of guerrilla forces in the field. By June 1980 Moscow could realistically claim only partial success. Members of both the Parcham and Khalq parties remained guerrilla targets; the security of many urban areas could only be assured in daylight; and the Mujahidin, though suffering heavy casualties during the spring offensive, were far from destroyed as a fighting force. For their part, the rebels were too weak to force a Soviet withdrawal, and though they had caused an estimated 8000 Soviet casualties by June, their successes, often daring and spectacular, were isolated. Six months after the landings at Bagram both sides were faced with a stalemate that neither could resolve without escalating the war.

The chief damage to the Soviet Union resulting from their military action was not any casualties or equipment losses the Mujahidin could inflict, but the disastrous diplomatic consequences of the invasion. Moscow had hoped to pass off the action as military support to an ally against an armed rebellion – a relatively respectable activity for a superpower. But instead world opinion perceived the event as a naked example of military aggression and expansionism. Both the process of detente with the West and the Soviet Union's image in the Third World suffered as a consequence. A prolonged guerrilla war was not to improve the Soviets' diplomatic standing in the years ahead. **Ian Westwell**

The Cold War ho

The decline in superpower relations, 1975-84

The Soviet intervention in Afghanistan in December 1979 marked for many observers the point at which the process of detente between the Soviet Union and the United States finally collapsed into a new Cold War. But although it became a constant target for anti-Soviet rhetoric, the Afghanistan invasion was only one element in a general pattern of worsening superpower relations – indeed, had relations not already deteriorated, the Soviet action would not have provoked such an uproar of protest in the West.

Detente had begun to falter in 1974. While US Secretary of State Henry Kissinger hoped that American willingness to negotiate with the Soviet Union on strategic weapons, trade and other issues would encourage Soviet abstention from interference in Third World disputes, the Soviet Union rejected any linkage between the two. Moscow insisted on supporting her Third World allies. She noted that the United States continued to strengthen her relations with Iran and suspected that Washington had supported the

overthrow of Allende's Popular Unity Government in Chile in 1973.

The prolonged Watergate scandal, which culminated in Nixon's resignation in August 1974, was bound to create doubts in Moscow as to the reliability and coherence of US foreign policy. Kissinger had managed to distance himself and the State Department from involvement in Nixon's predicament, and when Nixon's successor, Gerald R. Ford, confirmed Kissinger as his secretary of state, he ensured that there would be continuity in the conduct of US foreign relations. But detente suffered further set-backs in 1975 when the defeat of South Vietnam by the North Vietnamese Army was attributed in the United States to the generous Soviet provision of military aid to Hanoi – Kissinger complained bitterly that 'we shall not forget who supplied the arms which allowed North Vietnam to make a mockery of its signature on the Paris Agreements'. When civil war broke out in Angola in 1975 following the departure of the Portu-

Above left: President Ronald Reagan addressing US troops during a visit to South Korea in April 1984. The election of President Reagan in 1980 coincided with a serious deterioration in East-West relations.

1978

s up

Above: A Soviet mechanised unit advancing during exercises in Eastern Europe. The onset of a new Cold War in the late 1970s revived Western fears of Soviet conventional military superiority in Europe.

guese, the Soviets supplied arms to the left-wing Movimento Popular de Libertação de Angola (MPLA), while Cuba despatched troops to assist the MPLA in their struggle against pro-Western guerrillas and the South Africans. The pro-Western forces were deprived of American support when Congress, fearing involvement in another Vietnam, cut off all US aid to them.

These events did not, however, spell the end of detente. In November 1974 at Vladivostock, the United States and the Soviet Union continued the SALT negotiating process when they agreed in principle to a maximum of 2400 Inter-Continental Ballistic Missiles (ICBMs), Sea-Launched Ballistic Missiles (SLBMs) and long-range bombers each. Of the missiles 1320 could have Multiple Independently-Targetable Re-Entry Vehicles (MIRVs). However, SALT soon encountered criticism in the United States when ex-Governor Ronald Reagan of California, a contender for the 1976 Republican presidential nomination, attacked the entire SALT process as a means whereby the Soviet Union had been allowed to catch up with, and even overtake, the United States in missile production and deployment. He and his supporters described current satellite verification procedures as inadequate to prevent the Soviet Union from cheating over the number of MIRVs it possessed in its arsenals, pointed to the massive Warsaw Pact superiority over Nato in conventional arms as evidence of the aggressive nature of Soviet policy, and loudly condemned Soviet intervention in the Third World. Not only did Kissinger prohibit the use of the word 'detente' in official communications, but Ford decided to suspend further negotiations with the Soviet Union over SALT II until after the elections, so great was the outcry within his own party.

An administration divided

The election of Jimmy Carter as Democratic president in November 1976 led to a further period of delay and confusion as Carter and his new team worked out their policy towards the Soviet Union. Carter had been elected on a platform which had promised a return to the traditional theme of liberal morality in US dealings with the outside world – a concern for human rights, the Third World and a reduction in the arms trade – which he contrasted to the cynical and immoral policy of Kissinger. The new president also promised that he would personally oversee the conduct of US foreign relations, unlike Ford, who had tended to leave foreign policy to Kissinger. However, Carter's two principal advisers were bitterly divided in their approaches to foreign policy. Cyrus Vance, the secretary of state, represented the more liberal wing of Carter's foreign policy team, while National Security Advisor Zbigniew Brzezinski was a hardliner who distrusted the Soviet Union. Their conflicting advice and Carter's seeming inability to make a decisive choice between them gave rise to an impression of confusion and incoherence within the administration which baffled both allies and foes alike. Moscow's suspicions were kindled at the outset when, in March, Cyrus Vance arrived in Moscow with a new SALT II package which proposed deeper cuts in strategic weapons than had been proposed at Vladivostok while at the same time insisting that European theatre nuclear weapons, which the Soviets had demanded should be included in SALT II, should not be discussed. The Soviet Union was outraged by this

public demonstration of American inconsistency and made a firm stand for the figures agreed upon at Vladivostock to be honoured. Carter reluctantly gave way, leading the Soviet rulers to conclude that the new president was a lightweight figure who could not be taken seriously as a negotiator and who was unlikely to adhere to his stated positions for very long.

The Soviets were further angered by public attacks by Carter and other US officials on their civil rights record. In 1978 Carter abandoned this stance as counter-productive, and began to suggest that he had not intended any linkage between human rights and SALT II, but much damage and ill-will had been created by that time in East-West relations. While negotiations for SALT II had recommenced in Geneva in October 1977, these soon became entangled in a long controversy as to whether a new generation of weapons being developed by the United States – the mobile MX ICBM, the B-1 bomber, cruise missiles and the neutron bomb – should be included in the agreement. The United States countered by pointing out that the Soviet Union was developing new ICBMs and a new long-range bomber. When in 1978 Carter cancelled the highly expensive B-1 and postponed the production of the neutron bomb (although research on both weapons continued), he anticipated some counter-concession from Moscow, but none was forthcoming.

Aid and intervention

Relations between the two superpowers also deteriorated in Africa. A new area of hostility opened in 1978 when the Soviets provided arms and Cuban troops to assist Ethiopia in her war with Somalia over the disputed Ethiopian province of Ogaden. Carter had cut off US aid to Addis Ababa in protest at the regime's appalling human rights record and it seemed to his critics that the Soviet Union had taken advantage of this gesture in order to install herself in the strategically important Horn of Africa. The growing anti-Soviet hysteria in the United States was fed by the seizure of power by a communist government in Afghanistan in April 1978 which seemed to portend a Soviet forward move in Central Asia. Thus while a SALT II agreement was hammered out by the two superpowers in June 1979, broadly on the lines agreed to in the Vladivostock accords, and without the inclusion of theatre nuclear weapons in Europe, it was much too late: Carter decided against submitting it to Congress for approval since the intensity of anti-Soviet hostility there made its rejection certain.

Carter suffered a further blow in January 1979 when a popular revolt overthrew the Shah of Iran, one of the most loyal supporters of the United States in the Gulf, and set up an Islamic fundamentalist government which proceeded to demonstrate its anti-American credentials by seizing the personnel of the American embassy in Tehran and defying all Carter's verbal and military efforts to secure their release until January 1981, when they were freed in return for a large ransom. The despatch of Red Army forces to Kabul in December 1979, although designed to sustain a communist regime already in power, elicited the most vigorous US protests. It directly resulted in a US boycott of the Olympic Games in Moscow in 1980 which deeply offended the Soviet Union.

Apparently threatened by Soviet expansionism and Muslim fanaticism, the United States' position in the Third World seemed to be extremely precarious,

Left: President Jimmy Carter meeting Soviet leader Leonid Brezhnev in June 1979 for the signing of the Salt II Treaty in Vienna. US-Soviet relations were already strained, however, and the treaty was never ratified by the US Senate.

despite, or perhaps because of, Carter's well-meaning efforts to improve relations with the more progressive elements in Third World societies. Under these pressures after 1978, Carter's policy had begun to shift away from its earlier, more liberal, attributes and Brzezinski's influence in the administration had increased. Defence expenditure rose – a rapid deployment force was set up which could be despatched to the Persian Gulf in any emergency affecting oil supplies and more money was invested in outer-space anti-satellite weapons. Yet Carter's increasingly hard line towards the Soviet Union came too late to enable him to escape from his image in the eyes of many Americans as a weak and vacillating president. Reagan, Republican presidential candidate in 1980, found a ready response from many electors when he depicted Carter as a president who had allowed the Soviet Union to steal a march on the West in the Third World and whose reluctance to increase American defence expenditure had weakened US power and

prestige abroad. He could point to the rapid expansion of the Soviet fleet and the growth of the Soviet nuclear arsenal as examples of the threat to worldwide US interests.

Reagan's election in November 1980 was a clear repudiation of the tattered remnants of detente. During the campaign Reagan emphasised his determination to reverse the decline of US power and to redress the balance which he claimed had, under Carter, swung in favour of the Soviet Union. His administration increased defence expenditure well beyond Carter's levels – it rose by 13 per cent in 1982 and a further 17 per cent in 1983. Reagan reversed Carter's decision against deploying the MX in 1981, announcing that 100 of them would replace the ageing and vulnerable Titan and Minuteman missiles, although exactly how they would be deployed remained a matter of some controversy. He also authorised the production of the B-1 bomber and the neutron bomb. More money was also devoted to expanding conventional

Left: A US Pershing II nuclear missile, complete with warhead (right) and launcher unit (left) on manoeuvres in the United States. Nato plans to station Pershing IIs and cruise missiles in Western Europe provoked considerable opposition, particularly in West Germany and Britain.

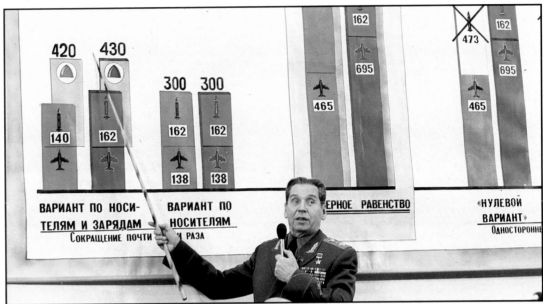

Above: The controversial MX missile, which came up against strong opposition in the United States, where plans for its stationing on land provoked public fears; some experts argued that it served no useful military purpose.

military strength and US naval power. The military space programme was speeded up – Reagan demanded the establishment of a complete US anti-missile system in space by the end of the century.

The new administration was determined to achieve decisive military superiority over the Soviet Union even if this entailed increasing budget deficits, high interest rates and the consequent abandonment of promised tax cuts. There was also much talk in US military circles of the possibility of 'winning' a nuclear exchange with the Soviet Union, either by destroying Soviet nuclear arsenals and command and control centres with America's increasingly accurate missiles, or by defeating the Red Army in Europe. Such talk, which alarmed opinion inside and outside the United States, was played down by the administration, suggesting as it did the first-use by the United States of nuclear weapons, but it obviously contributed to the deteriorating relations between the two superpowers. Nor were relations helped by Reagan's

public assaults on the evils of the Soviet system. For its part, the Soviet Union announced that it would not fall behind in the arms race, no matter what the financial sacrifices.

In the event, talks on the limitation of both strategic and intermediate missiles (START and INF) in Geneva had little hope of making any progress. The United States insisted on the reduction of land-based ICBMs to 850 each, which was totally unacceptable to the Soviet Union, since land-based ICBMs formed the largest component of her strategic nuclear forces. The United States also offered the so-called 'zero option', whereby the United States would not place Pershing and cruise missiles in Western Europe if the Soviet Union would withdraw her SS-4, SS-5 and SS-20 intermediate range missiles from west of the Urals. This was equally unacceptable to Moscow, since the offer ignored the existing manned bombers and land- and sea-based missiles at the disposal of Nato. The Soviet Union, after demanding in vain the

Above: Soviet chief of general staff, Marshal Nikolai Ogarkov, at a press conference in Moscow on 5 December 1983 where he presented figures which claimed to show that the West was attempting to gain military superiority over the Warsaw Pact. Left: President Reagan refers to a map showing the threat posed to Western Europe by Soviet SS-20 missiles. In the 1980s the propaganda battle between East and West took precedence over genuine attempts at negotiations.

inclusion of all 'forward-based' systems in Western Europe, broke off the talks in 1983.

The death of Leonid Brezhnev and the appointment of Yuri Andropov in his place in November 1982 made little difference to the relations between the two superpowers. If anything the repression of dissidents in the Soviet Union was stepped up after he came to power. His health was too poor and his time in office was too short to allow any initiative by the Soviet Union to try to reverse the downward trend in superpower relations. The imposition of martial law in Poland in October 1981 and the crushing of the independent trade union movement Solidarity by the Polish Army prompted the United States to impose economic sanctions on the Soviet bloc – chiefly in withholding further loans and banning exports of new technology – but the effect of these sanctions was much reduced by the refusal of the Western European countries to abandon the projected construction of a natural gas pipeline from the Soviet Union to Western Europe and by the angry protests of US Middle Western farmers at the possible loss of Soviet markets for their surplus grain.

During the election year of 1984 Reagan toned down to some extent his anti-Soviet utterances, but the Soviet Union and its partners refused to participate in the Olympic Games in Los Angeles in the summer. Reagan's supporters continued to accuse the Soviet Union of sending aid to the left-wing guerrillas in El Salvador, although since 1981 US military aid to Third World pro-American states, irrespective of the anti-democratic nature of most of their regimes, had been stepped-up. Reagan continued to insist that there would be no relaxation in the US drive for superiority. At Salt Lake City on 5 September 1984, while he called for balanced and verifiable arms treaties with the Soviet Union, the president made it clear that he would continue to modernise US armed forces and to push ahead with his 'Star Wars' programme. 'We have come a long way in restoring that margin of safety . . . we have completely reorientated American foreign policy, imbuing it with a new energy and moral purpose.' The increasing rigidity of Soviet policy under the ailing and divided leadership of Konstantin Chernenko, combined with Reagan's refusal to compromise his policy goals, suggested that little relaxation of East-West tension was in sight.

Michael Dockrill

Below: US Air Force F-111 bombers, capable of delivering nuclear weapons against targets in Eastern Europe and the western USSR from bases in the United Kingdom. As East-West relations froze, the prospect of successfully limiting nuclear arms became more and more remote.

Key Weapons

AIR-TO-SURFACE MISSILES

MISSILES

1983

The ASM (air-to-surface missile) is essentially a bomb with a rocket motor attached and is usually provided with an integral guidance system. ASMs serve in two roles: anti-shipping and ground attack. Both categories of missiles make use of a wide range of guidance systems, the most popular being some form of radio control – the control of the missile via a radio link with the launch aeroplane – by either joystick or radar. The favourite form of guidance for the anti-shipping missile is inertial control through gyroscopes until at close range when active radar-homing operates. Semi-active and passive radar homing and electro-optical (a televisual link with the launch aeroplane) guidance is also used.

The ASM is a development of two types of weapon that saw widespread service in World War II: the guided bomb and the unguided rocket. The Azon bomb was successfully operated by the US Army Air Force and rockets such as Tiny Tim and Holy Moses were used in the Pacific and European theatres, as well as seeing action with Skyraiders and early jet aircraft during the Korean War. It was a logical progression to seek to combine guidance with rocket propulsion. Designs that were being tested at the end of World War II were produced as research projects – the Gargoyle and the Gorgon for example – and it was from the experience gained in developing these that the foundations of the modern tactical ASM in the US armed services were laid.

In 1954, the US Navy requested a weapon that would combine the destructive power of a 113kg (250lb) bomb with rocket propulsion and a guidance system. Martin Marietta produced to the navy's specifications the AGM-12 Bullpup which entered service in 1959; manufacture of the series ended in 1970. The missile is guided by a switch on the control column of the launch aeroplane – the pilot steers the missile by keeping the twin rear tracking flares on the missile aligned with the target. The Bullpup was adopted by the US Air Force and Marine Corps as well as the Navy and was used extensively in Vietnam.

The major ASM in service with the US Air Force in the 1980s is the AGM-65 Maverick. Hughes Aircraft delivered the first rounds for service at the end of 1972 to the Tactical Air Command where they are carried

on F-4 Phantoms and A-10 Thunderbolt IIs. The Maverick is designed to attack fortifications, armoured vehicles, parked aeroplanes, radar sites and similar targets that require bombing. Originally produced as an electro-optically guided missile, the first IIR (imaging infra-red) Maverick using an infra-red seeker to send an IR image to the launch aircraft's cockpit display was delivered to the US Air Force in October 1983 and a laser-guided version for the US Marine Corps is to enter service in 1985; the US Navy

Previous page: A Harrier takes off from HMS *Illustrious* armed with a test version of the Sea Eagle missile. The Bullpup A can be carried by many types of aircraft such as the Phantom (top) and the P-3 Orion (above); it was extensively used in the Vietnam War.

Right: An F-111 with imaging infra-red (IIR) Mavericks. Below: The image transmitted to the pilot's cockpit display by the infra-red camera in the nose of an IIR Maverick.

Top left: A Harpoon anti-ship missile launched from a P-3 Orion. Top right: A HARM on an A-7C. Above: This F-105G is carrying Shrikes (outboard pylons) and Standards (inboard), both anti-radiation missiles like the HARM, over Laos in 1972.

is also to adopt the Maverick.

The US Navy's Maverick programme is intended to supplement its main air-launched anti-ship missile, the AGM-84A Harpoon. The Harpoon is perhaps more famous as an SSM (surface-to-surface missile) but it actually began as a project for an air-launched missile. Development of the air-launched version was slower than for the RGM-84A Harpoon SSM due to some difficulties with test missiles from 1975 onwards, but it is now in service with naval aircraft of the US, UK and Japanese armed forces.

A more specialised class of air-to-surface missiles in use with the US armed forces is the ARM (anti-radiation missile), designed to take out enemy radars. Three types are in service: the AGM-45 Shrike, the AGM-78 Standard and the AGM-88 HARM. The ARM operates by using an integral seeker unit to lock-on to enemy radar emissions which then guide the missile onto the target. The Shrike and the Standard have both been used operationally in Vietnam and the Middle East; the HARM (high-speed anti-radiation missile) entered service in 1983 and is expected to replace both the Shrike and the Standard.

The first ASM deployed by the Soviet Union known to Nato analysts was the AS-1 Kennel. Development of this large anti-ship missile was accelerated by using MiG-15 components. It employed either radio control or beam-riding (following the radar beam locked on to the target by the launch aircraft's radar) for initial guidance, making its final

attack with a crude active radar-homing device. The missile was withdrawn in the early 1970s.

Two ASMs were first displayed to the public on Soviet Aviation Day in 1961 – the AS-2 Kipper and the AS-4 Kitchen. The Kipper is carried by the Tu-16 Badger-C fitted with a nose radar; the missile is thought to be a beam-rider with active radar-homing in the attack phase. The AS-4 Kitchen was originally carried by the Tu-22 Blinder-B and since its introduction has been seen arming the Tu-26 Backfire-B. The Soviet armed forces appear to regard it as a successful weapon as indicated by a new programme to convert Bear-C and Bear-D aeroplanes into Kitchen carriers, identified by Nato analysts as the Bear-G. Guidance is initially by an inertial system, followed by either active radar or infra-red homing.

The AS-5 Kelt was the only Soviet ASM introduced in the late 1960s, entering service about 1967. Kelts were used during the Yom Kippur War by Egyptian Tu-16s against radar stations and supply dumps. Based on the AS-1 design, AS-5 uses a rocket motor in place of the AS-1's turbojet. The AS-5 may be used against either shipping or land targets using an autopilot for flight guidance and active radar-homing for the attack; the AS-5 can also be used in an anti-radiation mode against radar stations.

The AS-7 Kerry and other recent Soviet ASMs are shrouded in mystery. Very little is known about their appearance, guidance and purpose, and what is generally accepted should be treated with a certain amount of suspicion. The AS-7 is definitely an ASM and entered service in the late 1970s; Nato analysts believe it to be carried on the Su-24 Fencer and possibly on the MiG-27. At first guidance was thought to be by radio command but now the idea that it is a beam-rider is gaining acceptance, but both seem rather dangerous to the delivery aeroplane which would be forced to remain in the vicinity of the hostile target in order to command the missile. The US Department of Defense has identified the AS-8 as a Soviet version of its own Hellfire missile, carried on the Mi-24 Hind-D. There are also a number of other ASMs in various stages of development but even less is known about these, although one is suspected to be an anti-radiation missile.

In Western Europe, the largest producer of ASMs is France, which has been designing them since the mid-1950s. One of the first to enter service was the AS 12, a derivative of the AS 11 anti-tank missile, which is designed to operate in the anti-ship and anti-submarine role. A wire-guided missile, steering is done by line-of-sight, using either a gyrostabilised sight or night-vision equipment. The AS 20 and AS 30 missiles are near contemporaries and fulfil a similar role, differing mainly in size. Radio command line-of-sight guidance was originally used but later models of the AS 30 abandoned the joystick control, using instead an aeroplane-mounted IR seeker kept in alignment with the target to generate steering commands transmitted to the missile: this was known as TCA

(télécommande automatique).

The French Durandal is an unusual weapon designed to crater runways. A very light weapon, Durandal is dropped from the aeroplane like an ordinary free-falling bomb, but then a parachute opens at the tail, braking the bomb's fall and pitching it to at least a 20 degree angle; then a rocket motor fires and propels the bomb forcefully onto its target. As many as 16 Durandals may be carried by the Mirage 2000.

An early Anglo-French armaments project was the Martel ASM that came in two variants: the AJ168 electro-optically guided missile produced by British Aerospace and the AS 37 anti-radiation missile produced by Matra of France. The types have identical

Above: The AS-4 Kitchen, carried under a Tu-22M Backfire, is sometimes equipped with a nuclear warhead. Above right: Durandal missiles were designed to be carried in large numbers by fighter-bombers like this experimental F-15. Right: A runway cratered by Durandals.

Left: An AS 12 missile fitted to a Westland Wasp. This combination severely damaged the Argentinian submarine *Santa Fe* during the operation to recapture South Georgia island in 1982. Below left: The AS 30 missile carried on the centre wing pylons is the laser-guided version; its warhead is 240kg (529lb) of explosive with a choice of impact or delay fuzes. Below: The Martel AJ168 missile is the British contribution to an Anglo-French project; it is TV-guided.

structure, wings, fins, power system and solid-propellant boost motor and are carried on Buccaneers, Harriers, Atlantics, Jaguars and Mirage IIIs.

The notorious AM 39 Exocet is also one of the French family of ASMs. Lighter than the ship-launched version, the AM 39 has a longer range and can be launched from either helicopters or aeroplanes. The AM 39 uses inertial mid-course guidance combined with active radar-homing for the attack. It has a European-made competitor in the Messerschmitt-Bölkow-Blohm Kormoran, based on a Franco-German project of the early 1960s. These missiles aim to impact just above the waterline and have a special warhead designed to pierce the hull of the ship before detonating.

The British Aerospace Sea Skua is a semi-active radar-homing anti-ship missile that equips the Lynx helicopters of the Royal Navy. The missile was designed with the intention of giving helicopter-equipped ships a long-range defence against missile-armed fast attack craft. The Sea Skua saw action in the Falklands War when used in an attack on Argentinian

Top right: An Exocet fired from a Super Frelon helicopter of the French Navy. Above: A Tornado launches a West German Kormoran missile. Right: A Sea Skua missile being fired from a Royal Navy Lynx. This trio of anti-ship missiles represents one of the most dangerous threats to warships available. The Sea Skua was used against the Argentinian patrol boats *Alferez Sobral* and *Comodoro Somellara* in 1982, while the Exocet also demonstrated its combat capabilities to great effect during the Falklands War.

Left: An experimental Sea Eagle, on a Sea Harrier, used to attack the target HMS *Devonshire*.

Below: The Swedish Rb04 missiles on this Viggen are designed to attack seaborne invaders.

patrol craft. The Sea Eagle is a similar missile under development with British Aerospace; developed from the Martel, it is designed to be carried by Buccaneers and Sea Harriers.

The French and the Italians are also working on new types of air-launched missiles, the AS 15 and the Marte respectively. The AS 15 is a wire-guided missile, a system which is no longer fashionable now that semi-active radar guidance is available. The Marte is a development of the ship-launched Sea Killer missile to be used by helicopters and is radio-controlled by the helicopter's radar.

Some non-aligned nations produce their own ASMs. Sweden produces two, the Rb04 and the Rb05, both of which are anti-ship missiles. The Rb04 uses inertial guidance with active radar-homing in the attack phase of flight, while the Rb05 is radio-controlled. Argentina produces the Martin Pescador ('Kingfisher'), a radio-controlled ASM. The Mitsubishi Heavy Industries company of Japan is producing the ASM-1 anti-ship missile which uses inertial guidance with active radar-homing for the attack.

The development of precision-guided munitions and guided ASMs increases both the lethality and expense of tactical attacks by aeroplanes. The spread of radar-homing in place of the previous radio control is more evidence of the increasing military use of electronics. However, it seems expense and complexity will not deter developments in this field.

Air-to-Surface Missiles

Type	Length	Speed	Range
AGM-12B Bullpup	3·2m (126in)	Mach 2·4	11·3km (7 miles)
AGM-65A Maverick	2·5m (98in)	Mach 1·2	16km (10 miles)
AGM-84A Harpoon	3·8m (151in)	Mach 0·75	92km (57 miles)
AGM-45A Shrike	3m (120in)	Mach 2	40km (25 miles)
AGM-78 Standard	4·6m (180in)	Mach 2·5	56km (35 miles)
AS-1 Kennel	8·2m (324in)	subsonic	160km (100 miles)
AS-2 Kipper	9·5m (372in)	Mach 1·2	560km (350 miles)
AS-4 Kitchen	11·3m (444in)	Mach 3·5	460km (286 miles)
AS-5 Kelt	8·6m (339in)	Mach 1·2	230km (143 miles)
AS-7 Kerry	not available	Mach 1	11km (6·8 miles)

Type	Length	Speed	Range
AS 12	1·9m (74in)	Mach 0·27	6km (3 miles)
AS 20	2·6m (102in)	Mach 1·7	6·5km (4 miles)
AS 30	3·9m (153in)	Mach 1·5	11·3km (7 miles)
AJ168 Martel	3·9m (153in)	Mach ·9	60km (37·2 miles)
AM 39 Exocet	4·7m (185in)	Mach 0·9	70km (43.5 miles)
Kormoran	4·4m (173in)	Mach 0.95	37km (23 miles)
Sea Skua	2·5m (99in)	Mach 0·9	15km (9 miles)
R04	4·5m (175in)	subsonic	32km (20 miles)
R05A	3·6m (142in)	supersonic	9km (5·5 miles)
Martin Pescador	2·9m (116in)	Mach 2·3	9km (5·5 miles)

Warriors of Allah

The Afghan guerrilla fighters

Armed resistance to the Marxist regime established in Afghanistan by the April 1978 Saur Revolution developed rapidly during the winter of 1978-79. Indeed, central authority of any kind had never been widely accepted among the tribesmen and ethnic minorities of what was one of the poorest and most backward countries in the world. The efforts of officials of the ruling Khalq wing of the People's Democratic Party of Afghanistan (PDPA) to impose unpopular reforms and a programme of modern education and literacy on the traditionalist villages offended the conservative rural Mullahs, who encouraged resistance to what they saw as the godless communism which was being forced upon them.

Backed up by squads of soldiers, the Khalqi officials were soon resorting to summary executions of local religious and village leaders in an effort to suppress active opposition, but this merely provoked many of the peasant tribesmen, who jealously guarded their independence, to rebellion. Armed with ancient muskets and ·303 Lee Enfield bolt-action rifles, many of which were manufactured from poor materials in small workshops across the border in the Northwest Frontier Province of Pakistan, the Mujahidin, as the rebels were known, soon controlled large areas of the countryside, and posed a serious threat to the government of Noor Mohammed Taraki.

The Afghan Army, though well-equipped and trained by the Soviet Union, had itself been deeply divided by the communist takeover, which many nationalist officers opposed. Peasant conscripts were often unwilling to fight the Mujahidin with whom many of them identified, and poor morale led to a high level of desertion, often directly to the rebel side. Unable to contain the insurgency, both Taraki and his successor Hafizullah Amin relied totally upon Soviet assistance. The clear identification of the PDPA government with the Soviet Union, aggravated by clumsy measures such as the substitution of the red flag for the traditional red, black and green Afghan flag, led to its further isolation and strengthened the Mujahidin claim to be fighting a holy war of liberation against a foreign-dominated regime.

Ethnic and political divisions prevented the Mujahidin from developing into a unified national movement, however. The largest and traditionally dominant ethnic group in Afghanistan was the Pushtuns (or Pathans), most of whom lived in the south of the country. Their close links to the Pushtun tribes of Pakistan had been a cause of conflict between the two countries for many years, and successive Afghan governments had supported Pushtun separatism in Pakistan. Tension over this issue had contributed greatly to the strong links which Afghanistan had developed with the Soviet Union as a counter to the pro-American policy of Pakistan. The Pushtuns were heavily represented amongst the Mujahidin, but traditional rivalries with other ethnic groups, such as the Uzbeks in the north and the Tajiks in the north and northeast of Afghanistan, proved hard to overcome.

As the war spread, with government aircraft bombing rebel villages and inflicting heavy civilian casualties, many Afghans fled as refugees to the safety of Pakistan and Iran. Afghan opposition parties, dominated by religious leaders and urban intellectuals, also established themselves abroad, and many were based in the city of Peshawar in the Pakistani Northwest Frontier Province. The Pakistani government – which opposed the Kabul regime for traditional nationalist reasons as well as because of its opposition to communism on the basis of its own strict Islamic fundamentalism – encouraged these opposition groups.

They became the main channels through which Pakistan distributed the financial and military aid which began to be contributed to the Mujahidin insurgency by the conservative Islamic states of the Gulf and Saudi Arabia, as well as by the radical Libya

Above: An Afghan Mujahidin guerrilla looks out across the mountain valleys where the bitter war against Soviet forces has been waged. The Mujahidin first took up arms against the Marxist government in Kabul, but after the overthrow of Amin in December 1979 and the occupation of the country by some 85,000 Soviet troops, they continued to fight for an independent Islamic Afghanistan.

Mujahidin political groups

Hizb-i-Islami (Islamic Party)
Pushtun, fundamentalist; led by Gulbuddin Hekmatyar; nationwide.

Hizb-i-Islami (Islamic Party)
Pushtun, fundamentalist; led by Yunis Khalis; based in the Jalalabad area, Nangarhar and Paktia provinces.

Jamiat-i-Islami (Islamic Society)
Mainly non-Pushtun ethnic minorities; led by Burhanuddin Rabbani; military leaders include Ahmed Shah Massoud; based in northeast and northern Tajik and Uzbek regions.

Jabha-i-Nejat-i-Melli-Afghanistan (Afghan National Liberation Front)
Loyal to the Mujaddidi family of traditional Islamic leaders, small and ineffective; led by Sibghatullah Mujaddidi; based in the southeast.

Mahaz-i-Melli-Islamiye-Afghanistan (National Islamic Front)
Loyal to Gailani family, accepts need for compromise with USSR; led by Sayyid Ahmad Gailani; based in Paktia Province.

Harakat-i-Inqilab-i-Islami (Revolutionary Islamic Movement)
Party of moderate rural Mullahs; led by Mohammed Nabi Mohammadi; based in the northern province of Faryab.

Sazman-i-Nasr (Organisation for Victory)
Shi'ite, pro-Iranian; based in the northwest.

Shu'la-i-Jawed (Eternal Flame)
Tajik, pro-Peking; based in Badakshan Province.

Setem-i-Meli (Against National Oppression)
Maoist, Tajik; based in Badakshan Province.

Top: Gulbuddin Hekmatyar, leader of the fundamentalist Hizb-i-Islami. Above: Burhanuddin Rabbani, leader of Jamiat-i-Islami, whose most famous guerrilla commander was Ahmed Shah Massoud, active in the important Panjsher Valley.

of Colonel Gaddafi and the revolutionary Iranian Islamic Republic of Ayatollah Khomeini. The Peshawar parties were therefore in a position to impose their own conditions upon the Mujahidin rebels who came to them for support, and while they made the wildest claims for their own efforts in the war against Kabul, made only a negative contribution by injecting their own divisions and rivalries into an already disorganised internal resistance movement.

Though the Mujahidin resistance was unable to realise its full potential and remained uncoordinated and without clear leadership, it nevertheless was able to deprive the Kabul government of control of large areas. The inability of the Amin government to contain the insurgency was a direct cause of the Soviet military intervention of December 1979, which aimed to substitute a government of national reconciliation under the more moderate Babrak Karmal for the isolated and almost universally hated Amin. The occupation of Afghanistan by up to 85,000 Soviet troops only strengthened opposition, however, and the failure of the policy of conciliation left Moscow with no alternative but to accept the necessity of a protracted counter-insurgency war in Afghanistan while a strong central administration was slowly constructed in Kabul.

While under Taraki and Amin brutal repression had confined active opposition largely to the countryside, the Soviet intervention led to strikes and demonstrations in the cities, with bloody clashes between unarmed demonstrators and soldiers of the Afghan Army. The effect upon army morale was catastrophic, and from a pre-intervention peak of 80,000 men it soon collapsed to some 30,000, many of whom were poorly trained and unreliable conscripts, who deserted to the Mujahidin in whole units.

Mutinies and desertions provided the Mujahidin not only with recruits, but also with modern weapons, such as the Soviet-made AKM automatic assault rifle, large numbers of which soon supplemented the traditional Lee Enfield. International opposition to the Soviet intervention led to an increase in arms supplies from abroad, though many Mujahidin units, particularly in the north, remained largely dependent upon captured Soviet weapons or upon weapons supplied or sold by Afghan Army soldiers. China and Egypt, in particular, supplied large amounts of Soviet-type weapons, including assault rifles, ZU-23 anti-aircraft cannon, mines and RPG-7 rocket launchers, and President Reagan announced that the United States would also be prepared to provide assistance to the Mujahidin. It remained unclear, however, to what extent the Americans were prepared to become involved in Afghanistan, and US assistance appeared to

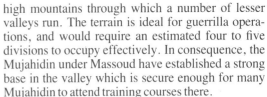

Above: Craftsmen produce copies of Lee Enfield rifles in a primitive workshop in Pakistan's Northwest Frontier Province. Even using such crude weapons, the Mujahidin soon managed to gain control of much of Afghanistan's mountainous countryside. Left: Rebel commanders such as Massoud (seated far left) were able to arm their men with captured AK assault rifles and with heavier weapons such as the Chinese-produced Type 52 75mm recoilless rifle (below). China, Egypt and the US all armed the rebels after the Soviet intervention.

be limited to organising and financing supplies from other sources.

Meanwhile, the Soviet forces had established control of the main towns and roads, and began to develop the infrastructure of occupation, with huge bases near the main towns in the seven military zones which they had established. From these bases 'search and destroy' operations were mounted against Mujahidin units which posed a threat to communications and the all-important supply route from Soviet Central Asia to Kabul. While maintaining this minimum military objective of preventing the collapse of the Karmal government and the victory of the anti-communist Mujahidin, the Soviet Union pursued the long-term strategy of reconstructing the Afghan armed forces under a new, pro-Soviet officer corps.

The Mujahidin were nevertheless able to capture a number of towns. Heavy fighting was reported around the southern city of Kandahar on several occasions, and even after heavy bombing and a large-scale Soviet-Afghan offensive in 1981, Mujahidin units remained active within the city. The control of the eastern town of Herat was also disputed, provoking a major Soviet offensive in the area during 1981-82, and the Mujahidin were able to seize control of Gulbahar, at the head of the strategically important Panjsher Valley, during July 1981.

The Panjsher Valley, to the north of Kabul and threatening the main supply-route to the Afghan capital from Soviet Central Asia through the Salang Pass, was the scene of continued fighting, and of a number of major Soviet offensives. The Mujahidin there were under the command of Ahmed Shah Massoud, a highly capable and popular guerrilla commander who had unified a number of small bands into a well-organised and efficient fighting force of some 2000-3000 men. The fighting in the Panjsher Valley, though more intense and coordinated than elsewhere, is typical of much of the war in Afghanistan since the Soviet intervention. The valley itself is almost 125km (80 miles) long, and is surrounded by high mountains through which a number of lesser valleys run. The terrain is ideal for guerrilla operations, and would require an estimated four to five divisions to occupy effectively. In consequence, the Mujahidin under Massoud have established a strong base in the valley which is secure enough for many Mujahidin to attend training courses there.

During 1980-81, there were a number of Soviet-Afghan Army offensives in the Panjsher Valley, but the heaviest fighting occurred in May 1982, when the Soviet command mounted Panjsher 5. The mouth of the valley was sealed on 10 May, and a combined air and artillery bombardment was concentrated on suspected Mujahidin positions. On 17 May, a Soviet battalion was helicopter-lifted into the area between Khenj and Dasht-i-Rawat. Simultaneously, a strong ground force advanced up the valley with the aim of reaching the positions occupied by the heliborne troops.

Blocking Soviet progress

Massoud's Mujahidin, however, inflicted heavy losses on the exposed heliborne battalion, and, forewarned of the Soviet advance by a forward reconnaissance unit, were able to block the progress of the 360 'Nevel-Polotsk' Motor Rifle Division and the Afghan 444 Commando Brigade. An armoured column of T62 tanks and BTR-60 PB armoured personnel carriers (APCs), advancing from Rokka, came under continuous attack and failed to deploy off the highway, falling victim to Mujahidin ambushes and minefields. The Soviet troops failed to exploit their superiority in equipment, and the Mujahidin were able to concentrate their inferior forces against the head of the advancing column, inflicting heavy casualties and preventing the relief of the helicopter-borne battalion.

A second Soviet offensive in August 1982, code-named Panjsher 6, showed that the Soviets had learned a number of lessons from the May disaster. Greater attention was paid to the preparatory bombardment, which was carried out by Su-25s, MiG fighter-bombers and Mi-24 Hind helicopter gunships. Coordination of the air support operation was conducted from airborne command posts in An-12 aircraft, whose presence overhead soon became a warning signal to the Mujahidin of an impending Soviet attack. The main offensive commenced on 30 August, and Soviet troops advanced up the valley from Rokka, consolidating each stage of the operation by secondary attacks into the Panjsher's side valleys, into which the Mujahidin withdrew.

Soviet tactics still displayed a number of weaknesses, however. Infantry showed a marked unwillingness to advance from the protection of their APCs to engage the Mujahidin at close quarters, and tank commanders also seemed reluctant to deploy across country, therefore remaining dangerously dependent upon the narrow mountain roads where they were vulnerable to Mujahidin ambushes.

While the Soviet Army was unable to eliminate the Mujahidin of Massoud, the 1982 offensive had taken the war into the heart of a previously secure rebel base area, and had prevented Massoud from expanding his operations and threatening communications through the Salang Pass. By late 1982, both sides evidently found it in their interests to conclude an unofficial truce, which left the Panjsher in Mujahidin hands, but allowed the Soviet and Afghan Armies to

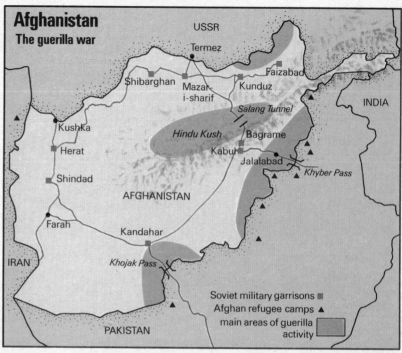

Afghanistan
The guerilla war

USSR

Termez

Shibarghan · Mazar-i-sharif · Kunduz · Faizabad

INDIA

Salang Tunnel

Kushka

Hindu Kush · Bagrame

Herat · Kabul

Jalalabad

Khyber Pass

Shindad

AFGHANISTAN

Farah

Kandahar

Khojak Pass

■ Soviet military garrisons
▲ Afghan refugee camps
main areas of guerilla activity

PAKISTAN

IRAN

Above: A Mujahidin guerrilla picks his way down towards a burning Soviet convoy, ambushed on a remote mountain road.

Below: Rebels man a Soviet 12·7mm DShK heavy machine gun against surprise attack by Soviet helicopter gunships.

concentrate on other threats to security.

By April 1984, however, Massoud felt strong enough to return to the offensive, and his men mounted a number of operations along the Salang-Kabul road, involving several units of up to 500 men each. The attack found Soviet troops prepared, however, and many of Massoud's men were killed in a helicopter-borne Soviet counter-attack near the Salang Tunnel. The Mujahidin attack provoked a renewed Soviet offensive into the Panjsher, carried out by a combined Soviet-Afghan force of some 15,000 men. The success of this offensive was indicated by persistent rumours that Massoud himself had either gone into hiding or had been killed.

While neither side was able to impose a military solution to the conflict in Afghanistan, attention was periodically diverted to a number of diplomatic initiatives which sought to discover a political formula which might achieve a Soviet withdrawal and an end to the war. The Soviet position remained that a withdrawal would only take place if the Karmal regime achieved international recognition, and if Afghan security was guaranteed by an agreement between Afghanistan and the neighbouring states of Iran, Pakistan and China.

The continued war in the Gulf between Iraq and Iran, with its potential for direct involvement of the superpowers, remained a principal reason for Soviet

Left: Mujahidin keep watch over the rooftops of Herat. Despite their objective of maintaining control over Afghanistan's main cities, the Russians have been unable to prevent guerrillas operating in the urban areas.

Below: An Afghan government soldier captured in an ambush is menaced by a rebel's highly-decorated Lee Enfield. Most government or Soviet soldiers taken prisoner by the Mujahidin suffered an unpleasant death. Bottom: A band of guerrillas move swiftly across country, passing a pylon brought down by a sabotage attack.

willingness to pay the military and diplomatic costs of its occupation of Afghanistan. The creation of an American Rapid Deployment Force, whose charter lays down its theatre of operations as stretching from the Horn of Africa in the west to Afghanistan in the east, clearly reinforced the Kremlin's suspicions of Western intentions in the region, and added to fears of a new threat to Soviet security from the south. With relations between Moscow and Washington frozen in a new Cold War, the prospect of an early diplomatic solution to the Afghan crisis remained remote in 1984, and a prolonged Soviet occupation and a continuing bitter guerrilla war seemed inevitable.

Robin Corbett

Hit and run

A Mujahidin attack

At about 1700 hours on 6 August 1980, a small contingent of Mujahidin guerrillas prepared to move out from their base to launch an attack against the Soviet garrison in Jalalabad. For two days the group, which was a part of a Mujahidin force some 500 men strong, had been lying up in the buildings of a deserted village several miles from Jalalabad. The village had proved to be a particularly useful staging point for the guerrillas, providing protection from aerial observation, and its mountain location made it easily defensible against any enemy attack. During their time at the village the guerrillas had carefully gone over the plans of the forthcoming operation. They had also spent a considerable amount of time on weapons maintenance; their limited arsenal consisted mainly of Lee Enfield rifles and captured Soviet AK assault rifles and rocket launchers.

The first stage of the operation was to reach a safe house where they could rest and eat before moving into Jalalabad during the hours of darkness. The group descended from their mountain in typical hill tribesman fashion, darting from cover to cover, rarely ever presenting a target to a possible enemy and employing the protection given by dead ground and natural cover to the full. The only major threat to the guerrillas during the daylight journey was that posed by the constant patrol of Soviet gunships. Whenever these passed nearby, scattering mines and anti-personnel devices, the guerrillas would remain absolutely still. The speed of the helicopters made it quite difficult for pilots actually to notice a man on the ground.

As dusk fell, the guerrillas reached their first safe house, that of a farmer, and awaited the arrival of a second group of Mujahidin. Shortly after, the second group arrived – though they had been delayed and forced to take a far longer route because Soviet troops had blown three important bridges the previous day. The assault force now numbered 23 men. After the distribution of arms and ammunition, the group's leader Engineer Mahmoud (who had received training with the Afghan Army), gave the orders for movement.

As the group approached the outskirts of Jalalabad, Engineer Mahmoud deployed 10 men from the group to hold a narrow iron bridge over a canal which they had just crossed. The detachment was to maintain constant surveillance of the approaches to the bridge and to hold it until the fire party returned. Landmines, salvaged from Soviet ammunition trucks, were to be dispersed in a wide arc around the bridgehead with particular concentration on the main approaches. Members of the fire party quickly acquainted themselves with the approximate positioning of the mines and established two routes which they would use to return along in order to avoid scoring 'own goals'.

As soon as the 10-man group had established itself at the bridge, Engineer Mahmoud moved out with the

Above: An Afghan guerrilla fighter proudly displays a captured Soviet RPG-7. The rebels have been able to augment their limited arms supplies through the capture of Soviet arms and ammunition. Right above: Mujahidin, armed with much-prized Soviet assault rifles, scramble down a mountain pass. The harsh terrain has contributed greatly to the military survival of the Mujahidin.

Right: Soviet vehicles, victims of a successful rebel ambush, lie burnt-out and abandoned at an isolated outpost north of Kabul. The vulnerability of vehicles to ambush, emphasised by the Russians' inflexible ground strategy, was quickly exploited by the Mujahidin forces who were able to launch lightning attacks and then disappear.

main fire party and pressed on into the suburbs of Jalalabad. The group had arranged to take a further rations break at the house of a sympathiser and reached the location undetected. Once there, food was distributed, prayers said and the final weapons checks were made. The AK assault rifles carried by some members of the group were highly valued; the 30-round magazine and semi-automatic action compared very favourably with the bolt-action Lee Enfields with which most of the guerrillas were armed, particularly since the Lee Enfield only held a five-round magazine. The guerrillas had also learned a new trick from their Soviet enemy – the use of hollow-nosed rounds, the effect of which was literally to blow a man apart. Even if the round only hit your forearm it would be capable of removing the entire shoulder.

Leaving the safe house

At 2300 hours the assault group left the safe house and made its way towards a pre-selected ambush site; Engineer Mahmoud carried a captured Soviet rocket launcher. The group reached its objective, a walled garden, and deployed quickly and quietly. Eight men remained by the entrance, while the rest moved along a bomb-damaged wall which overlooked a main road leading into the centre of Jalalabad. Several lorries passed along the road but the guerrillas were waiting for a more substantial target, reluctant to waste valuable ammunition. The tactics were standard guerrilla practice: a small, lightly armed force with standby support deploying into the heart of an urban area where it could select a known target, destroy it and melt away into the countryside. As the group waited in the garden a two-man foot patrol stopped for a cigarette on the other side of the road. The guerrillas maintained their positions and were unperturbed by the enemy presence. They were not anxious to engage

the troops. Lack of medical facilities meant that if you were hit in a firefight there was a high probability that you would die.

At about 2330 hours, the familiar squeaking rumble of tracked wheels signalled the approach of either an APC or a tank. Engineer Mahmoud placed his rocket launcher, an RPG-7, through a hole in the wall of the garden. As the vehicle crossed his sights he fired the round at point-blank range. The explosion was deafening. For a moment there was silence and then the screams of the victims filled the air.

Immediately the group retreated at speed through the garden. Shots rang out as Soviet troops pursued the attackers. Almost in the same instant the guerrillas stopped, turned and released a volley at their pursuers. At the gates of the garden the two guerrilla sections joined up and ran down a street out into open fields. The Russians opened up with machine guns and sent up flares to illuminate the area. But the retreating guerrillas proved very difficult targets and, while still fleeing, returned sporadic bursts of fire. With automatic fire filling the air, the fire party rendezvoused with their support at the canal bridge.

Engineer Mahmoud quickly deployed his men, giving them new arcs of fire, and prepared to engage any Soviet troops following. The Russians, however, seemed reluctant to follow the guerrillas into the countryside away from the safety of their garrison. Shortly afterwards, the group recrossed the canal and made its way to the safety of the farmhouse, where the guerrillas rested until 0300 hours. Still under cover of darkness they made their way back into the hills. Intense air activity immediately following dawn, from Soviet helicopter gunships, forced the rebels to keep low, but there were no ground troop movements. Engineer Mahmoud's group had fulfilled its objective – one Soviet target for one RPG round.

Alexander McNair-Wilson

In the Afghan trap

The Soviet Army's techniques in Afghanistan

It is a long-established feature of the Soviet attitude to warfare that military action must be strictly subordinated to political goals. In Afghanistan, the Soviet military involvement has consequently been carefully limited by the Kremlin's conception of its policy objectives. Their counter-insurgency effort has not attempted to establish control over the whole of Afghanistan – in any case an impossible goal – or to deter the guerrillas from continuing fighting by imposing a high level of casualties, on the principle of the US 'body-count' in Vietnam. Instead, they have committed the minimum force required to hold essential points – basically the main towns and major communications routes – while attempting to reconstruct the Afghan Army and state into a self-sustaining entity. Even in pursuing these limited objectives, however, the Soviet forces have encountered enormous difficulties.

The main cause of the Soviets' initial military set-backs in Afghanistan was their total unpreparedness for counter-insurgency warfare. Prior to 1980 the training of the entire Soviet Army was based on the concept of either a war with Nato in Europe or a conflict with the Chinese in Asia. They were as

unprepared for mountain warfare as they were for counter-insurgency. Also, some deeply-ingrained features of the Soviet Army made it a flawed instrument for its task. Good radio communications, the use of personal initiative and a high standard of junior leadership are all essential ingredients in any counter-insurgency strategy. Initially, therefore, the Russians' performance was merely a reflection of an army in which only senior officers have access to radio sets, maps are restricted documents issued to officers only, subalterns are not permitted to exercise their judgement and sergeants, far from being the respected figures who form the backbone of Western armies, are mere administrative cogs. This, then, is the difficult background against which Russian efforts in Afghanistan should be seen.

The adaptation to the conditions of warfare in Afghanistan was a painful process for the Soviet Army, and much of its performance was decidedly unimpressive, but the Soviets did slowly get to grips with the problem. Some of the worst casualties of the first year arose from the use of tanks to escort convoys. The most serious flaw in Soviet tank design is the continued use of a low, domed turret in which elevation and depression of the main armament are strictly limited. This meant that tanks were often unable to engage their attackers on the inaccessible

Left: Smoke billows over a village in the Panjsher Valley during a bombing strike by Soviet aircraft. Soviet and Afghan government forces relied heavily upon their total command of the air to strike at Mujahidin bases and villages which had aided the rebels. Civilian casualties were high, and many fled to the safety of refugee camps in Pakistan and Iran. Below left: A Mujahidin fighter surveys the ruins of a village destroyed by an air attack.

high ground, a fact which the guerrillas quickly recognised and put to good use in their choice of ambush sites. A more formidable response was provided by the quadruple cannon of the ZSU-23-4 self-propelled anti-aircraft system, but the vehicle's limited ammunition capacity would not support a protracted engagement. The effect on morale of a situation in which the only vehicles to survive an ambush belong to the escort can well be imagined. The tanks were withdrawn, many being shipped back to Russia, and their place was taken by armoured personnel carriers (APCs), the crews of which could make a mounted or dismounted response as the position demanded.

To cope with the demands of mountain warfare, the Soviet Union turned to its mountain races, notably from the Caucasus. In the drastic re-examination of method which followed the early set-backs, men from such areas were drafted into the 104th and 105th Airborne Divisions, which serve by rotation in Afghanistan. These two divisions, upon whom much of the fighting fell, are now acknowledged to be mountain divisions in everything but name. Even the Motor Rifle divisions, which form the bulk of the Soviet garrison, now receive training in mountain warfare techniques, including the different performance of weapons at high altitude, before taking their turn.

Calling down an airstrike

As time went on, Soviet methods came in some ways to resemble American techniques used in Vietnam. This entailed, for example, a gradual improvement in communications which enabled embattled convoy commanders to request artillery fire support from within the fortified base camps, provided these were within range, or to call down an airstrike from the considerable air contingent present. The air contingent is based mainly at Bagram, Kandahar, Shindand and Herat, and there is therefore nowhere inside the country that is more than a few minutes flying time from its airfields; if necessary, further strikes can be mounted from air bases across the Russian frontier. The Soviet fixed-wing ground attack strength within Afghanistan itself is estimated as being 68 MiG-21 Fishbed light strike aircraft; 30 MiG-23 Flogger strike aircraft; 10 armed-reconnaissance versions of the MiG-25 Foxbat; and 65 Sukhoi Su-17 and Su-20 Fitter close-support attack aircraft. To this must be added the Afghan government's own air force which on the eve of the Soviet invasion was said to include 40 MiG-21s, 50 of the older MiG-17s, 24 Su-7BM close-support aircraft and 45 Il-28 Beagle light bombers. It is not known how much of the Afghan Air Force remains operational.

Together, these aircraft deploy a formidable array of air-to-ground weaponry, yet the application of airpower in this way has not produced the desired results. There is nothing wrong with the Soviet theory of ground support: senior air force officers locate their headquarters beside those of senior ground-troop commanders to ensure the closest possible cooperation at the strategic and tactical levels, while air controllers strive to devise yet more efficient means of target indication. The difficulty is that flying fast jet aircraft among the mountains in uncertain weather demands intense concentration which leaves very little time available for identifying the precise area of the target which has been indicated, especially as the

A soldier's story

There is very little glamour about the war in Afghanistan for the young Soviet citizen who is drafted to serve there. It is a nasty war at the best of times, and the Russian soldier lives in constant fear of being picked off by an Afghan sniper or captured by a band of guerrilla fighters. The story of one Soviet soldier who ended up in the West gives an idea of the state of morale in the army.

Yuri Vashchenko had just left school when he was called up in 1982. From his birthplace in Kansk in Siberia he was sent to Omsk for training. 'It was tough and the food was very bad. We were always hungry,' he said. By the end of the year he was in Afghanistan.

Above: A group of Soviet soldiers, armed with AKS-74s.

'Morale among the troops was very low. They would talk only about where it was safe to go, where there was shooting and what was on sale in the markets – jeans, radios and so forth. But the atmosphere was always tense, and no one trusted anyone else.'

Yuri decided one evening to go for a stroll round the town and was immediately captured by the Afghans. He was lucky not to be killed on the spot – the usual fate for Russians taken prisoner. He was eventually taken to a Red Cross post inside Pakistan.

Above: A Soviet soldier is exhibited to the press by his Mujahidin captors. The rebels varied greatly in their sophistication, but some were well aware of the value of propaganda.

Right: A Mil Mi-24 Hind helicopter gunship on a counter-insurgency mission in the Afghan mountains. The Hind undoubtedly proved its effectiveness, but flying conditions in Afghanistan were often hazardous.

guerrillas are expert at concealing themselves. Consequently, much of the payload is wasted, and occasionally a pilot will fly his aircraft straight into the ground, to the delight of the Mujahidin. Seeking better results, the Soviets resorted to the use of napalm and, allegedly, chemical warfare weapons, both of which cover a hillside rather than a specific area. In addition, in an attempt to isolate the guerrillas from local support and supplies, villages in areas where they are operating are razed by concentrated air attacks. The result of this policy has been to depopulate entire valleys, increase anti-Russian feeling and swell the number of refugees in Pakistan.

Helicopters formed part of the Soviet order of battle in Afghanistan from the outset, but the failure of ground troops and fixed-wing aircraft to contain the guerrillas has led to their use on an ever-increasing scale. The versions employed most frequently in Afghanistan are the Mil Mi-8 Hip and the Mi-24 Hind, joined recently by the giant Mi-26, all of which can serve either as troop carriers or gunships mounting a variety of sensors and ground-attack weapon systems. These have given the Russians access to the vital high ground and have enabled them to inflict losses on the Mujahidin where they have previously been unable to do so. If, for example, a guerrilla group is located in the hills some Russian units will be lifted into blocking positions to cut off their retreat while others will be air-landed on a dropping zone from which an assault can be launched after the objective has been softened up. Similarly, during large-scale cordon-and-search operations in wild country the use of helicopters as flying command posts has enabled senior officers to coordinate the movements of their troops as never before.

Although the use of helicopters has produced results for the Russians, the story has not been one of unqualified success. At high altitude, thin air and uneven thermals can both prove fatal, and machines serving in Afghanistan have now been modified to cope with these conditions. Occasionally, too, helicopters crash among the high peaks after being caught in a deadly 'white-out' blizzard. To counter the threat posed by rotocraft the Mujahidin first put up a barrage of smallarms fire, but this was largely ineffective as Soviet designs are capable of absorbing more punishment than most. The guerrillas then acquired shoulder-launched heat-seeking surface-to-air missiles, including the Russians' own SA-7 Grail. The fact that Soviet helicopters now regularly release a series of decoy flares when overflying doubtful territory suggests that some machines at least have been hit.

There is no indication that the Soviet Union has made any serious progress towards its political goal of a stabilised Afghanistan permitting the withdrawal of Soviet combat forces. Support for the guerrillas remains constant. The Russians are able, however, to entrust most day-to-day military operations on the ground to the Afghan Army, reserving their own forces to the defence of major bases and occasional major operations against guerrilla concentrations. The first five years of Soviet operations in Afghanistan undoubtedly witnessed an immense improvement in Soviet counter-insurgency techniques, and there was some evidence that the Russians were taking advantage of the situation to give their forces real combat experience – for example, imitating the Americans' practice in Vietnam of rotating officers regularly, thus sacrificing efficiency in the immediate counter-insurgency campaign to the longer-term goal of officer training under combat conditions.

Drunkenness, drug-taking and desertion

There has also been a resemblance to Vietnam in the effect of the Afghan conflict on Soviet troops. There has been a decline in morale and efficiency, provoked by bad living conditions and disenchantment with the cause, which has manifested itself in a variety of ways, including drunkenness, drug-taking, desertion, widespread crime, the sale of army property to civilians, and the murder of unpopular officers. In contrast, the Mujahidin have suffered no such crisis of morale and have acquired a growing expertise in the use of the more sophisticated weapon systems. It is certainly true that by involving yet more divisions the Kremlin could reduce guerrilla activity to an acceptable level, but how many divisions and at what cost is an open question.

Bryan Perrett

Below: Trucks drive through the wreckage of an ambushed convoy. The single most important objective of Soviet operations in Afghanistan was to keep open the main supply routes, but this proved a far from simple task. Even under armoured escort, convoys were never safe.

Rotors against rebels

The helicopter in counter-insurgency operations

The first large-scale military use of helicopters took place during the Korean War, where they were extensively employed for Casevac (casualty evacuation, also known as Medevac or medical evacuation) and also served in a limited role as troop transports. The ability of the helicopter to operate over difficult terrain previously accessible only to infantry on foot was highlighted by experience acquired at this time. Insurgent forces often operated in forests, jungles, mountains or swamps and it was realised that the helicopter would be a useful instrument in the surveillance of insurgents and the rapid deployment of troops onto their positions.

Initially, a poor power-to-weight ratio that left very little spare lifting capacity imposed a serious limitation on the use of helicopters. This was due to the low horsepower of the air-cooled radial engine, the lightest and therefore the best engine available. However, a major technical breakthrough was achieved in 1955 by the Sud-Aviation and Turbomeca companies of France, who produced the Alouette II helicopter powered by a gas-turbine engine. Thereafter, turboshaft propulsion was universally adopted and this

speeded up the spread of helicopters in military service.

The French Army made limited use of the helicopter in the counter-insurgency role in Indochina, but the first major use of helicopters for counter-insurgency operations was by the British in Malaya during the Emergency in the 1950s. The poor transport infrastructure and rugged jungle terrain severely limited infantry mobility in operations against the Malay communists, but the arrival of troop-carrying Westland Whirlwinds in 1953 provided an invaluable increase in tactical reaction enabling soldiers to reach remote areas before word of their approach could be passed to the guerrillas. Although useful as a transport, the helicopter was not suited to large-scale tactical operations in Malaya because its noise gave warning of approach, and good cover for the alerted guerrillas was given by the thick jungle growth. However, although the jungle hindered the landing of helicopters, it was found that a simple landing zone could be quickly cleared by either chain-saws or explosives.

The more open terrain in Algeria provided the

Above: Bell UH-1Ds of the US 1st Cavalry (Airmobile) landing troops near Bong Son in South Vietnam. The employment of helicopters against insurgents on a large scale was characteristic of the Vietnam War. Top right: Inside a helicopter gunship over Vietnam; the gunship has proved highly effective in counter-insurgency operations.

Right: A British Westland Wessex lowers a 105mm pack howitzer for a firebase in the Radfan. Helicopters can lift heavy equipment to regions other forms of transport cannot reach.

scene for the first use of mass helicopter tactics. The Morice Line along the Algerian-Tunisian border, built by the French to prevent guerrilla infiltration, had numerous sensory devices emplaced along it and when these detected the crossing of the line by guerrillas, paratroopers would be flown by Sikorsky S-55s to the vicinity of the infiltration in platoon or company units. The French also fitted every helicopter with a mounting to take a 20mm machine gun, to be used when the rotocraft was not carrying troops to provide mobile fire support of forces in the field.

In the 1960s in the Radfan, north of Aden, and along the Malaysian-Indonesian frontier in Borneo, the helicopter and the British Army resumed their successful cooperation as in the recently-ended Malayan Emergency. Although the terrain was very different in the two cases, the helicopter played a similar role in both. As in Malaya, it was used to deposit troops close to the positions of enemy forces and to evacuate casualties. The extremely small numbers of troops involved in these conflicts kept the number of helicopters used on any single operation low.

The arrival of helicopter gunships

The American involvement in Vietnam saw the mass tactical use of helicopters for counter-insurgency operations at its height. The 16,000-strong First Cavalry Division (Airmobile) entered the combat zone in August 1965 equipped with 428 helicopters, amounting to some 40 per cent of all American rotocraft operating in Vietnam; one of the lessons that the US Army drew from the French experience in Indochina was that movement of troops on the ground in vehicles was very vulnerable to the ambush tactics of the insurgents – hence the deployment of an enormous number of helicopters by the standards of previous counter-insurgency operations. Early actions revealed that helicopters were vulnerable to fire from the ground and the army requested a more heavily armoured and armed helicopter to give more firepower to airmobile operations. Two designs for helicopter gunships were produced and one, the Bell Huey Cobra, became the standard model for all the US armed services.

Helicopters were essential to the tactics of 'search and destroy' which the Americans employed. Search and destroy operations involved as a first step the location of guerrilla forces, either by sensory devices or aerial observation, including the use of scout helicopters. Once the enemy was located, ground forces would move in and seek to engage him and pin him to one position. Meanwhile, airlifted troops supported by helicopter gunships would be set down in landing zones around the enemy positions and would seek to complete an encirclement. The enemy would then theoretically be destroyed by firepower.

Casevac remained an essential helicopter function during the Vietnam War, operating so efficiently that remarkably few soldiers died of their wounds, even when fighting far from their main base. The CH-47 Chinook played a vital role in the setting up of artillery firebases in otherwise inaccessible areas, and in maintaining supplies to far-flung units. It was also used to drop CS gas on known enemy strongholds, the drums being rolled through the machine's rear door. No use of helicopters on the scale of the US effort in Vietnam has been attempted since.

The Rhodesian Army became possibly the most

Below: A Rhodesian Fire Force 'stick' goes into action from an Alouette III. Bottom: A British Westland Whirlwind in Malaya; the Malayan Emergency was the scene of the first extensive use of helicopters in counter-insurgency operations.

experienced counter-insurgency army in the world during 14 years of fighting against black guerrillas. At first, in the 1960s, the number of guerrillas crossing into Rhodesia was small and it did not stretch the capacity of the Rhodesian forces to operate against them; helicopters simply airlifted an infantry patrol to track down the insurgents. However, from 1972 there was a steady increase in guerrilla activity that spread throughout the country and severely strained the resources of the Rhodesians. In response to this increasing intensity of operations, the Rhodesian armed forces implemented a new tactic involving 'Fire Forces'. A Fire Force typically comprised four helicopters, including a gunship and a command vehicle. If a contact was made with guerrillas the troops on the ground would radio for help and a Fire Force would respond. The helicopters would circle the guerrillas' position and the gunship would engage them while the commander summoned further air support. The ground troops aboard the remaining two choppers would be deployed in such a way as to cut off the guerrillas' escape routes and a firefight would then ensue which theoretically would destroy the guerrillas. These tactics proved a very effective use of helicopters against insurgents.

The relatively small-scale counter-insurgency operations of the British Army in the border areas of Ulster in the 1970s and 1980s brought a further variant on the use of helicopters. As in other conflicts they showed their worth as an alternative to ground movement where even armoured patrols were vulnerable. Their speed of response was exploited to bring troops rapidly to the scene of an incident, and they were used to set down and pick up foot patrols. Reconnaissance, entrusted primarily to the lightweight Sioux, was gradually enhanced by the introduction of improved sensors. Given the nature of the Northern Ireland situation, however, there has never been any question of introducing helicopter gunships – they would be provocative and in any case highly inappropriate to the low-level insurgency being faced.

Since 1979 the chief example of helicopter-borne counter-insurgency has been the Soviet campaign in Afghanistan. The Soviets gradually recognised their need for an extensive use of helicopters in the mountainous Afghan terrain, where their armoured vehicles proved extremely vulnerable to ambush and suffered great problems in achieving any cross-country mobility. Using the Mi-4 Hound, the Mi-8 Hip and the Mi-24 Hind, they developed a by now standard range of counter-insurgency techniques, placing combat troops to the rear or flanks of guerrilla positions, using gunships to provide mobile fire support for troops on the ground, and exploiting the strength of the helicopter as a reconnaissance vehicle – its ability to achieve good ground observation. For heavy lifts the Soviets have employed the Mi-6 Hook, the Mi-10 Harke and the Mi-26 Halo, currently the largest helicopter in the world.

The helicopter has clearly demonstrated its worth as an essential piece of counter-insurgency equipment, although it has yet to prove itself on the high-technology battlefield. **Paul Szuscikiewicz**

Key Weapons
LANDMINES

The landmine is a cheap and versatile weapon which has seen a great deal of action in conflicts since 1945. The first true mines were successfully developed in the mid-1930s, helped by advances in techniques of fuzing, arming and explosive filling. In World War II both Allied and Axis forces laid extensive minefields and their continuing usefulness in war has been demonstrated as recently as the Falklands conflict, during which the Argentinians laid thousands of mines on the islands.

Landmines fall into two basic categories: anti-tank and anti-personnel. All types usually comprise a case, a fuze and an explosive charge. The fuze is normally located at the top of the mine, generally detonating the device in response to pressure. The required activating pressure can vary greatly: 8-50kg (18-110lb) for an anti-personnel mine and 200-250kg (440-550lb) for an anti-tank mine. An anti-personnel mine usually has a charge of 75-100 grams (2·6-3·5oz), compared with a charge of 5-10kg (11-22lb) for an anti-tank mine. The case varies in shape, composition and size depending on the role the mine is intended to fulfil.

Anti-tank mines are usually laid in carefully chosen positions to channel attacking vehicles into areas where the defenders will have a good chance of destroying them. It is effective as an anti-tank weapon

Previous page: As the PLO left Beirut in 1982, their minefields were cleared by the Lebanese Army; the anti-tank mines are Soviet TMN-46s. Right: These anti-tank and anti-personnel mines laid by the Argentinian Army and dug up by the Royal Engineers on the Falklands are of Spanish and Italian, as well as Argentinian, origin. Below left: This Yugoslav TMA-3 anti-tank mine has no metallic parts. Below right: An M80 mine, the practice model of the US M19 anti-tank mine. Bottom left: Two Afghan guerrillas hold up a Soviet TM-62P plastic anti-tank mine. Bottom right: A Soviet TMN-46 metallic anti-tank mine.

primarily because it can strike against the two weakest parts of the vehicle: the tracks and the thinly-armoured underside (or 'belly'). Anti-tank mines are classified by the method of attacking the vehicle, giving three distinct types: those which attack the tracks and roadwheels, those which attack the belly, and the off-route mine which attacks the tank from the side, like an automatic anti-tank gun. The tracks and running gear can be disrupted by any strong blast, but belly-attack and off-route mines need to use a shaped charge to penetrate the tank's armour. Of course, a belly-attack mine will also tend to damage a tank's running gear if its charge is large enough.

The anti-tank mine fuze also comes in a variety of forms. The simplest is the single-impulse fuze, requiring only the correct amount of pressure to detonate it; although it is vulnerable to simple counter-measures, its cheapness has made it the most common fuze on anti-tank mines in the world. Double-impulse fuzes are more complex and aim at defeating one of the simplest counter-measures, the mine-clearing roller fixed to the front of a tank. The first pressure of the roller fails to detonate the mine but the second pressure of the tank does; if the tank is without rollers the first roadwheel acts as the first impulse and further pressure detonates the mine.

A special type of fuze for the belly-attack mine is the vertical tilt rod. This sticks up out of the mine, and, when broken or bent by a tank, will detonate after a short delay. Other types of fuzes are the influence fuze, which uses thermal, magnetic, acoustic or seismic electronic sensors to detect the tank, and tripwires for the off-route attack mine. The mine may also employ an anti-disturbance fuze to counter being lifted either by hand or by an anti-mine plough. Examples of anti-tank mines include the British Bar Mine, the French Model 1952 MACI vertical tilt rod mine, the Soviet TM-46 and the American M-19.

The primary aim of the anti-personnel mine is to inflict casualties on infantry (it can also disrupt wheeled transport). Anti-personnel mines are deployed in a number of ways – in conjunction with anti-tank mines to prevent a crossing on foot, along routes likely to be used by an advancing enemy, and to protect a prepared position. Mines are very effective at harassment when scattered about randomly in the path of the enemy.

Anti-personnel mines come in two categories: individual-attack and mass-attack. As the name implies, individual-attack mines are designed to injure one man and have a small blast radius. They are either methodically emplaced on the ground or scattered by a dispenser on a vehicle or helicopter. The scatterable mine lies on the top of the ground, avoiding detection through its very small size and through having camouflaged material attached. Mass-attack mines are modern equivalents of cannister and grapeshot, like them discharging hundreds of steel pellets or balls up to 100m (110yds) away. They are normally detonated about a metre (one yard) above the ground; to achieve this they are either mounted on a stake or have a central section blown into the air by a small charge before the main charge explodes. They are usually triggered by a tripwire or foot switch. Some mass-attack mines, such as the American M-18 Claymore, are designed to propel the fragments in a specific direction rather than attempting to achieve an all-round effect. Examples of anti-personnel mines include the British Ranger mine, the US M-3 and M-14

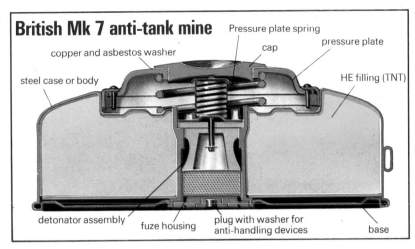

British Mk 7 anti-tank mine

copper and asbestos washer — Pressure plate spring — cap — pressure plate
steel case or body — HE filling (TNT)
detonator assembly — fuze housing — plug with washer for anti-handling devices — base

Right: The Soviet PMD-57 anti-personnel mine is made of wood. The firing pin is placed through a hole in the bottom half of the box. Wooden mines were first developed during World War II.

Right: The interior of an M18 Claymore comprises 700 steel balls embedded in a plastic matrix with C-4 plastic explosive behind the spheres.

Below: The Ranger anti-personnel mine is made of polycarbonate plastic; it has a diameter of only 62mm (2·45in) and a thickness of 32mm (1·25in).

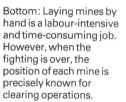

The Ranger anti-personnel mine system uses a highly flexible, multi-barrelled projector that can be mounted on APCs (left), small boats (centre) and trucks. The projector holds 72 disposable tubes each containing 18 mines that are fired up to a range of 100m (330ft).

Bottom: Laying mines by hand is a labour-intensive and time-consuming job. However, when the fighting is over, the position of each mine is precisely known for clearing operations.

and the Soviet POMZ-2.

Both anti-personnel and anti-tank mines are used by most armies in the world and improving counter-measures have led to demands for more complex variants; these demands are forcing the cost of manufacturing up, making landmines a less economic way of harassing the enemy. An increasing number of mines are being constructed from non-metallic materials – plastic in the Israeli No. 10, wood in the Soviet TMD-B anti-tank and PMD-6 anti-personnel mines. These are very difficult to detect with electronic devices.

The manner of laying mines is as varied as the types of mines themselves. Before and during World War II, minelaying was done by hand – a time-consuming and tedious process. For larger minefields most armies now use some form of mechanical minelaying (minelaying by hand may still be done when either time is available or for small minefields). The standard method uses an agricultural disc to cut the earth, a plough to lift it, a device to arm the mine, and a chute through which the mine is dropped into the earth. There are also smoothers to replace the earth, in this way camouflaging the mine. When there is not sufficient time to use mechanical methods, some form of surface laying is used; this can be done by a mechanical layer, but the scatterable system is more popular. Scattered mines are fired from tubes which can be mounted on specialised variants of APCs, or attached to helicopters, or even in a device which looks like a suitcase. Artillery, such as the US M198 155mm howitzer, can fire munitions containing mines, and rockets, such as the US Multiple Launch Rocket System, can do the same.

Some examples of scatterable systems either now in use or in development are the British Ranger anti-personnel mines, the West German MSM/MW (Minestreumittel-Werfer), the Italian Valsella VS/MD scatter-dropping mine system and the US M128 Ground-Emplaced Mine-Scattering System

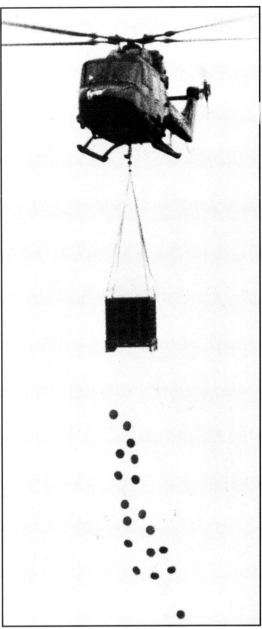

(GEMSS). The Ranger system consists of 72 disposable tubes, each containing 18 plastic mines, mounted on a special rack. By using manual firing each tube can be fired independently and the mines, dispersing in flight, scatter randomly over the ground; a total of 1296 mines can be laid in just over one minute and the mines arm themselves automatically after 15 seconds on the ground. The MSM/MW is being developed for defensive mining at short range using the Dynamit Nobel AT2 hollow-charge mine; the launchers contain 100 mines and can be installed on a helicopter or on the M548 tracked carrier. The Valsella VS/MD system looks like a large crate suspended beneath a helicopter and carries 1920 anti-personnel or 200 anti-tank mines, or a combination of both. The M128 GEMSS holds up to 800

The Technovar DAT scatter-dropping mine system can drop either anti-tank or anti-personnel mines from a height of 100m (330ft) and at a speed of 200km/h (125mph). The container (above) is slung below a helicopter (right).

Below: A Bar Mine layer operates in wintertime conditions. The smoothers at the rear cover over the mines dropped down the chute.

mines and is mounted on the M794 trailer which can be towed by any suitable vehicle.

Clearing mines is a difficult and dangerous task; it is either done by hand or using engineering vehicles equipped with rollers, flails or ploughs. The mines are detected either by prodding the ground with a bayonet or specially-designed prodder, or by using a mine-detector. Mine-detectors use a low-frequency electrical current to detect changes in the magnetic field caused by the mine's metal casing; the mine-detector can be defeated by a non-metallic mine, but newer models using certain radio frequencies or operating on a whole radio frequency band are capable of detecting non-metallic mines. A quicker way of clearing mines is by using a plough attached to the front of a tank. The plough skims off the topsoil in front of the tank tracks, pushing it to one side together with the mines; this method imposes a great deal of strain on the tank structure. Another mechanical method is the use of a roller which seeks to detonate the mine by exerting the required pressure; the rollers themselves are virtually indestructible. Flails work on a similar principle. However, all these methods are flawed: influence fuzes can destroy the mine plough tank, while the double-impulse fuze would defeat the flail or roller-equipped tank. Mines can also be cleared by using a rocket hose. A rocket trailing an explosive length of hose is fired across the minefield; the hose is then detonated and the mines, which are very sensitive to such a detonation, will also explode.

The ability of ground-scattering technology to lay mines rapidly has allowed them to play a major role in a fluid, mechanised war. Their simplicity and effectiveness at ambushes makes them useful in guerrilla warfare. Predictions of the landmine's demise have been premature.

Mine-clearing operations can be carried out by microwave detectors (below), mine ploughs (centre left), hand probes (centre right), or mine rollers (bottom). It is a dangerous task to perform, even in the absence of enemy action.